A Surgeon with Custer at the Little Big Horn

A Surgeon with Custer at the Little Big Horn

JAMES DEWOLF'S DIARY AND LETTERS 1876

Edited by
TODD E. HARBURN

Foreword by
PAUL ANDREW HUTTON

University of Oklahoma Press ❦ Norman

James DeWolf's diary and letters were originally published in *North Dakota History* 25, nos. 1 and 2 (1958): 33–82. Edward S. Luce's introduction to the diary and letters is reprinted by permission of the State Historical Society of North Dakota.

LIBRARY OF CONGRESS CATALOGING-IN-PUBLICATION DATA
Names: DeWolf, James M., 1843–1876, author. | Harburn, Todd E., editor.
Title: A surgeon with Custer at the Little Big Horn : James DeWolf's diary and letters, 1876 / edited by Todd E. Harburn.
Other titles: James DeWolf's diary and letters, 1876
Description: Norman, OK : University of Oklahoma Press, [2016] | "James DeWolf's diary and letters were originally published in North Dakota History 25, nos. 1 and 2 (1958): 33–82." | Includes bibliographical references and index.
Identifiers: LCCN 2016041688 | ISBN 978-0-8061-5694-1 (cloth)
 ISBN 978-0-8061-6310-9 (paper)
Subjects: LCSH: Little Bighorn, Battle of the, Mont., 1876—Personal narratives. | DeWolf, James M., 1843–1876—Diaries. | DeWolf, James M., 1843–1876—Correspondence. | United States. Army—Surgeons—Biography. | United States. Army. Cavalry, 7th. | United States. Army—Military life—History—19th century. | Physicians—United States—Diaries. | Physicians—United States—Correspondence. | Frontier and pioneer life—Dakota Territory.
Classification: LCC E83.876 .D355 2016 | DDC 973.8/2—dc23
LC record available at https://lccn.loc.gov/2016041688

The paper in this book meets the guidelines for permanence and durability of the Committee on Production Guidelines for Book Longevity of the Council on Library Resources, Inc. ∞

Copyright © 2017 by the University of Oklahoma Press, Norman, Publishing Division of the University. Paperback published 2019. Manufactured in the U.S.A.

All rights reserved. No part of this publication may be reproduced, stored in a retrieval system, or transmitted, in any form or by any means, electronic, mechanical, photocopying, recording, or otherwise—except as permitted under Section 107 or 108 of the United States Copyright Act—without the prior written permission of the University of Oklahoma Press. To request permission to reproduce selections from this book, write to Permissions, University of Oklahoma Press, 2800 Venture Drive, Norman, OK 73069, or email rights.oupress@ou.edu.

To my wife, Shirley Lynn Harburn
With many thanks for her enduring Love and Faith,
for being my Best Friend,
and for always being there for me

Contents

List of Illustrations	ix
Foreword, by Paul Andrew Hutton	xi
Preface	xiii
Acknowledgments	xix
Introduction: James Madison DeWolf of Mehoopany, Pennsylvania	3
1. Fort Seward, D.T.: March 10 to April 14, 1876	29
2. Fort Abraham Lincoln, D.T.: April 16 to May 14, 1876	71
3. Misjudgment and the Trail to Disaster: May 17 to June 24, 1876	95
4. "If He Had Gotten a Few Feet Further . . .": The Retreat to Reno Hill	125
Epilogue	147

APPENDIXES

A. Account Book Pages of DeWolf's Diary	149
B. DeWolf's Early Diary Entries, October 1875	153
C. Edward S. Luce's Introduction to DeWolf's Diary and Letters, 1958	157
Notes	163

Bibliography 233
Index 249

Illustrations

FIGURES

Achsah Clapp DeWolf Fisk	2
DeWolf-Robinson and Pearson (Pierson) family cemetery	6
Mehoopany, Pennsylvania, 2013	7
James Madison DeWolf, around age seventeen	8
Dogan Ridge, Bull Run National Battlefield	11
Camp Lyon, Idaho Territory, 1866	14
New Camp Warner, Oregon, c. 1870	17
Fannie Downing DeWolf with her sister and brother	18
Harvard Medical School, c. 1878	21
James Madison DeWolf	22
DeWolf's U.S. Army contract	25
Fort Totten surgeons' quarters	26
Lieutenant Colonel George Armstrong Custer	31
Brigadier General Alfred H. Terry	32
Brigadier General George Crook	35
Dr. Henry R. Porter	36
First Lieutenant George E. Lord, assistant surgeon	38
Colonel John Gibbon	39
Lieutenant Colonel Lewis Cass Hunt	45
Dr. Henry H. Rugar	46

Captain John Henry Patterson	47
Jamestown and Fort Seward, Dakota Territory, 1877	49
Edward H. Lohnes	50
Officers' quarters, Fort Seward, Dakota Territory, c. 1880	53
DeWolf's medical report, March 31, 1876	58
Ernest Brenner	64
Bismarck, Dakota Territory, c. 1873	72
Surgeons' quarters, Camp Hancock	75
Steamboat *Denver*, Fort Abraham Lincoln	76
Major Marcus A. Reno	79
Fort Abraham Lincoln, c. 1875	82–83
Captain Frederick W. Benteen	87
DeWolf's sketch of Fort Lincoln, May 8, 1876	88
DeWolf's journal entries, June 12–14, 1876	118
Second Lieutenant Benjamin Hodgson	122
Second Lieutenant Charles Varnum and companions	132
Second Lieutenant George D. Wallace	134
DeWolf's death site, 2013	135
James Madison DeWolf	139
David and Emma Hall's house, Norwalk, Ohio	144
Graves of James Madison DeWolf and Fannie DeWolf	145

MAPS

Reno Scout	117
Valley and timber fight areas and Reno's retreat	128

Foreword

Paul Andrew Hutton

Few subjects in American history have attracted quite so much attention as the June 25, 1876, Battle of the Little Big Horn. Five companies of the Seventh United States Cavalry, under the immediate command of Lieutenant Colonel (Brevet Major General) George Armstrong Custer, were wiped out by an overwhelming force of Sioux and Cheyenne warriors on that day. Custer's Last Stand immediately captured the imagination of the world, and that fascination has lingered to this day. Michael O'Keefe's two-volume bibliography, *Custer, the Seventh Cavalry, and the Little Big Horn*, published by the Arthur H. Clark Company in 2012, annotated over 10,000 items for Little Big Horn research, 3,000 of which were books. Over the years many of the world's best historians and writers have been attracted to the saga of Custer and his last battle, from such celebrated novelists as Ernest Haycox, Thomas Berger, Mari Sandoz, Evan S. Connell, and Michael Blake, to such noted historians as Robert M. Utley, Jay Monaghan, Paul Hedren, Jerome Greene, James Donovan, Nathaniel Philbrick, and T.J. Stiles (who received the 2016 Pulitzer Prize for his *Custer's Trials*). Why has this familiar story remained such catnip for both writers and readers?

It is, of course, the universal human dimension of the story that so draws us to it. On the one hand, you have heroic Native peoples making a stand for a threatened way of life, and on the other hand, the gallant Seventh Cavalry soldiers unwittingly marching to their doom. Death stalks us all, and we are pulled, much like moths to the flame, into the romantic tragedy of this tale, for it resonates with our own mortal fears. The defiant Sioux and Cheyenne warriors and the doomed troopers of the Seventh, so perfectly locked in a fateful dance of death, are impossible to resist.

It is that human dimension that Todd Harburn captures in his careful editing of the diary and letters of Dr. James DeWolf. While DeWolf's diary has long been available to students of Custer's final campaign, it is the letters, and Harburn's meticulous annotations, that make this volume so invaluable. These letters are incredibly poignant, for they encapsulate the human dimension of the Little Big Horn fight that has so long captivated readers. It is truly heartbreaking to read the lines written by this fine young doctor to his beloved wife as they plan a future that we know will never come. Harburn brings to life the real stuff of history: not abstract theories of mass social movements, but the raw emotion of the human condition. The dreams of this young couple are dreams we can all share.

As a distinguished orthopedic surgeon, Todd Harburn fully comprehends the problems that confronted young Dr. DeWolf. Harburn provides countless insights into the issues faced by the young doctor. One of the most fascinating aspects of this book is DeWolf's transition from raw Civil War soldier, to untrained hospital steward, to Harvard-trained contract surgeon. It really is a fascinating American success story—at least until DeWolf reaches the Little Big Horn. It is the great irony of the story that DeWolf's realization of the American dream leads him directly to Custer's Last Stand.

Todd Harburn brings the past to life with his skillful editing of James DeWolf's story, a tale of soaring achievement and devastating tragedy. It is, in fact, the ultimate American story.

Preface

ON JUNE 25, 1876, at the Little Big Horn River in Montana, Lieutenant Colonel George Armstrong Custer and five companies of the Seventh United States Cavalry under his direct command were killed fighting against a force of more than two thousand Lakota and Northern Cheyenne warriors. Controversy and debate among professional and skilled amateur historians, researchers, students, and interested readers have continued over the nearly 150 years since the battle. Hundreds of books, essays, and articles have been written, a flood of information that will most likely continue indefinitely. Among the many well-recognized historical figures who fought that day—on both sides—were several who are less well-known today. One such individual was Acting Assistant Surgeon James Madison DeWolf, one of the three physicians and surgeons assigned to Custer's column.

A civilian contract doctor with army experience, DeWolf is perhaps best known for keeping a diary of the 1876 expedition against the Indians through the night of June 24, that is, until he was killed in the battle the next day. The diary was retrieved by his colleague and friend Acting Assistant Surgeon Henry Rinaldo Porter, also a civilian contract surgeon and the only physician of the three with Custer's troops to survive the battle.[1] Porter eventually sent the diary to DeWolf's wife, Fannie. Aside from his diary, Doctor DeWolf is perhaps less well known than his medical colleagues at the Little Big Horn. Nonetheless, the preserved correspondence to his wife and the diary he kept during the expedition are important because they contain his behind-the-scenes observations, his commentary and opinions about officers and enlisted men, and his observations about military protocol and social aspects of the 1870s West. As an educated man with army experience, DeWolf left behind writings that provide insight into some of the personalities, perceptions, and emotions of people with varying backgrounds who made up the 1876 expedition. His descriptions of terrain, weather conditions, and campsites on that fateful journey not only provide additional perspective but also correlate with many of the other surviving primary writings by those who witnessed these events with him. His letters show him to have been a compassionate doctor of temperate personality but someone suited to the rigorous society of the army and the western frontier.

DeWolf's diary along with a collection of letters he wrote to his wife, Fannie, were donated to the Custer Battlefield National Monument in 1941 by Verne Adams Dodd (Fannie DeWolf's son from her second marriage). Fannie had remained at Fort Totten while DeWolf traveled with Custer and the Seventh Cavalry. The DeWolf diary and letters have been published only once before: in 1958, by Major Edward S. Luce, former superintendent of the Custer Battlefield National Monument (as it was designated then), in *North Dakota History*, the journal of the State Historical Society of North Dakota.[2]

The idea for this book came about in 2008 during my first visit to the Little Bighorn Battlefield National Monument (as the site is now designated). Like so many others, I have always had an interest in the Little Big Horn story. Because no biography or major work had been written on DeWolf aside from Luce's work with *North Dakota History* nearly six decades ago, a new printing of these documents with more in-depth annotation and additional biographical information on DeWolf seemed as if it would be useful to researchers who shared my interest. After making initial inquiries, I received permission from the administrators of the State Historical Society of North Dakota and Little Bighorn Battlefield National Monument to reprint the DeWolf diary and letters with more extensive annotation than Luce's minimal footnoting of 1958.

I approached that task with the intention of making these important contemporary documents more readily available to historians, researchers, and interested readers. Luce's original 1958 publication is difficult to locate today. Other contemporary journals of the 1876 expedition have been published in various forms, including Brigadier General Alfred H. Terry's letters to his sisters, edited by James Willert; Mark Kellogg's diary and newspaper journal, edited by Sandy Barnard; Private Charles Windolf's accounts; and the meticulous studies and mapping of the expedition's trail by John M. Carroll and Frank L. Anders and more by recently Laudie J. Chorne, to name a few. James DeWolf's letters provide further confirmation of and supplemental information about many of the camp sites on the trail to the Yellowstone and the Little Big Horn.[3] This work is intended to add commentary to DeWolf's perspective of those sites, what happened along the way during the expedition, and some of his nineteenth-century medical perspectives. Moreover, as Edward Luce indicated in his introduction to the original printing, the doctor's letters to his wife supplement the actual diary with many more details about what happened each day, as well as the behind-the-scenes social and cultural issues DeWolf and Fannie found in military life. In addition, this volume presents some previously undiscovered or unpublished information on his personal life and ancestry, his Civil War service, and his funeral and final interment in Ohio at his wife's family plot.

The book has been divided into four chapters. The introduction presents DeWolf's ancestry and early life, Civil War army career, and experiences in the years leading up to his eventual medical school matriculation. Although the letters to his wife follow in chronological order over the four months of the 1876 spring expedition, I have chosen to group these in appropriate sections pertaining to each segment of the journey for easier reviewing: chapter 1 contains those letters corresponding to his diary entries at Fort Seward, chapter 2 contains letters from his stay at Fort Abraham Lincoln, and chapter 3 includes those letters during the final days of the journey to the battle of the Little Big Horn. Chapter 4 reviews and correlates all known references to DeWolf's death during the retreat from the timber fight at the onset of the attack at the Little Big Horn and his final journey for interment in Ohio.

Portions of Luce's original editing notes (which totaled only twenty-seven brief identifications) have been amalgamated with my own endnotes and are designated as such. However, other information in the endnotes and annotations reflects my own research as well as some previously published information. Luce's original introduction is included as appendix C. The surviving original diary consists of fifty-one unnumbered pages measuring 4 1/4 × 6 1/2 inches in two small pocket-sized notebooks. Luce presented the diary portion immediately following his introduction, but I have chosen to include the diary entries with letters of the same date to provide an easier correlation of the events described. I hope the endnote format will prove more accessible than traditional footnote format, which would have extended and broken up the letters excessively, making reading more difficult. Luce noted in his original introduction that DeWolf did not capitalize the beginning of each sentence and misspelled words at times. DeWolf's punctuation and occasionally his grammar are indeed less than exemplary. For the sake of authenticity and historical tradition, I nevertheless chose to leave punctuation, spelling, and capitalization in DeWolf's diary and letters as he wrote them. The doctor used italics in place of underlining to emphasize words, as well as brackets on occasion to clarify others, and these styles have been retained.

Luce also noted DeWolf's poor penmanship, which is at times difficult to decipher—perhaps that is not surprising, in light of the notorious handwriting of physicians and surgeons today. Regardless, Dr. Verne Adams Dodd painstakingly deciphered and transcribed the thirty-two letters (nearly forty-seven letters if multiple entries during the same day are counted) when he donated them to Major Luce and the Little Big Horn battlefield archives in 1941. Dodd's work and the State Historical Society of North Dakota's printing of Luce's work in 1958 made this current presentation much easier to write. Still, it was a thrill to see and hold DeWolf's original diary in my own hands, a courtesy very generously afforded by the National Park Service historians and archivists at the Little Big Horn battlefield.

Reading his long letters to his wife reveals that DeWolf was well liked by his colleagues and peers, had a pleasant personality, and was diplomatic in his dealings with others, though he could be firm when necessary. His letters also reflect quite a good sense of humor. Some authors have commented that he was probably the least experienced of the three surgeons with Custer's column, as Porter had served in the Arizona Indian campaigns and in private practice and First Lieutenant George Edwin Lord had served at Fort Buford prior to this 1876 expedition. Whatever the case, DeWolf was a capable and competent surgeon performing his duties and was well suited to the rigors of military campaigning; he was not simply an academic physician. Also readily evident in the letters are DeWolf's deep love, respect, and adoration for Fannie.

While annotating the diary and letters, I benefited from having access not only to the many primary sources, including post returns and special orders, that have been preserved in various archives and museums but also to the enormous volume of published books and articles on the Indian wars period and the Little Big Horn story. Such readily available resources made writing this book much easier, though it was still a long and involved process. That said, I assume all responsibility for any factual errors contained here, including those of omission. I also recognize the existence of differing interpretations of many (if not all) of these events. Therefore, I have refrained from simply reiterating most of the controversial aspects of the expedition and battle. I have limited my personal interpretations to the context of DeWolf's participation in the battle and have strived to keep those to a minimum, with the intent of reminding readers that these controversies exist and referring readers to some of the well-known previously published sources for additional reading so that they can formulate their own opinions. Furthermore, in referring to the battle itself, I have chosen to use the term "Little Big Horn," as that spelling is in keeping with the U.S. Army's historically preferred spelling and title of the battle, rather than the more popular modern terms "Little Bighorn" and "Custer's Last Stand."[4]

The diary and letters of James Madison DeWolf and his own story are, without question, an important part of the 1876 expedition and events at the Little Big Horn. It is my hope that this book will be seen as a worthy effort to expand our understanding of that significant time and place in history.

Acknowledgments

No AUTHOR is the sole contributing source for any book of this type, and I extend my sincere appreciation to the following individuals, institutions, and organizations for their assistance. If I have inadvertently missed anyone, it is unintentional, and my greatest apologies are extended.

Without question, this monograph would not have been possible were it not for the kind permission of the administrators of the State Historical Society of North Dakota (SHSND) and the Little Bighorn Battlefield National Monument to edit the 1876 diary and letters of James Madison DeWolf. I am indebted to Kathy Davison, now retired but the former editor of the State Historical Society of North Dakota, for permission to use and reprint Edward S. Luce's original transcription and editorial notes of DeWolf's diary and letters from the society's journal in 1958 (the first and only printing of these entire documents until this endeavor) and for her enthusiastic support of this project. I owe a great debt also to Sarah Walker, research archivist, and Jim Davis, historian and archives specialist at the SHSND, both of whom provided me with their undivided attention and assistance during my research visit to the archives. Ms. Walker was especially generous with her time and patience concerning my numerous e-mail inquiries, requests, and telephone calls over the past eight years for her assistance in locating documents and information in the society's collections.

Likewise, National Park Service administrators and historians at the Little Bighorn Battlefield National Monument were equally helpful and supportive of the project. I am indebted to Sharon Small, curator, and John Doerner, the former historian at the monument, for their permission to publish the original DeWolf diary and letters from the Little Bighorn archives and use of other documents and photos from the park's White Swan Library collections. Moreover, I am especially thankful to them for unselfishly taking time out of their schedules to meet with and assist me during my research visits, which always seemed to occur at the busiest time of their season, during the week of the annual June 25 anniversary of the battle. I will be forever grateful to Ms. Small for providing me with a lifetime memory in being able to hold and review DeWolf's original diary in my own hands during one of those visits. I also owe sincere thanks to John Doerner and to the supervisor of park rangers, Jerry (Gerald) Jasmer, for their most generous permission to make arrangements for me to visit the site of DeWolf's death at the Reno retreat pathway from the Timber Fight, a section of the battlefield that is not accessible to the general public. More recently, Ms. Cindy Hagen, cultural resources specialist at the park, has also been most generous in taking time out of her busy schedule in providing answers to my questions regarding resources available and permission to use images from the Little Bighorn collections.

I am greatly indebted to the historian Henry Timman of Norwalk, Ohio, former director of the Firelands Historical Society and Museum, who unselfishly provided me with previously unpublished personal information regarding James DeWolf and his wife, Fannie, from the museum's collections. His hospitality during my visits to his town is also appreciated. It was with Henry's encouragement that I went forward with this book project. We all owe Mr. Timman the deepest of gratitude as well for his efforts in securing a new official U.S. military veterans headstone for DeWolf's grave in Norwalk's Woodlawn Cemetery.

Of course, my book benefited enormously from the numerous published books, studies, and articles on Custer and the Little Big Horn from the long list of distinguished historians and authors who have paved that way over the years. Among those on that voluminous list, I extend my sincere appreciation to Paul Hedren, Paul Andrew Hutton, Sandy Barnard, Ron Nichols, and James Brust. Hedren and Hutton, both historians and authors of several

Acknowledgments

excellent works pertaining to the Little Big Horn and related topics in western history, took time from their extremely busy personal schedules (including during the course of writing their own newest books) to assist me in bringing this book to fruition. Hedren reviewed several drafts of my manuscript, offering critiques and important suggestions for revisions in several areas. Holding me to his high standards of historical scholarship in several areas saved me from what would have been some very embarrassing inadvertent errors. In addition to his unselfish sharing of his expertise concerning the 1876 campaign, the Little Big Horn, and the Plains Indian wars, his encouragement to me for this project has been a great inspiration. Likewise, Paul Hutton reviewed portions of the manuscript and graciously contributed the foreword to this volume. Ron Nichols and Sandy Barnard, also author-historians of the Little Big Horn story, have always been very kind to me during my visits with them at their annual book fair in Hardin, Montana, as well as in our occasional correspondence. I am indebted to Mr. Nichols for his kind permission to reprint two maps from his excellent biography of Major Marcus Reno, *In Custer's Shadow*. I also thank him and Mr. Michael O'Keefe of the Custer Battlefield Historical and Museum Association for their permission to quote information from *Men with Custer*, the immensely helpful and updated volume of biographies of the Seventh Cavalry soldiers and other combatants involved in the Little Big Horn expedition that Mr. Nichols edited and which was published by that organization. I also am grateful to Little Big Horn author-historian Dr. James Brust, who kindly offered his expertise and critique of the earliest draft of the manuscript, which was extremely helpful. Both he and Mr. Barnard continually offered their support and encouragement for my project.

Additionally, I also extend my sincere appreciation to another distinguished historian, Keith Widder, my longtime friend and colleague. Dr. Widder, former curator of history at Colonial Michilimackinac for the Mackinac State Historic Parks, former senior editor for the Michigan State University Press (now retired), and author of numerous books and articles on Mackinac's military and colonial history, reviewed an early draft of the manuscript. He shared his expertise in editing, style, and content as well as historical research presentation, all of which were very helpful suggestions.

Director Paula Radwonski and Dick Squires, researcher and docent, both of the Wyoming County Historical Society and Genealogical Library in Tunkhannock, Pennsylvania, near DeWolf's hometown of Mehoopany, went out of their way to make my very short "blast trip" to their wonderful library extremely productive and enjoyable. Moreover, I greatly appreciate their patience and willingness for further assistance in providing me with additional information during my multiple subsequent inquiries and requests to them. Likewise, John "Jack" Giblin, director (and a longtime friend and colleague to me), Rodney Foytik, research specialist, and Thomas Buffenbarger, library technician, all of the amazing U.S. Army Heritage and Education Center's museum and archives in Carlisle, Pennsylvania, were extremely helpful, as they extended their hospitality to me during my trip out and back to their facilities. Author-historians James Donovan, C. Lee Noyes, and Glen Swanson were helpful and offered encouragement for my book project. Other historians and personnel at various archives and museums were additionally helpful and more than generous with their assistance in requests for information or permission to use material from their institution's collections and with their time during the course of my research. These include Aaron Barth, director of the Fort Abraham Lincoln Foundation; Mary Carabin, director of the Firelands Historical Society, Norwalk, Ohio; Luisa Dispenzirie, museum curator, Fredericksburg and Spotsylvania National Military Park; Jack Eckert, public services librarian at the Harvard Medical School, Francis A. Countway Library of Medicine and Center for History of Medicine; the late Alice P. Gayley, Civil War author-historian of Pennsylvania; John Griffith, Vista, California; Coi Drummond-Gehrig, Digital Images Collection administrator, Denver Public Library; Scott Gipson, president, Caxton Press, Caldwell, Idaho; Steve Lent, museum historian, Bowman Museum, Prineville, Oregon; Jenny McElroy, reference librarian and permissions contact, Gale Family Library, Minnesota Historical Society; Keith Norman, Fort Seward Interpretive Center and *Jamestown Sun*, Jamestown, North Dakota; and the library staffs at the National Archives in Washington, D.C., Mackininaw City, MI Public Library and the Norwalk Public Library in Norwalk, Ohio.

I owe a very special thank you to my good friends Jeff Headley and Jim Trump. Both of these gentlemen were crazy enough to each twice endure long-distance driving trips with me out to the Little Big Horn, including putting up with all my incredible (but true) stories along the way. Jeff, who is the father-in-law of my youngest daughter, Stacey, is an excellent photographer, and several of his photos from our trips grace my den at home, providing great memories. I am grateful for that sharing of his talents. Thank you also to Jeff's wife, Pam, who allowed him to go on these trips with me and for her encouragement of my book project. Jim, a veteran reenactor and also the author of several serious historical novels, including one on the Seventh Cavalry's Company A at the Little Big Horn, has been most supportive of my book and has offered his encouragement. I also am grateful to Tim and Sheri DeWolf of Mehoopany, Pennsylvania, who kindly shared with this stranger the history of their family farms during my visit to the area. Tim is a third-generation grandson of James DeWolf's uncle Amasa Robinson DeWolf. Gene and Ann DeWolf Erb (Ann is a distant cousin of James DeWolf), authors of the insightful historical novel about James and Fannie DeWolf, *Voices in Our Souls*, provided a wonderful meal for me and Jim Trump on one of our trips back from the Little Big Horn, while unselfishly sharing some fruits of their research in their book during our visit to their home in Iowa.

Special thanks is also due to Charles (Charley) Warner of Milton, Pennsylvania, and my longtime friend Greg Teysen of Mackinaw City, Michigan. Charley, an experienced, serious collector and evaluator of original nineteenth-century images (daguerreotypes, ambrotypes, and tintype images), kindly shared his knowledge about these types of early photographs from his private collection, which includes a few Seventh Cavalry soldiers in civilian settings. Greg, who is a professional photographer and art gallery owner, unselfishly provided me with copies of various photographs during the planning stages of my book as well as his unwavering support of my book.

I would be remiss in not acknowledging the many other friends who provided encouragement, support, and assistance in various ways. These include Steve and Sandy Alexander, Rod Beattie, Chuck Brew, Mike Clark, Ros Cottrill, Mike Crane, Mike DeJonge, Brian Dunnigan, Mike and Kathy Fausell, Larry Gibson, Stan and Doris Graiewski, Matthew Headley, Michael Headley, Steve Held, Jaeger Held, Peggy and the late Everett Horn (Everett was responsible for rekindling my interest in the Little Big Horn story and introduced me to many of his friends and colleagues who live in Hardin, Montana, and near the battlefield), John Inatello, Brian Jaeschke, Jonnie Jonckowski, Andrew Kercher, James McGaughey, Andrew Miller, John Milteer, Daniel O'Connell, Julie O'Dell, John Pearson, Wesley Perry, Phil Porter, Pat Sulser, Tom Tocco, Terry Todish, Tim Todish, Harvey and Charlene Warren (former owners of the Fort Custer site), Phil Whitlow, and Craig Wilson.

I owe an enormous debt of gratitude to Charles "Chuck" Rankin, associate director and editor-in-chief of the University of Oklahoma Press, for taking a chance on publishing a book by a lesser-known historian and author such as me. His continued encouragement, sound advice, and expertise helped take this book to the next level, and his recommendations for some revisions of an early draft of the manuscript, particularly of the first chapter, were most insightful. Additionally, the professionalism, generosity, and teamwork approach that Chuck and his staff—including Sarah C. Smith, manuscript editor, and editorial assistants Brittney Berling and Bethany Mowry—have shown me during the publishing process have been of the highest level and another example of why their press is among the forefront of leading publishers of U.S. western history. I am also very grateful to freelance copyeditor Sally Boyington, whose skillful insight and expertise refined this author's too often overzealous and wordy prose into a readable and smooth-flowing narrative. A special thank you is also extended to the three anonymous reviewers for the University of Oklahoma Press of the earliest (unfinished) draft of my manuscript. Their insights and expertise in the Little Big Horn and Plains Indian wars, as well as their constructive criticism and suggestions for improvement and revisions to portions of the manuscript, were extremely helpful and are greatly appreciated.

As is true of most authors, I am fortunate to have the love and support of my family. My two beautiful and wonderful daughters, Stacey and Shannon, along with their husbands, my great sons-in-law, Michael and Luke, all have been encouraging to me, as always, during this long project. They have also helped their dad with computer issues and eased his frustration regarding the same when those situations arose periodically, forcing me to take a timeout during the game. Michael, who holds a master's degree in military history, reviewed portions of the manuscript and offered helpful suggestions in addition to his Internet and technology skills. Last but not least, I owe a great personal debt of thanks to my wife, Shirley, for her support and encouragement, once again, during another book-writing project. I appreciate her kindness (perhaps more than she may know) for her listening to my repeated recitations of various sections of the manuscript and offering her suggestions. She was also a most forgiving traveler as I dragged her some two hundred miles out of the way and eighteen hours driving in one day to tour and do some research at Fort Totten for the book on one of my trips out west. Yet while she has been unselfish in allowing me to take long-distance trips out to the Little Big Horn several times in addition to my numerous research trips, what I am most thankful for is her enduring love and friendship, for which I will forever be grateful.

A Surgeon with Custer at the Little Big Horn

ACHSAH CLAPP DEWOLF FISK
Achsah, mother of James DeWolf and her second husband Jonathan Fisk. They married after the death of their first spouses, his first wife being Achsah's sister, Sara "Sally" Clapp. Photographer, M. H. Eberhart, Wyoming, Iowa. *Courtesy of Suzi Saxman, Spicewood, Texas.*

INTRODUCTION

James Madison DeWolf of Mehoopany, Pennsylvania

JAMES MADISON DEWOLF was born on January 14, 1843, in Mehoopany, Pennsylvania, to Mark Anthony (1813–65) and Achsah Clapp DeWolf (1817–1907). He was the second-oldest surviving brother among their nine children, with only four living siblings during his early childhood years: a sister (Mary, b. 1845) and three brothers (Edwin A., 1840–after 1902; Erastus L., 1851–1917; and Archibald, 1857–after 1880). Another younger brother (William, b. 1844) died when James was three years old. Before James was born, three other siblings had also died in infancy (Amanda, 1837–37; Edward P., 1838–39; and Ormin A., 1840–43).[1]

James's father was a farmer, having followed in the family tradition of the DeWolfs who had migrated to the Mehoopany region from Connecticut. Mehoopany, a small farming town in present-day Wyoming County, Pennsylvania, was first settled in 1775 by several men from the Connecticut colony, some of whom eventually fought in the American Revolution, including the nearby infamous Wyoming Valley Massacre of 1778. Mehoopany was named for the creek that local Indians called Hopeny, meaning "place of the wild potatoes"; the creek is a tributary of the larger Susquehanna River. Farms around the original Mehoopany village were established as the area became more populated after the Revolutionary War and before the War of 1812. Additional nearby villages eventually formed among those farms within the original larger Windham Township.[2]

The DeWolf family's origins have been traced from some of the oldest aristocratic European family lines in Belgium, France, and

3

Livonia (of the Russian Baltic provinces).³ James Madison DeWolf's first documented American ancestor is recorded as Balthasar De Wolf (also spelled de Woolfe), of Lyme, Connecticut, who appears in the records in Hartford, Connecticut, in 1656 and from whom the New England families descended.⁴ From Balthasar and his wife, Alice, originated the main branches of the DeWolf family in America, primarily in Connecticut, Rhode Island, Pennsylvania, and Nova Scotia, although DeWolf descendants today are scattered all across the United States.

A tangential, though interesting, note is that the Rhode Island branch of the family, whose descendants were involved in the merchant shipping business of the old seaport town of Bristol, was also heavily involved in the slave-trading business. According to recent research and the publishing of a controversial book by family descendants, this Rhode Island faction has been found to be the largest slave-trading family in U.S. history from 1769 to 1820.⁵ However, there is no evidence that the Pennsylvania lineages of the DeWolf family ever held slaves, as that state had banned slavery in 1780.⁶ As such, it is not surprising that James Madison DeWolf would eventually join the Union cause with others from his state during the American Civil War. Moreover, his demeanor and personality, as evidenced by his later Big Horn expedition letters and diary, provide no evidence of racial undertones or beliefs.

There were two lines of the DeWolf family in Pennsylvania. The lineage from the Mehoopany area was originally established by James Madison DeWolf's great-grandfather Charles (1747–1814).⁷ Charles had married Elizabeth Walbridge of Connecticut, and they had seven children: five sons and two daughters. After originally residing in Brooklyn, Connecticut, Charles moved his family to Mehoopany circa 1780.⁸ Although he was a hatter by trade, his children and their families were farmers. Most of his sons married in Mehoopany, and many of his descendants live in that area and the surrounding towns today.⁹

Charles "The Hatter" DeWolf had large tracts of land in the outlying Mehoopany area, which extended west of the village proper. He trapped beaver for the pelts to be made into hats, which were eventually sent east. His sons inherited or were deeded his lands and remained in the Mehoopany and surrounding areas, establishing their own farms and families.[10] His oldest son, Amasa (1778–1850), who was the grandfather of James Madison DeWolf, married Diantha Robinson (1792–1853) of New York. Amasa had also initially been a hatter but later became a school and music teacher, owning a sawmill while also engaging in farming. Amasa and Diantha had eleven children, including five sons. Their first child was Mark Anthony, the aforementioned father of James Madison DeWolf, and he likewise continued in the family farming business.

Little is known about the early family life of James Madison DeWolf, other than that he had the usual conventional schooling of the era and helped out on the family farm. His true birthplace is known to be Mehoopany; however, the literature at times has erroneously listed the nearby villages Jenningsville or Forkston instead. This confusion is most likely inadvertent, due to the numerous DeWolf relatives living in these surrounding areas.[11] By 1850, there were six farms in the area of Mehoopany village (now Mehoopany Township), comprising about 756 acres of farmland, among the total of 895 farms in the county, which had 10,655 people according to the 1850 U.S. Census of Wyoming County.[12] Mehoopany Township has not changed much since DeWolf's childhood days, remaining a rural agricultural area with a population of 892 people, according to the 2010 U.S. Census of Wyoming County.

Civil War Years, 1861–1865

James seemed destined to continue in agriculture, helping his father in maintaining the family farm. However, with the outbreak of the Civil War, at the age of seventeen DeWolf was among the many Pennsylvanians who answered the call of the Union. He joined a local volunteer company "raised without authority" on April 23, 1861. The local newspaper noted that "on Saturday evening, a large and enthusiastic meeting convened at the Court House," and over the next few days, some forty men had enrolled as volunteers for the

DeWolf-Robinson and Pearson (Pierson)
Family Cemetery

DeWolf's father, grandfather, uncles, and other relatives are buried in this cemetery, located at the Mehoopany Township/Forkston Township line on SR 87 about two to three miles from Mehoopany village proper. His parents' farmland is in the background; Mehoopany Creek lies beyond that, along the tree line. *Author's collection.*

company, electing James B. Harding as their captain.[13] This began DeWolf's lifelong army career.

DeWolf's company went to Harrisburg, Pennsylvania, where he and his fellow volunteers were eventually assigned to the newly authorized Pennsylvania Reserve Corps. He was officially enlisted in the First Pennsylvania Light Artillery Volunteers, Battery A with the rank of private on May 29, 1861, by that company's commander, Captain Charles T. Campbell.[14] DeWolf's official Army Service Record provides information as to his physical stature and appearance—"5 feet, 7 1/2 inches in height, of fair complexion,

Introduction 7

Mehoopany, Pennsylvania, 2013
Hometown of James DeWolf. The building at the front left is believed to be where DeWolf's initial Civil War company was enlisted. *Author's collection.*

with grey eyes and sandy color hair"—and an initial occupation of "farmer/laborer."[15] There are also three existing photographs that are purported to be of DeWolf. Although some question remains concerning the provenance of each image, there are significant similarities of several features in the physical appearances to support a correlation between all three images. One is a tintype that most likely dates from his late teens, just before his early army service; the second shows DeWolf as a young man; and the third shows him in his later years.

The First Pennsylvania Light Artillery Volunteers, Battery A was actually part of the Forty-Third Regiment of Pennsylvania. In April 1861, Philadelphia citizen James Brady had called for a light artillery regiment, and around 1,300 volunteers responded

JAMES MADISON DEWOLF
Original tintype, previously unpublished. This was probably taken about the time he enlisted in the Civil War at age seventeen. Tintype attributed to Thomas Jefferson Trapp, photographer, Williamsport, Pennsylvania. *Author's collection.*

from companies already formed in several counties from the eastern portions of the state.[16] Because of the usual politics between the regular federal army commanders and the state administrators, more than half of the volunteers ended up joining regiments from surrounding states, while the eight remaining companies, including the Mehoopany company, were sent to Harrisburg. The regiment was clothed and equipped by the State of Pennsylvania, organized into batteries, and then ordered in August 1861 to report to Camp Berry, near the Capitol in Washington. The various batteries were then assigned to different corps and divisions of the federal army, with DeWolf's Battery A assigned to Brigadier General George A. McCall's Pennsylvania Reserve Division, Army of the Potomac.[17] A few months before Battery A's first engagement, Captain Campbell would be promoted to lieutenant colonel and be in command of the entire regiment, with Captain Hezekiah Easton replacing him as Company A commander.

Although his father remained a civilian at home, records show that James's older brother, Edwin, and his uncle Amasa also served in the

Civil War. Both men enlisted in the Fifty-First Pennsylvania Volunteer Regiment later that year; they were the only other members of James's direct family lineage who served in the war.[18] One of his other uncles, Lafayette Erastus DeWolf, was drafted along with nine other men from the nearby North Branch Township on September 30, 1863; however, Lafayette never ended up entering the army.[19]

During the years DeWolf served with the artillery company, his unit received high praises from superior officers for the gallant conduct of its men. Battery A was involved in several early battles of the Civil War in Virginia, which DeWolf listed on his personal summary of his army services. These included the Battle of Dranesville, December 20, 1861; Mechanicsville (Beaver Dam Creek), June 26, 1862; Gaines' Mill, June 27, 1862; and the Second Battle of Bull Run (Manassas), August 29 to 30, 1862.[20] At Dranesville, which was situated on the Leesburg pike between Leesburg and Alexandria, Battery A suffered no casualties. However, it inflicted heavy losses on the opposing Confederate batteries, so much that "the road was strewn with men and horse; two caissons, one of them blown up a limber, a gun-carriage wheel, a quantity of artillery ammunition, small arms, and an immense quantity of heavy clothing, blankets, &c.," as Brigadier General McCall wrote in his official report. He particularly noted the "evidence of the fine artillery practice of Easton's battery."[21] Their action at Dranesville also received commendation from Lieutenant Colonel Thomas L. Kane, commander of the rifle regiment known as "The Bucktails" or Kane's Rifles, the Thirteenth Pennsylvania Reserves in the Pennsylvania Volunteer Reserve Corps, which supported the battery there. In his report, Kane noted "the admirable conduct of Captain Easton and the brave artillerists with him, who served the guns of Battery A."[22]

The following summer, DeWolf's battery was involved in portions of the Seven Days Battles of the 1862 Peninsula Campaign. This series of battles was part of General George B. McClellan's unsuccessful attempt to take Richmond. Still under McCall's Pennsylvania Reserves division in the Army of the Potomac, Batteries A, B, and G of the First Pennsylvania Light Artillery Regiment were placed in the artillery section, along with the Fifth U.S. Artillery,

Battery C.²³ At Mechanicsville, Battery A initially covered the bridge at New Bridge, about one-half mile away. However, it was subsequently placed in front of Beaver Dam Creek, which emptied into the Chickahominy River over a two-hundred-yard-wide swampy area. Supported by the Eighth and Ninth Pennsylvania Reserve Regiments under Brigadier General John F. Reynolds and Brigadier General Truman Seymour, respectively, the battery blasted Confederate forces as they attempted to cross the swamp in front of the battlefield.²⁴ At Gaines' Mill the next day, Battery A was ordered to fall back and position itself on a hill near the Gaines' house, facing a dense forest. Despite a gallant defense, it was overwhelmed by a ferocious Confederate charge but was able to withdraw. Battery A suffered some losses, including the heroic death of Captain Easton and "their battery of four guns [12 pounders] and two caissons."²⁵

Battery A was reorganized shortly thereafter and received new guns in time to be engaged at the Second Battle of Bull Run (Manassas) at the end of the following month. By the time of this encounter, First Lieutenant John G. Simpson (from Franklin County, Pennsylvania) had succeeded the late Captain Easton as commanding officer of Battery A, and DeWolf had been promoted to corporal.²⁶ McClellan's recent threat to Richmond having been thwarted, this second Bull Run engagement marked the Confederate offensive campaign by Robert E. Lee and his Army of Northern Virginia against Major General John Pope's newly created Army of Virginia. After suffering a second defeat on the same battlefield as the year before, the Union army continued its withdrawal toward Washington. As part of the Third Corps of Pope's army, DeWolf's Battery A and its fellow Batteries B and G were again placed with the Fifth U.S. Artillery, Battery C, in the artillery contingent of General Reynold's Reserves section under the overall command of Captain Dunbar R. Ransom.²⁷

The Pennsylvania batteries took part in the three days of intense fighting at this second Manassas encounter, particularly on the final day. Battery A was among the huge massing of forty guns on Dogan Ridge when Reynold's Reserves were ordered there as the climactic portion of the battle began to unfold.²⁸ Late in the day, as the Union

DOGAN RIDGE AT BULL RUN NATIONAL BATTLEFIELD
Battery A was among a huge massing of forty guns on this ridge in Brigadier General John Reynold's Reserves section on the last day of the Second Battle of Bull Run (Manassas) on August 30, 1862. DeWolf was wounded here. *Author's collection.*

artillery continued its heavy bombardment of the surging Confederate forces, DeWolf was wounded in the right arm (specifically, the ulna). The extent of his injury is described in detail in his eventual invalid army pension certificate: "while in the service aforesaid, and in the line of his duty, [DeWolf] was wounded by a Musket or rifle ball, in the 'Battle of Bull Run' on the 30th day of August 1862; about 5 o'clock PM; the said ball entering the right arm on the front & about 3 inches lower than the elbow & then transversing directly through the arm after passing diagonally through about 5 inches of the arm there. That he was admitted a Patient into Finley Hospital Washington DC on the 1st day of September 1862."[29]

DeWolf spent the next two months recovering from his injury at Finley Hospital, one of the larger war hospitals in the Washington area during the Civil War.[30] While there he received a medical discharge from the army on October 29, 1862, due to "necrosis of ulna from gunshot wound, degree of disability one third."[31] Being "incapacitated from field service," he served as a contract nurse at Finley over the next year. It was during this time that he most likely acquired his interest in the medical field before going on to serve as a hospital steward in his later army service. DeWolf also applied for and was granted an invalid army pension for disability in 1863.[32] Upon improving over the next several months and "partially regaining the use of his arm," however, he resigned his pension on September 21, 1864.[33] Thereafter, he reenlisted in Company A of the First Pennsylvania Light Artillery Volunteers as a private, joining the battery in late March of 1865. He participated with his regiment in the April 3 taking of Richmond, and the battery was subsequently involved in dismantling the city's Confederate defenses over the next few months.[34]

DeWolf's return to active service suggests that his ulnar wound was not as serious as it could have been, both because he was allowed to reenlist in his regiment and because he never mentioned it in his later letters or in his diary of the Little Big Horn campaign. Many soldiers who sustained forearm injuries during the Civil War that were initially perceived as severe were able to function quite well, returning to either active service or daily activities requiring use of the injured limb in later life. Many documented cases attest to the capability of some of the better army surgeons, but because the more refined aspects of surgery were in their infancy, amputation was more often the standard treatment at the time.[35]

The end of the Civil War was in process after the surrender of the Confederate Army of Northern Virginia at Appomattox Court House on April 9, 1865. The jubilation surrounding James's eventual homecoming was cut short, however, by his father's death in Mehoopany on May 3, 1865, a month before James's discharge from Battery A on June 13.[36] Mark Anthony was buried in the DeWolf-Robinson/Pearson family cemetery on their farmland beside the road (present-day State Route 87) between the village of Mehoopany and Forkston at the township line. James most likely stayed on at the family farm during that summer to help his mother and siblings. At some point he decided that a return to civilian life as a farmer was not his calling, however, and that a career in the army as a medical steward was. Perhaps stimulated to do so by his injury and subsequent experience as an army nurse during the recent war, he joined the regular U.S. Army later that fall.

On August 28, 1872, his mother, Achsah, married one of the local neighboring farmers, Jonathan Fisk, whose farm was just north of James's uncle Amasa's farm.[37] Jonathan's first wife, Sara "Sally" Clapp (d. 1872), was Achsah's sister. While some of the family's original farmland was passed on to her other children, Achsah eventually sold the remainder to several Robinson family members and other local farmers.[38] She and Fisk moved to Wyoming, Iowa (in Jones County), by 1882, sometime after James died at the Little Big Horn. This would partly account for why she is not buried with her first husband in the aforementioned DeWolf-Robinson/Pearson family cemetery.[39] In 1890, Achsah applied for James's army pension.[40] After Jonathan's death in 1896, she returned to Pennsylvania to live with her oldest son, Edwin, and his family in Wyoming County, where she died in 1907. She is buried in Wyoming Cemetery.[41]

Postwar Years, 1865–1873

At twenty-one years old, having decided to leave his family and native Pennsylvania, DeWolf enlisted in the regular army's Fourteenth U.S. Infantry, Second Battalion, Company E, on October 5, 1865 in New York City, New York.[42] During and after the Civil War, U.S. expansion continued along the Bozeman Trail through Wyoming to Montana, along the Oregon Trail in the Northwest to Idaho and Oregon, and from California as well. This progressive influx of white settlers brought further confrontations with the region's various Indian tribes. These conflicts included the Snake

CAMP LYON, IDAHO TERRITORY, 1866
Courtesy of Caxton Press, from Mike Hanley, Owyhee Trails
(Caldwell, Idaho: Caxton Press, 1973), 115.

War (1864–68) in southeastern Oregon and southwestern Idaho, involving the Northern Paiute, Shoshone, and Bannock tribes living along the Snake River. DeWolf was assigned to that western region with his infantry unit.[43]

He first served at Fort Vancouver, Washington Territory (present-day Oregon), from December 1865 until June 19, 1866.[44] His duties were initially as a hospital attendant (regular company privates serving as nurses or cooks), although he was promoted to hospital steward on May 17, 1866.[45] He was transferred to Fort Boise, Idaho Territory, in July of that year,[46] serving "with an expedition against Indians" during his three-month stint there.[47] DeWolf was then ordered to Oregon Territory at Camp Lyon, where he arrived on October 21, 1866.[48] Established on June 27, 1865, Camp Lyon was

Introduction 15

among several U.S. military forts and camps built to protect settlers, miners, lumbermen, and stagecoach roads from Indians.[49] DeWolf was the lone "medical" personnel at the small, crude, and isolated post (an atypical occurrence) when he was ordered to "take charge of the Hospital Department" at Camp Lyon and to "enter upon his duties at once" by the post commandant, Captain James C. Hunt of the Fourteenth Infantry.[50] He served at Camp Lyon for the next two years and reenlisted there in the Fourteenth Infantry for another three years on October 5, 1868, the same day he was discharged from his initial 1865 three-year enlistment.[51] Whether he was involved in any further military actions during the Snake War is unknown, but it seems unlikely, because DeWolf never mentioned such activity in his surviving correspondence. He appears to have served only in his hospital steward duties.

After serving the ensuing winter months at Camp Lyon, DeWolf was ordered "without delay" to Camp Warner, Oregon Territory, where he arrived on June 5, 1869, and served for the next five years.[52] Located at Honey Creek in south-central Oregon, Camp Warner was the second post of the same name built in 1867 during the Snake War. It had been moved from its original site some thirty-five miles away and was used as a supply depot and the headquarters of Lieutenant Colonel George Crook for the last portion of the war. While the soldiers referred to it as Fort Warner, the U.S. Army never actually designated it as a fort, and it is known officially as the New (or Second) Camp Warner.[53]

During his time at Camp Warner, DeWolf visited California in the course of his hospital duties. In May 1871, he was ordered to pick up a Private William Perkins of Company I, Twenty-Third Infantry, at the Insane Asylum in Stockton and turn him over to the medical director in San Francisco at the Military Headquarters, Division of the Pacific/Department of California.[54] In a quick communique to Lieutenant F. L. Dodge, the post adjutant at Camp Warner, DeWolf also requested in advance a "three day delay in his arrival at Stockton, California for the purpose of Visiting Friends in San Francisco."[55] Just who these friends were, how DeWolf knew them, or whether his request was granted is not known. Although not exactly a vacation for DeWolf, it most likely was a welcome interruption of the monotonous routine of his hospital duties at Camp Warner. It was also a chance to see another part of the country. Upon his eventual return to the post, DeWolf served as hospital steward for the next two years.[56]

At Camp Warner, DeWolf met a young woman who became the love of his life. Frances or Fannie J. Downing was born in 1852 at Norwalk, Ohio (just south of Sandusky), to Thomas (1814–75) and Elvira (c. 1817–58) Downing. Her legal name is recorded on documents as "Fannie," but she always signed her name as "Fanny." Her parents were farmers, as were most of the residents in that region of north-central Ohio.[57] One of three siblings, Fannie had a natural sister and eventually a stepbrother, Frederick. Her older sister, Emma, married twenty-three-year-old David T. Hall (1832–1906), a Norwalk resident, in 1856 at the age of sixteen. Hall later served in the 123rd Ohio Volunteer Infantry during the Civil War and eventually became an insurance agent and fireman in Norwalk.[58] Fannie would remain close to her sister and brother-in-law throughout her life.

Not much is known about Fannie's early years. Her mother died on October 6, 1858, when Fannie was about six years old. Local records show that her father, Thomas, married Nancy Wadsworth at Norwalk on October 4 of the following year.[59] The U.S. Census of 1860 regarding Norwalk records Fannie and her new six-month-old stepbrother, Frederick, as dependents in the Downing household.[60] By 1870, she had completed her schooling and became a schoolteacher.[61] Apparently, her stepmother had not treated her well while she was growing up, and in her search for a fresh beginning, Fannie took a job homeschooling the three children of a widowed rancher in Oregon.[62] Boarding at his home proved less than satisfactory, though, as the rancher made known his personal intentions of marrying her.

Luckily, Fannie became acquainted with James DeWolf during a couple of monthly trips to the trader's post at Camp Warner to obtain provisions for the ranch. The two fell in love and were soon married at Camp Warner on October 3, 1871, by post chaplain

NEW CAMP WARNER, OREGON, C. 1870
Courtesy of A. R. Bowman Museum, Crook County Historical Society, Prineville, Oregon, no. 6106K.

Reverend M. J. Kelly.[63] Shortly thereafter, she was appointed a hospital matron at the post. Fannie DeWolf was apparently the type of woman who could adapt and survive life in the military. As was the case with all the other army wives she would meet during her life with James, however, she was subject to occasional fears and anxieties that the hardships of the West presented. That their marriage was perhaps the closest to an almost-perfect consummate union as can ever be is evident by James's surviving letters to her. Those writings reveal his consoling encouragement in the occasional times of melancholy while she awaited his return from the Little Big Horn expedition.

The newlywed couple served in the hospital department at Camp Warner for the next two years. During this time, James became

FANNIE DOWNING DEWOLF
Fannie, the wife of James DeWolf *(seated at right),* with her sister, Emma Downing *(standing),* and brother, Fred Downing *(seated at left). Courtesy of Firelands Historical Society, Norwalk, Ohio.*

so interested in the medical profession that he decided to pursue a career as physician. In May 1872, he petitioned the surgeon general: "I have prepared myself for the study of Medicine as far as practicable without the benefit of medical Lectures and I desire, if possible to be stationed so that I may attend these lectures without interfering with my duties as Hospital Steward. I am willing to refund to the United States the cost of my transportation, should that be a barrier to the change of station."[64]

Although he lacked any previous formal higher education, his request was granted, and he was admitted to Harvard Medical School. Having acquired the physical skills and a good medical background from his hospital steward duties during the past six years, DeWolf was also well liked by his superior officers, all factors that supported his requests. He was highly recommended by the acting assistant surgeon, C. W. Knight, with whom he worked at Camp Warner, who wrote a letter of recommendation stating, "I have known Hosp. Steward James M. DeWolf since October 1868, and his character has been most excellent both officially and morally. He has ever been diligent and attentive, is very accurate in his accounts, and a thoroughly temperate man. One of his objects in making the request is to enable him to attend medical lectures after office hours, for which I consider him thoroughly prepared."[65]

In March 1873, DeWolf received a letter from Assistant Surgeon General C. H. Crane of the War Department relating, "In view of your long service in the Army as Hospital Steward, you are requested to inform this office whether you desire a change from your present station to one in the Department of the East or Department of the Lakes." Crane added that he could "not promise an assignment to any particular post in either of those Departments." Nonetheless, DeWolf's petition to the army for a transfer to the Department of the East in New York City, and then eventually to Watertown Arsenal in Boston so that he could concurrently attend classes at Harvard, was granted in April 1873.[66]

Medical School Years, 1873–1875

James and Fannie moved to Watertown in September 1873, residing at the arsenal. He enrolled in medical school classes while continuing his duties on active service as a hospital steward at the arsenal, which was not far from campus.[67] At that time, Harvard Medical School consisted of a single building on campus at North Grove Street, in use from 1847 to 1883. The first floor housed rooms attached to the laboratory as well as the janitor's apartments, while the second floor held two large lecture rooms, the chemical laboratory, and the library. A third floor housed the theatre used for formal lectures and professors' and demonstrators' rooms. The dissecting room was in a separate hall attached to the main building. The Grove Street Building also housed the Warren Anatomical Museum, named for Dr. John Collins Warren (1778–1856), a retired teacher who had donated over one thousand specimen anatomical collections to Harvard.[68] The university replaced the medical school building with a larger, expanded structure of "modern" design in 1883.

Until 1871, medical school training in the United States consisted of a two-year program, which seems strange in comparison to today's standard four-year medical degree program. However, Harvard was one of the first universities to advocate "higher standards of preliminary [medical] education with concentration on the sciences," and as a result, the training of physicians and surgeons at its medical school was increased to a three-year program, instituted that same year.[69] Unlike most conventional medical students, who lacked practical experience, DeWolf was able to use his advanced didactic experience in treating patients out in the field as an army hospital steward to his advantage. He graduated in two years instead of three, the medical school administrators making an exception to the extra year requirement since he did exceptionally well and had also taken extra classes.

At the time of DeWolf's matriculation, the medical school had 170 students.[70] While some researchers have stated that DeWolf was not listed among the students, written documentation confirms that he was a student.[71] On February 17, 1875, the dean of Harvard Medical School, Calvin Ellis, certified "that J. M. DeWolf has

Introduction 21

HARVARD MEDICAL SCHOOL BUILDING, C. 1878
DeWolf attended medical school classes here.
Author's collection.

passed the required examination in the medical school of Harvard University and will receive his degree at the usual time in June." Subsequently, R. H. Fitz, the secretary of the medical school, noted on June 12 that "James M. DeWolf has been attending the course of Surgery at this school, as open to graduates in medicine, during the present term." Finally, the professor of clinical surgery, David W. Cheever, noted in a letter to the surgeon general, "I have pleasure in stating that I have known Mr. James M. DeWolf as a good and persevering student of medicine and surgery; and that he has paid special attention to the latter branch having taken on extra course of instruction in Superficial Anatomy and Operative surgery, as a graduate, besides all the usual and required instruction in the medical school of Harvard University."[72]

JAMES MADISON DEWOLF
This photograph of DeWolf was probably taken after his Civil War years. Year and photographer unknown. *Courtesy of Firelands Historical Society, Norwalk, Ohio.*

That DeWolf handled a full-time job as hospital steward at the arsenal while attending classes and studying is no small feat. Much like today, medical school training in the 1870s consisted of both formal lecture classes and time spent in group observations of autopsies and dissections performed by medical school professors and surgeons. DeWolf also enrolled in a separate graduate class that provided actual direct individual experience in anatomical surgery and dissection. This additional study, along with his previous experience as a hospital steward on the frontier during the preceding years, undoubtedly helped James successfully complete the rigorous Harvard curriculum. DeWolf passed his final examinations at the Grove Street Building on February 9, 1875, and was awarded his graduate medical degree from Harvard Medical School in June.

Although busy with his duties at the arsenal and medical school, during the two years he and Fannie spent in the Cambridge and Watertown area, DeWolf became a Freemason and joined the Pequossette Lodge. The lodge was one of two masonic lodges in Watertown, the other being the Bethesda Lodge.[73] DeWolf attended regularly and became a well-respected member of the lodge, as evidenced by the comforting letter of condolence and high praise of her husband that Fannie received shortly after the lodge learned of his death at the Little Big Horn.[74]

After his graduation from Harvard, DeWolf sought to obtain a commission as a medical officer in the army. Three months prior to his graduation, he petitioned the surgeon general at the War Department in Washington, D.C., inquiring about the possibility of an exemption to sit before the Army Medical Examination Board. At age thirty-two, he was considered too old to officially qualify for potential service as a military physician. U.S. Army policy at that time limited the top age of candidates to twenty-eight, believing that younger men were more fit for the rigorous demands of military medicine.[75] One can only imagine DeWolf's elation when he read the March 13 letter from the Surgeon General's Office informing him, "[I]n view of your service in the Army, the limit of age in your case will be extended."[76] DeWolf and Fannie made a trip back to his Pennsylvania home after his graduation and completion of the short-term graduate surgical course. He received a letter from the assistant surgeon general of the U.S. Army, C. H. Crane, on August 28, 1875, addressed to him at Forkston, inviting DeWolf to appear before the Army Medical Examination Board on October 4 "for the examination of candidates for appointment in the Medical Staff of the U.S. Army" in session in New York City.[77] Apparently confident that he would be successful in his appearance before the examining board, DeWolf resigned his position as hospital steward at the Watertown Arsenal and was discharged from the army on September 18, 1875.[78]

DeWolf failed the army examination, but that was not uncommon: nearly three of every four applicants failed. Nor does it indicate that DeWolf was incompetent or not qualified to serve as an army surgeon. Although one historian has suggested that the Harvard Medical School examinations were apparently not as difficult as the army medical board examinations, this is unlikely in DeWolf's situation. Administrators at Harvard Medical School, led by faculty member Professor James C. White and President Charles William Eliot, had ardently proposed and instituted significant educational changes in the curriculum in 1871, including stringent, tougher examinations, in addition to the aforementioned increase to the three-year course study required for a degree.[79] Even Lieutenant George Lord, who, like DeWolf, died at the Little Big Horn, nearly failed his own army medical board examination. Of the four candidates who sat in front of the examining board at the same time as Lord, two withdrew and the third failed. While Lord passed, the board recommended that he be "directed to devote special attention to physics, physiology and chemistry, in which branches his examination was not fully satisfactory."[80] Not unlike medical board exams today, there was often much esoteric information that, while appropriate and essential during the formal medical school years of training, had no bearing on or effect for the practice of medicine in the military field or with the general public. The ability to recite the details of the physiology of bile, which was one of Lord's oral exam questions, certainly has no relevance for an army surgeon performing an amputation in the field.[81] Some administrators have summarized this general situation and held to the dictum that "neither in civil or military practice . . . any more than in any other avocations in life, is scholarship the measure of ability."[82] By this measure, both Lord and DeWolf demonstrated more than adequate performance and knowledge of their surgical skills in their actual military field duties and were anything but incompetent.

An Army Contract Physician

While undoubtedly disappointed by his failure of the army medical board examination, DeWolf remained steadfast in his desire to continue serving the army. He quickly petitioned the Surgeon General's Office to request a position as a civilian contract physician. This was granted on October 16, 1875, when he received a reply from Assistant Surgeon General Crane informing him, "In reply to your communication of the 12th Instant, Inclose herewith a contract (in duplicate) for duty in the Department of Dakota, which you will please sign and return with copies to this office, together with the Oath of Office duly executed."[83]

(Form 24.)

Contract with a Private Physician.

This contract, entered into this __23rd__ day of __October__, 1875, at __Forkston__ in the State of __Pennsylvania__, between __the Surgeon General__, of the United States Army, and Dr. __James M. DeWolf__, of __Forkston__, in the State of __Pennsylvania__ witnesseth; that for the consideration hereinafter mentioned the said Dr. __DeWolf__ promises and agrees to perform the duties of a medical officer, agreeably to Army Regulations, __in the Dept of Dakota__ [or elsewhere (1°),] [and to furnish the proper medicines, (2°)]; and the said __Surgeon General__ promises and agrees, on behalf of the United States, to pay, or cause to be paid, to the said Dr. __DeWolf__, the sum of __One hundred__ dollars for each and every month he shall continue to perform the services above stated; [and if he serve west of the Mississippi River, or at a small-pox hospital, or on quarantine duty, or with troops on marches or on transports, he shall receive one hundred and twenty-five dollars per month (3°)]. He shall also receive the fuel and quarters of an Assistant Surgeon of the rank of First Lieutenant, and actual traveling expenses when traveling under orders and not with troops; and when serving west of the Mississippi River he shall receive one daily ration in kind. [And if the said Dr. _____ shall be required to furnish his medicines, he shall be compensated therefor at the rate of _____ per cent, on his monthly pay, to be determined by the Surgeon General, (4°)]. And it is furthermore agreed, that at the expiration of his term of service, the said Dr. __DeWolf__ shall receive actual traveling expenses to the place of making the contract; provided said contract is not annulled for misconduct or neglect of duty, in which case no traveling expenses will be furnished. All of which shall be his full compensation, and in lieu of all allowances and emoluments. This contract to continue at least __One year__ if not sooner determined by the General commanding the Military Division or Department, the Medical Director, or the Surgeon General.

In this contract (1°) (2°) (3°) (4°) have been stricken out.

Signed, sealed and delivered in the presence of

__Jno. Wilson__

__For the Surgeon General__
__C. H. Crane__ (SEAL)
__asst Surgeon General U.S. Army__

__J. M. DeWolf, M.D.__ (SEAL)

NOTE 1.—Accounts arising under this contract will be paid by the Pay Department. Those clauses in [] not applicable to this contract shall be stricken out before signature and so noted.
NOTE 2.—Contracts with private physicians, made by the Surgeon General or the Medical Director of a Department, will be annulled only by the direction of those officers, or by that of the Commanding General of a Military Division or Department. (General orders, No. 3, War Department, Adjutant General's Office, Washington, D. C., January 21, 1862.)

DeWolf's U.S. Army contract
Courtesy of the National Park Service, Little Bighorn Battlefield National Monument (LIBI_00007_04889), "Dr. DeWolfe's Contract as Army Contract Physician, 10/23/1875."

ORIGINAL FORT TOTTEN SURGEONS' QUARTERS
Surgeons' quarters at Fort Totten, Devil's Lake, Dakota Territory (now North Dakota). Doctor DeWolf and his wife, Fannie, lived in this building during their time at the fort. *Author's collection.*

A candidate's lack of endorsement by the military examining board did not indicate that he was unqualified to serve in the profession. In fact, as there was still a shortage of physicians, the army utilized civilian physicians, including many who had been denied by the military examining boards and who were thus signed on as contract physicians.[84] On the surface, this might appear as a strange dichotomy, implying that the army considered those physicians who did not pass the military board examination good enough to be contract surgeons but not good enough to serve as "commissioned" surgeons with the same position and responsibilities. These contract surgeons were given the title of acting assistant surgeon and were considered part of the official army medical staff at any post to which they were assigned. The only practical difference was that by regulations, army contract physicians were not entitled to wear army uniforms. The standard contract offered a pay rate of $100 per month, unless the physician was assigned to serve west of the Mississippi River or served in the field during a time of war, for which the pay was $125 per month. DeWolf's contract, assigning him to the "Dept. of Dakota" and thus qualifying him for the higher monthly pay rate, became effective as of October 23 "for at least one year." It also contained the standard stipulations that he was to "receive . . . the fuel and quarters of an Assistant Surgeon of the rank of First Lieutenant, and actual traveling expenses when traveling under orders and not with troops."[85]

During this time, DeWolf and his wife appear to have resided in his hometown area of Mehoopany and Forkston, presumably staying with his mother and siblings. The fact that all of his correspondence with the War Department was addressed to him at the Forkston area supports this theory. Also, DeWolf's notebook and diary do not start at the beginning of the 1876 expedition in March of that year but rather in October 1875. The first eight pages contain entries documenting his successful treatment of his first civilian patients as a new physician and surgeon, all of whom appear to be residents of the Forkston/Mehoopany area. The conditions he treated included a urinary tract irritation problem, a headache, and a febrile episode; he also delivered a baby.[86]

Soon after they received confirmation from the Adjutant General's Office that his contract surgeon arrangements were complete, James and Fannie traveled to the Department of Dakota's Headquarters at St. Paul, Minnesota. Whether they made a quick stop in Norwalk to visit Fannie's sister and brother-in-law, Emma and David Hall, is unknown, although it seems reasonable that they would have done so. After reporting to headquarters on November 5, 1875, DeWolf received orders from the commanding administrative staff there, assigning him to duty as acting assistant surgeon at Fort Totten, Dakota Territory.[87] The DeWolfs arrived at Fort Totten late on the evening of November 14, 1875, "in the midst of a driving snow storm having travelled all the way from Fargo D.T. by team a most unpleasant journey at this season of the year," as the post surgeon, Doctor James Ferguson, noted in his log.[88] During DeWolf's nearly four-month stay at the post, Doctor Ferguson's entries into the official Fort Totten medical log relate the various common conditions that he and DeWolf encountered during the winter, including "3 cases of acute diarrhea, 1 of chronic dysentery, one of constitutional syphilis, [and] one of terminal tubercular dissemination of the lungs" along with various "contusions and abscesses."[89] The freezing deaths of two drunken soldiers who had become disoriented and were lost in blizzard conditions also gave witness to the perils of the harsh Dakota winters.[90]

There is a gap in DeWolf's diary for the next four months after he left Pennsylvania, and he did not resume writing again until the beginning of the 1876 campaign in early March. However, DeWolf's later letters to his beloved wife, supplementing his own diary entries on the eventual Little Big Horn expedition, provide an interesting glimpse of some of the people he and Fannie came to know at Fort Totten. The DeWolfs settled in for the winter of 1875–76 at this remote post in northeastern Dakota Territory for the next phase of their life together, which, unfortunately, would be the last.

CHAPTER I

Fort Seward, D.T.
MARCH 10 TO APRIL 14, 1876

"[S]UCH A TRIP IS LIKE PLACING ONE ON THE BRINK
OF A PRECIPICE & GIVING HIM A PUSH"
[BUT]
"WE HAVE A JOLLY TIME AND ARE HAVING
AS NICE A TIME AS WE COULD ANYWHERE EXCEPT AT HOME."
Doctor James DeWolf,
letters of March 14 and March 16

AT ITS ONSET, the western U.S. military campaign of 1876 was a culmination of events from the immediate preceding years. After the Civil War, westward expansion of settlers increased, with further encroachment on Indian tribal lands. The Fort Laramie Treaty of 1868 had been signed after the conclusion of Red Cloud's War (1866–68), which had occurred as a result of transgression on Sioux (Lakota) lands in the Powder River region, as well as the construction of the Union Pacific railroad through Wyoming Territory. Among the provisions of this treaty was the stipulation that the U.S. government would not allow whites to settle on the Indian lands encompassed by the Great Sioux Reservation.[1] This new reservation comprised some 25 million acres of land for the various Sioux bands in Dakota Territory and spanned lands west of the Missouri River, including the Black Hills, between the forty-sixth and forty-third parallels of north latitude (the latter being at the northern border of Nebraska). The treaty also permitted those Sioux bands to hunt an unceded area "east of the summits of the Bighorn Mountains" in Wyoming and Montana Territories and "country north of the North Platte River" in Wyoming Territory and Nebraska during the peoples' expected transformation from hunters to agriculturalists, in compensation for their removal to the reservation. To carry out this process of "civilizing the Indians," the federal government established agencies on the reservation to set up schools to educate the children; provide food, clothing, and blankets; and encourage the spread of Christianity among the Lakotas.[2]

While some Lakota bands moved to their designated regions of the reservation, not all of the Sioux factions recognized the Fort Laramie Treaty, and many continued to both live and hunt in the unceded territory. Two prominent leaders among these nonreservation bands promoting defiance toward the federal government were Sitting Bull of the Hunkpapas and Crazy Horse of the Oglalas, neither of whom signed the 1868 treaty. Over the next five years, whites' disregard for the treaty contributed mightily to its eventual nonenforcement by the government. Among many transgressions, as perceived by the Sioux, was the encroachment of Northern Pacific railroad, despite the treaty stipulation permitting the peaceful construction of any railroad not passing over their reservation.[3] This was due in part to the northern boundary of the reservation not being specifically defined, although it was later assumed to be the Yellowstone River. By the early 1870s, Northern Pacific had begun construction of its railroad from Duluth, Minnesota, across northern Dakota Territory to Bismarck. However, further westward expansion by Northern Pacific came to an abrupt halt at Bismarck in 1873 because of a lack of funding that year, partly a result of the severe national economic calamity known as the Panic of 1873.[4]

During the following year, a Black Hills expedition ordered by the government to explore that region and locate a new military post incidentally discovered gold, triggering a mad rush by white prospectors that further enraged the Indians.[5] This expedition was led by Lieutenant Colonel George Armstrong Custer. Already famous for his many Civil War cavalry exploits, including his promotion to the rank of brigadier general and then major general with the U.S.

LIEUTENANT COLONEL
GEORGE ARMSTRONG
CUSTER
*U.S. Army Heritage and
Education Center, Carlisle,
Pennsylvania.*

Volunteers, Custer had gained further notoriety after his assignment to assist troops fighting Indians during the postwar western expansion.[6] The flamboyant officer and his Seventh U.S. Cavalry had also taken part in Colonel David S. Stanley's military escort during the previous year's Northern Pacific Railroad survey expedition along the Yellowstone River.

In addition to the invasion of their unceded lands, many bands occupying the Great Sioux Reservation had legitimate complaints of poor treatment, mismanagement of resources and supplies, food shortages, and corrupt Indian agents, the latter of whom were under the auspices of the Department of the Interior.[7] Then, in September 1875, the federal government failed in its attempt to purchase the Black Hills, which by then had been overrun with miners in the early stages of the gold rush, from the Lakotas.[8] In response to these developments, the Department of the Interior issued an ultimatum to the Sioux living in the unceded areas beyond the Black Hills: return to the reservation by January 31, 1876, or be labeled as hostile and face war and a forced return. This directive emerged from a

Brigadier General
Alfred H. Terry
Library of Congress, Prints and Photographs Division, LG-DIG-cwpbh-00588.

private meeting held at the White House on November 3, 1875, which included President Ulysses S. Grant; his new secretary of the interior, Zachariah Chandler; Lieutenant General Philip H. Sheridan, commander of the U.S. Army's Division of the Missouri; Secretary of War William W. Belknap; and Brigadier General George Crook, commander of the Army's Department of the Platte. General William T. Sherman, commander of the entire U.S. Army, was not in attendance, in part because of his long-standing political feuding with Belknap. Those who were in attendance agreed to a course of war.[9]

Although Sherman was the army's commander, Sheridan oversaw operations against the Indians, since the majority of the action would take place within his Division of the Missouri. From November 1875 to February 1876, Sheridan and his department commanders, Brigadier General Alfred H. Terry and Crook, devised a campaign to locate the roaming bands of Indians living outside the reservation and force their return.[10] The overall concept was for forces of converging columns to confront the Sioux. One column, to be commanded by Crook, would be formed of troops from posts in his

Department of the Platte in Wyoming Territory and Nebraska. A column of troops from Dakota Territory, which Terry had initially intended Custer to lead, were to move westward from Fort Abraham Lincoln. Colonel John Gibbon of the Seventh Infantry, commander of the District of Montana, was to lead a column of troops from the Montana posts. Although these columns were not necessarily intended to act in concert with one another, their simultaneous actions were expected to achieve the intended objectives. Having completed plans for the expeditions in the three months after President Grant's private meeting, Sheridan received authorization to commence the campaign on February 7, 1876.[11] As the army's plan for the 1876 campaign was set in motion, Doctor James DeWolf found himself involved.

While Sheridan and the other commanders planned their offensive, DeWolf had attended to his duties as acting assistant surgeon at Fort Totten. He and Fannie had settled in the cozy confines of the surgeon's quarters, which they shared with Doctor Ferguson and his wife, at the isolated and snowbound post on the shores of Devil's Lake. Outside of his hospital duties, James and Fannie were welcomed into the elite social class of the officers at the fort, becoming good friends with the Fergusons and with the fort's commandant, Lieutenant Colonel Lewis Cass Hunt (breveted a brigadier general for his services during the Civil War), and his wife. To pass the long, cold winter evenings, the officers and their wives engaged in various social activities commonly held at army posts during the Victorian era, such as card game clubs and performances at the Fort Totten post theatre. DeWolf's descriptions of these weekly gatherings in his later letters to Fannie provide an interesting and often entertaining glimpse of the army's upper social class. However, this winter routine was abruptly interrupted on March 2, 1876, when DeWolf received Special Order No. 27 from General Terry, ordering him to accompany the Seventh Cavalry Companies E and L from Fort Totten to Fort Abraham Lincoln and "report in person" to Custer. Although slightly melancholy about leaving his wife and the comfortable confines of Fort Totten, DeWolf prepared for the start of what would become his last campaign.[12]

The start of the 1876 operations was hampered and delayed by the severe weather conditions of the late winter season, even though it had been purposely planned for that time in an attempt to surprise the Indians in their winter camps. General Crook's Wyoming Column was the first to actually begin operations in the field, on March 1, and the first to engage in fighting with the Indians. This initial column under Crook, one of two commanded by him early in the campaign, included soldiers of the Second Cavalry, Third Cavalry, and Fourth Infantry (troops from the Ninth Infantry would be added during his second deployment later that spring).[13]

While Crook supervised this Big Horn expedition, as it was designated, the actual field command of the troops was delegated to Colonel Joseph Reynolds of the Third Cavalry. Two weeks into the expedition, Reynolds and troops of the Second and Third Cavalry attacked an Indian village discovered on the Powder River in Montana Territory. This was actually a winter camp of the Northern Cheyennes and not that of Crazy Horse and his followers, as anticipated. The Indians were initially scattered, but Reynolds lost the herd of Indian horses he was to destroy in a counterattack by the warriors and withdrew. Enraged after this initial debacle, Crook decided to return his column to Fort Fetterman.[14] Although the Northern Cheyennes had been allies of the Sioux, they had remained peaceful. The Fort Laramie Treaty of 1868 had provided no specific reservation for the Northern Cheyennes, yet it had allowed them a choice of either the Great Sioux Reservation or the Southern Cheyenne and Arapaho reservation established in Indian Territory, between the Arkansas and Cimarron Rivers, by the Medicine Lodge Treaty of 1867.[15] However, this March 17 engagement, which became known as the Powder River Fight, caused them to join in the hostilities.

Terry's Dakota Column was also delayed in deploying in the field, as a result of several unexpected developments. Besides being dependent on the arrival of additional troops at Fort Abraham Lincoln, the departure was also delayed by severe snowstorms, as well as some political folly involving Custer. During late February, Terry and Custer had worked together to plan their portion of the campaign. Thereafter, Custer was to resume command at Fort

Brigadier General George Crook
Photograph by D. S. Mitchell, taken at the time of the Reynolds court-martial in January 1877, Cheyenne, Wyoming Territory. *Courtesy of Paul L. Hedren.*

Abraham Lincoln and lead the column in early April. But after leaving Terry's headquarters in St. Paul on March 6, Custer and his wife, Elizabeth, were stranded on the train for a week, stuck in massive snowdrifts on the Dakota plains west of Fort Seward. At the same time, alleged scandals in President Grant's administration were developing; these would eventually affect the proposed army command structure for the 1876 campaign. In late March, a congressional hearing was convened in Washington, D.C., to hear and address allegations of financial corruption in the Department of the Interior, which also involved the secretary of war's appointment of traders at various western posts, including Fort Abraham Lincoln. These hearings became known as the Clymer-Belknap Hearings, named for the Democratic congressman Heister Clymer, who headed the investigation, and Secretary of War Belknap. As the former commandant at Fort Abraham Lincoln and of the Seventh Cavalry (the latter of which he had been for much of the preceding years, in absence of the regiment's Colonel Samuel D. Sturgis, who attended to administrative duties), Custer was summoned

Dr. Henry R. Porter, ACTING ASSISTANT SURGEON DeWolf's friend and colleague on the Little Big Horn expedition. *Courtesy of Denver Public Library, Western History Collection, 1 B-607, D. F. Barry Collection.*

back to Washington, D.C., to testify at the hearings.[16] Although mostly hearsay, his testimony implicated Belknap and President Grant's brother Orvil Lynch Grant in the alleged improprieties. Not surprisingly, this infuriated the president, and he retaliated by suspending Custer from command of the Seventh Cavalry and the planned Dakota Column of the 1876 campaign, forbidding him to leave Washington, D.C., for the time being. Only after the cautious intervention of Custer's military colleagues and friends—Terry, Sherman, and Sheridan—did President Grant relent and eventually allow Custer to participate in the campaign. However, Grant added the stipulation that Custer serve under the command of Terry, who was to lead the overall Dakota portion of the campaign, the latter being the honor Custer had coveted and believed he deserved. Custer had been both Terry's and Sheridan's original choice to lead the Dakota Column, but the political jousting with President Grant prevented that from becoming a reality.[17]

The Clymer-Belknap Hearings had further delayed the start of Terry's originally intended departure date of April 5 for the Dakota

Column, as Custer was not able to return from his Washington, D.C., ordeal until May 10. During the preceding weeks, additional troops had slowly trickled in to Fort Lincoln. DeWolf's detachment arrived on April 17 from Fort Seward. Five days later, Company C of the Seventeenth Infantry arrived from Fort Wadsworth, Dakota Territory, soon followed on April 25 by Company L of the Twentieth Infantry from Fort Ripley in Minnesota. The remaining Seventh Cavalry companies arrived in the next week and a half. Companies B, G, and K, which had been serving in the Department of the Gulf, and Companies H and M, from Fort Rice, Dakota Territory, arrived May 1 and May 5, respectively. All of these troops would join the companies already garrisoning Fort Abraham Lincoln to constitute the Dakota Column. The final contingent included Seventh Cavalry companies A, C, D, F, and I, although eventually all twelve companies of the regiment would be involved; soldiers from the Sixth Infantry (Company B) and Seventeenth Infantry (Company G); and a battery consisting of a provisional Twentieth Infantry company armed with three Gatling guns.[18]

After arriving at Bismarck and spending a day there, DeWolf took the ferry across the Missouri River to Fort Lincoln. Once there, he joined the current medical staff at the post, from which physicians would be chosen to accompany the Dakota Column. DeWolf's letters to Fannie provide not only descriptions of the post and the inner workings of daily activities there but also some interesting observations and comments regarding the various rumors of the aforementioned political and military conflicts on the national scene, as well as the petty jealousies among regimental officers and the medical staff all jockeying for positions in the upcoming campaign. Soon after Custer's arrival, the latter assignments were finalized. When it left Fort Abraham Lincoln, the Dakota column numbered 886 men; 50 officers; a veterinary surgeon; 4 contract surgeons; 39 Indian scouts; more than 150 wagons; about 175 teamsters, guides, and interpreters; 35 pack mules; and more than 100 cattle.[19] Assistant Surgeon John W. Williams had accompanied Terry from St. Paul after Terry appointed him to serve as the campaign's chief medical officer. Elbert Clark, Isaiah Ashton, Henry

First Lieutenant George E.
Lord, assistant surgeon
*Courtesy of Denver Public Library,
Western History Collection, 1 B-534,
D. F. Barry Collection.*

Porter, and DeWolf made up the contingent of contract surgeons for the column.[20] Clark had been serving at the Cheyenne River Indian Agency, while Ashton had just entered into his first army physician contract. Porter had recently served as contract physician for the army at Camp Hancock in Bismarck after being in private practice there. This would be his third army contract, after previous experience in the Arizona campaigns with Crook.[21] Porter and DeWolf quickly became close friends, and Custer would later choose both men to serve on his medical staff for the final trek to the Little Big Horn. They would be joined by George Lord, a commissioned first lieutenant and assistant surgeon in the army, who most recently had served as post surgeon at Fort Buford in Dakota Territory. Of the three, only Porter would survive the battle of the Little Big Horn.

The Dakota Column was to rendezvous with Colonel Gibbon's troops from posts in western Montana, including soldiers from the Seventh Infantry and Second Cavalry battalions and an artillery

COLONEL JOHN GIBBON (BREVETED BRIGADIER GENERAL AND MAJOR GENERAL, CIVIL WAR) Gibbon was the commander of the District of Montana and the Montana Column. *Library of Congress, Prints and Photographs Division, LC-cwpb-04455.*

detachment.[22] It was hoped that Gibbon's column and the Terry-Custer troops would locate Sitting Bull's Hunkpapas in those regions and push them south of the Yellowstone River and west toward the Big Horn River. During the preceding two months, Crook had also prepared his reorganized column to set out again, heading north from Fort Fetterman.[23] This column's objective was to prevent any southward movement of the Indians from the Powder, Tongue, Rosebud, and Big Horn River regions, where Crazy Horse's band of Oglala Sioux were assumed to reside.[24]

With the arrival of spring weather, all three columns were in the field by May 29 when Crook again left Fort Fetterman. Gibbon had departed Fort Ellis in Montana on April 3, and Terry and Custer had begun on May 17. Crook's second deployment (the Big Horn and Yellowstone expedition) would eventually engage the Indians at the Battle of the Rosebud in southeastern Montana on June 17, after which Crook would halt his advance. Just over a week later, on June 27, Terry and Gibbon would discover the disaster that had occurred at the Little Big Horn.

After the Dakota Column left Fort Abraham Lincoln amid great fanfare, with the Seventh Cavalry band playing Custer's favorite march, the old Irish drinking tune "Garry Owen," Acting Assistant Surgeon DeWolf would chronicle the daily movements in his diary. His personal letters to Fannie in between describe scenes of great adventure: the beautiful scenery along the way, the various camp sites after each day's march, and detailed summaries of the happenings that occurred on the journey. Yet perhaps his diary and his letter accounts of the severe blizzard conditions on the initial journey from Fort Totten to Fort Seward were an omen for the disaster that would befall DeWolf and his colleagues. His diary and letters thus begin with a description of his final campaign upon leaving Fort Totten.

Diary Entry, March 10, 1876

Two miles from Totten[25] my horse fell crushing my right foot

Diary Entries, March 10 and 11, 1876

March 10th 1876 in camp left Totten at 9 A.M. 10° below zero arrive at the Sheyenne (Davises')[26] at 2 P.M. one man a teamster frosted the tips of his fingers   Commenced snowing at 1/2 past two P.M. one team broke down   all chilled when we arrived but no one of the Command suffered severely   Three had their feet frozen one had finger frozen & several others had hands & feet chilled   it continued snowing & blowing till after night fall March 11th in camp 7 A.M. Broke camp   the wind blowing furiously the guide after going about one mile could not find the road   went on 3 miles and the wind increased & continued snowing so that objects were invisible at very short distance. Turned back and with great difficulty followed our trail back to old camp   numerous were the frosted noses & faces but none very severely   frosted my face slightly   my foot is painful but not disabled.

Diary Entry and Letter, March 12, 1876

12th Left Davises at 8 arrive at Beland[27] 1 p.m. fair day little wind but very cold   no mishap

Davis Ranch
8 a.m. [March] 12th 76

Darling
On leaving camp every thing went all right to 2 1/2 miles when my horse fell on my foot but is now all right again   Arrive here at 2 p.m. you know how it snowed   we did not learn from Maj. Smith what we might if we had stopped & had a talk so the Genls letter was the first intimation that we might have delayed. Yesterday we started out four miles and could not follow the road   turned back and & nearly all had face nose or ears touched by the Icy hand but none injuriously   they are only slightly sore this morning, that is the ears & noses   we shall start from here in a few minutes & go to Beland today   Brown[28] Carpiti[29] Caldwell[30] & Sergt Zimmerman[31] are quite severely frostbitten (feet)   all are in good spirits   we can keep warm at night & day our clothing is ample as clothing can be so you need not fear for me   I can stand it all right   hoping you will have a happy time this summer & don't fret about me at Lincoln. Good bye darling   love & kisses from your loving Husband J. M. DeWolf

Diary Entry, March 13, 1876

13th Left Beland at 6:25 a.m. Arrive at Seward at 8 p.m. Halted 10 minutes at the springs   many were frozen their noses faces fingers &c.   were well received & provided for.

Diary Entry and Letter, March 14, 1876

14th Remaining at Seward at Mr. DuBrays quarters.

Fort Seward[32] D.T.
March 14th 76

Darling wife

We arrive here last night on leaving Davises Sunday morning   we had a nice day & as our supplies were running close and expecting storms we on Monday marched from Beland   starting from Beland at 6.25 A.M. and arrive about 8 P.M. making a halt of about 10 minutes at Iron Springs [Grasshopper Hills][33] it stormed & blew so we thought it better to march than camp   we marched till dark. As the trail could not be seen during the day except on hills & places where the wind swept off the snow in most of the places the snow was near two feet & every valley was full of drifts ahead of everything. (by the way I could not hold him & keep behind on the trail as I would have liked)   well darling you can imagine how we feel with our noses frozen for Capt.'s & mine are in a very highly colored condition   I have got Cleaned up shaved and hope to call on some tonight   Capt. Patterson[34] has very kindly provided for us all   I have a bed in Mr. DuBrays[35] quarters & mess with Mr. Maize[36]   we are having good time   we are not sure of the road being open   they expect the train from the East tomorrow   it is a work train   Genl Custer was snowed in between here & Bismarck but has now moved on in Sleighs   this train he was on is expected to get to Bismarck tonight[37]   we may be here for a week but I think not longer   the men are nearly all frozen to some extent   many are just the tip of a finger nose or ear or face but scarcely one escaped entirely but there are none I think that will be dis-abled by it. I will find out tonight just how many there are touched by the icy hand   such a trip is like placing one on the brink of a precipice & giving him a push   of course we met the telegrams   they seemed like mockery though the men nearly perished to reach us but of course no one is to blame except the first telegram should have some discretionary power but now I think I can stand as much as any human being. Tell Mrs. Fletcher[38] I was sorry I did not let you act upon her suggestion & make me a hood   my foot is swollen yet but has ceased to be lame[39] but you know how lame horseback riding makes me   Capt & his frozen nose points from across the table to mine as we write   his eyes are quite inflamed from the light   my eyes are all right but nose is like a boiled lobster   Mr. DuBray says the mail has arrived from the East by stage   I will stop my letter this mail   Give my regards to Genl & Mrs. Hunt[40] Dr. & Mrs Ferguson[41] and all tell Mrs. McD. that Capt's [McDougall][42] & my nose mates well   hoping you are having a nice time   do not worry about me in the least for I am in good company and am well provided but hope we shall not leave Lincoln till warm weather   it seems I am omitting something but if I have perhaps Captain will inform you. You must write every mail of course   you may not have much news but I want to know you are well & happy. Do now try and cultivate the acquaintance of Mrs. Hunt, as I think you will find she will help you in your music and do try & enjoy yourself & be careful of your company (now don't pout because I tell you that)

I will write what there is to say every week   from your loving Husband

J. M. DeWolf

Diary Entry, March 15, 1876

15th Remaining at Seward, D.T.

Letter, March 16, 1876

Fort Seward D.T.
12 M March 16th 1876

Darling
I learned this morning that the mail had not left for Totten yet   it stormed & blew so the 14, 15, and still continues that it is almost

impossible to go out doors   it was lucky that we arrived the 13th   the roads are & will be blockaded for a week or two   I am going to wait here for directions & shall not make any only my regular reports   there were 41 frozen coming here and no doubts others that were so sleight as not to report   none I think will be permanently injured. *It is thought* that this expedition will fail to go out. That [Brevet] Genl. Custer will be promoted & taken from Command of the 7th Cav and from the command of this expedition and that there may be some small parties or one or two companies sent out but part of this are only surmises and not to be trusted explicitly[43]   Mr. Craycroft[44] & Dr. Ruger[45] have been & paid me a long visit this morning   Capt McDougall's eye is much better this morning   he had been ill & written to Mrs. M. I hope you & Mrs. McDougall are having nice times. Captain some expects to be relieved here but has not heard as yet   I attend my sick at call 7 1/2 & visit those in the hospital[46] at 10 and again at retreat   I am living with the mess Capt. Maize, Mr. DuBray & Capt McD. We have a jolly time and are having as nice a time as we could anywhere except at home. The Teams from Totten started out yesterday broke down & came back & it was very lucky for them that they did for I never witnessed such a storm in my life   they will start again as soon as the elements will permit   my two shirts I think will do me by having them washed often though if I have two more good ones you may send them by the mail next. Major Smith left here by stage yesterday morning. I cannot see how he could possibly get through   if not he must have a rough time of it   yesterday a Mr. Echerson[47] or such a name was up & spent the day with us and a good time you bet (*don't fear my drinking* for you have no reason)   Cards are not played here   they all of officers &c have been occupied the winter in the study of French Telegraphy &c and are   I will say bye bye darling   if I learn anything more before the mail leaves I will write it in

from your Husband
J. M. DeWolf

After dinner 5 1/2 Captain McDougall has received a telegram stating that Genl Custer has been ordered to send an officer to relieve

Lieutenant Colonel Lewis Cass Hunt (breveted brigadier general, Civil War)
Courtesy of John Griffith collection (also available at the Library of Congress, LC-DIG-cwpb-04472).

him here if one can be sent   Mr. Craycroft is also some expecting to be relieved here but no definite knowledge of such   the wind & snow is blowing at a terrific rate   I hope by next mail there may be some definite knowledge of what is to be done   give Dr. & Mrs. Ferguson my regards   hoping you are having a nice time from your loving Husband J.M.D.

Letter, March 19, 1876

Fort Seward D.T
Sunday 6 p.m. March 19th 1876

Darling wife
I will try & tell you how I am spending my time. I go to Sick Call at 7 1/2   breakfast 8 1/2 to 9 1/2 I went down to town returned about 11. gas & chat in my qrs or Capt. Maize's till dinner at 3 1/2 to 4 1/2 then chat until now   Capt McD & Maize are going Sleighing. I

Dr. Henry H. Rugar, acting assistant surgeon
Rugar was the post surgeon at Fort Seward in March 1876. He later became a prominent citizen around Fort Totten and a state legislator in the North Dakota government. DeWolf assisted Doctor Rugar during his stay at Seward before going on to Bismarck for the expedition. *Courtesy of State Historical Society of North Dakota, A2015-00001.*

have called at Capt. Pattersons twice Dr Rugers several times & last evening Capt. McDougall Maize, Mr. DuBray & myself went & serenaded Mrs. Forbes[48] or rather Capt M & M & DuBray with his Guitar done the serenading & I played dummy, went in & had a nice time staid till 10.[49] No one plays cards here and no drinking.[50] I wrote a letter for you last Thursday but the mail left before I knew & failed to take it so you will get it this mail. Capt. M & Mr Cray. I suppose will be along when you receive this—I admire Capt. McDougall the more I know him but Cray. I cannot say I do. Patterson is splendid & Maize to but of different type. Mr DuBray is an Englishman and is like all of his countrymen English he reminds me of Smith. I was at the P.O. & find a letter from Mich. for. I did not open it as the mail comes in Tuesday I will open any them are for us & send them in as I did last mail that Deed ought to be along this mail and the books from Carleton & Co I will finish this up before tuesday night

March 20. A most lovely morning. my patients are all doing well. A Courts Martial convenes today[51] am looking forward to tomorrow

Fort Seward, D.T.

CAPTAIN JOHN HENRY PATTERSON
Patterson, of the Twentieth Infantry, was the commander of Fort Seward in 1876. The photograph was taken when he was a first lieutenant in the Eleventh U.S. Infantry in 1861. *Courtesy of the National Park Service, Fredericksburg, and Spotsylvania National Military Park, "First Lieutenant John H. Patterson of the 11th United States Infantry," 1861, FRSP 2689.*

hoping to hear you are happy. I expect to learn something about the expedition when Calhoun[52] (who is coming to relieve Craycroft) arrives   suppose he will be here tomorrow   I find that this Calhoun is a person that I have seen in *Old* Camp Warner ten years this next October   I stopped at his quarters & had a good time   he was then a first Sergeant of D 23rd Infty so you find I will have some one that I can talk to about Oregon. He was examined by a board of old C W & recommended & finally examined at San Francisco Cal. Capt Henton[53] tried after his examination to prevent his Commission I think or at least they had a row   I will after I know what is to be done try & find out what assignment will be made with me, after the expedition for now I am inclined to think it will go out   they have fair collars at Kelly's in Jamestown for 12 1/2 cts[54] I will send you sufficient to Liquidate Bremmers amount soon but do not mention this to others or about the price of C at this point as I do not want to hurt his trade   I saw you got the samples [*the letter is torn and part is missing at this point*] it seems to me my pay was never so small   I want so many things   I have not spent any only for papers & the march coming down, but my mess & wash here will be something & when I get to Lincoln I must have some collars   now I have [*part of letter is missing*] that I did not bring more as I have not very plenty room for what I have. DuBray is going to try for a commission and think he may be able to get it   he is very hopeful

21st 10 A.M. news came yesterday that Gen'l Custer has been promoted and left Bismarck going east & that officers are coming with him to relieve Capt. M[cDougall] & Cray. as the mail does not go down from here after the eastern mail comes in I will have to close this now   Capt M. will no doubt be at hand by the time this reaches you to tell you the balance I cannot tell what effect the promotion of Custer will have upon the expedition's going out   it is thought by some that it will not start but it very likely will go. Hoping you are having a nice time and are not discontented   love & kisses from your Husband

J. M. DeWolf

Letter, March 21, 1876

Seward D.T.
March 21st 1876

After dinner

Darling wife
I have just read your splendid letters   they find me with a headache today but only from Seidletz Powders as I had to take one this morning.[55] I have been eating to much I feel all square since dinner   the eastern mail got in today at 12. The books from Carleton & Co have come   I looked them over but do not admire them much except their covers which are very nice   Gen'l Custer is looked for every moment   I suppose I may hear something later from you when Lunis[56] comes in but shall not be disappointed much if I do not   you have written you two   one I wrote that should

**JAMESTOWN, DAKOTA TERRITORY,
WITH FORT SEWARD IN THE BACKGROUND, 1877**
The town had numerous hotels and saloons, the latter of which often caused tension between the soldiers of the fort and the proprietors of those establishments. One reported calamity occurred when some rambunctious soldiers thrown out by a saloon keeper returned to the fort and fired one of the artillery pieces to blow the saloon's outhouse into oblivion! *Courtesy of State Historical Society of North Dakota, A1615.*

have went last mail. every body are asleep now Capt M, Maize, & DuBray smoking   the wind is commencing to blow   I am sick of writing about the road being open   the train from may arrive here tomorrow from the East but then the road will not be open only to the Cheyenne [Sheyenne] about half the distance. The west end the snow bound train the one that Custer left some two weeks ago or near that I believe got through to Bismarck yesterday and will turn & work back this way it is very uncertain when the road is clear if no more storms   perhaps in from 5 to 7 days I suppose Capt & Cray will be there to tell you all the particulars   I am so

EDWARD H. LOHNES
Lohnes operated an express service between Jamestown–Fort Seward and Fort Totten and later became a prominent citizen in the Devil's Lake area. *Courtesy of State Historical Society of North Dakota, Orin G. Libby Collection, 00105-00566.*

glad you are having such good times   tell Mrs. Hunt Mrs Fletcher & Mrs Ferguson & Dr that I am very grateful for their kindness to you and Mrs. McDougall that I admire her bravery   I am very sorry to hear that General Hunt is sick and hope he is improving and well before this   I have this mail received a notice of the death of a member, Edward Walker[57]   I sent the money to pay the assessment   you will receive the card again in in due time stamped Received Payment but if you receive any that are not stamped so send the dollar as I directed you to   I sent my application to the association of Greenfield Mass. today[58]   I am going down town by and by to mail this   hoping you are well and happy   I once more assure you that my anxiety & trouble are all and solely for you my darling wife   from your loving husband   love & kisses

J. M. DeWolf

My letters I think contains all that would interest you. we have beer but I only drink one glass a day & no whisky since the first day

Letter, March 22, 1876

Wednesday March 22nd Afternoon

Darling wife
I rec'd your letter of the 19th   it finds us all well   Genl Custer left this morning for the East. he has not been promoted that I know of but is going on unknown business to us, and is expected back in about two weeks   the expedition seems to be going to go out sure, & will perhaps be out until sept and of that there is now no definite knowledge   Capt & Cray. are turning over their companies. they have just gone down now. What do you mean about the P. and about Mrs Hunt   isn't it killing and the idea of his going to the President! I do not know what you mean   I have not heard anything about them. I hope you will have good times at the Doctors. Capt. Mc will deliver this. It seems to me a rather loose way of doing business   issue an order to go on the 10th then send directions what supplies to take after one has been gone from the post a week   Capt M & Cray leave tomorrow   it will be lonely when Capt. M. leaves   Cray will not be here to deliver his high flown phrases but I then am with careful cautious men who weigh well what they say. I have been giving DuBray a lecture on Harvard University. I have got him nearly sick telling him about the dissecting room.[59] Give my kind regards to Dr. & Mrs Ferguson   tell Mrs Fletcher I am very sorry to hear she is so afflicted & the General I am sorry to hear is sick in case you get entirely sick of Totten you must not feel that you are compelled to remain there for I will let you go home if becomes unpleasant for you there but if we cant stand it this summer I think it will be different next winter. my Package from Boston has not come yet you perhaps will get it when I am out on the Yellowstone   I think you will get no less than three or four letters from me this mail & one I think I forgot to seal thinking I might want to put in a few more words   the Telegraph operator is off drunk I suppose and so there is no news of the trains today   no wonder he gets drunk   I should think he would get crazy as all the officers go down & buzz him till he cannot attend to his business or anything else   they

play with his aparatis & really run him   well darling I must close for this mail   hoping you are happy & content as your happiness is my happiness   love & kisses from your loving husband

James M. DeWolf

Letter, March 25, 1876

Fort Seward D.T.
March 25th 1876

Darling wife

I sent you several letters last mail & one by Capt McD. Since then it seems rather dull but everything move on "L" Co has about as many in the G. H as usual. my sick call is more interesting from day to day inebriation being the cause of most of the suffering since the frostbites are nearly well.[60] though the seven cases one whose time expired will loose part of two toes & one other will perhaps loose some of his first toe which at the time of my other letters were apparently going to live.[61] It has been thawing very fast yesterday & day before. last evening the train from the east came in about 8 p.m. and this morning have started *East* to try and finish opening the road to Fargo   if they succeed in getting through to Fargo they will get a new supply of men & material. Engines &c and will open the road west pretty rapidly but if it continues freezing it will make it difficult   it is some talked of our marching to Lincoln. We shall have to next week if the road is not open as the Forage & hay &c will be out here & then the horses will have to leave or starve   all the hay & grain at James town has been bought & it will only last to the last of next week   Maj Smith (who relieved Cap M) talks of sending a team back   if he does send me some shirts white & all the collars I have   I think I told you to send some by Lunis but I am not sure however   I am doing very well   we all walk down town after dinner to go to the telegraph office get the news & return (no drink since the Mc & Cray left among the officers which suits

Fort Seward, Dakota Territory,
officers' quarters, c. 1880
*Courtesy of Minnesota Historical Society, no. 6794,
F. Jay Haynes, Photographer.*

me well do not mention this to any body)   I have opened Elmira's letter[62] and as the envelope will cost another stamp I will put it in with this without the envelope   I will open your letters while I am here so I can get the news (of course you are willing)   I wish months were shorter. Maj. Smith some recruits & officers was on the train that came in last night I am told   expect they will be up to this Post today. My Pocket inkstand broke coming   the ink froze & busted as I forgot to carry it in my pocket everything looks now as though I might be sent to Totten next winter   I will try & send you some funds from Lincoln   I think I ought to get the deed for the farm this mail. If it comes I will sent it on to you   you many send me my lodge notices as they come to hand and look through all of my Masonic Books Bylaws & notices and see if you can find the number of Pequosse the Lodge[63]   it begins to brighten up & think it may not freeze up yet   hope to get a long letter from you next Tuesday   you cannot imagine how much I feel our separation this time and hope it will not be necessary again. everything is like a dream to me   I do not like rooming with tobacco consumers   such a room as we keep you ought to see three guns in one corner one in another two pistols hung on the wall   our dressing table or Buro has everything you can think of on it in confusion   the window is full of Cartridge shells powder Flask hammer gloves wristlets &c &c   every corner is full of old Boots   the walls are dorned with hats caps Bridles styrups riding whips Guitar Boots smoking pouches pants overcoats &c &c in fact it is the place of a hunter. The quarters are some like the rooms at Totten   we occupy the room as our dining room   the front room has a table & stove & a lot of truck & is our passage way to our paradise though we are happy[64]   love & kisses darling from your loving Husb J. M. DeWolf

Second Letter, March 25, 1876

Fort Seward D.T.
March 25th 1876

9 P.M.

Darling wife
I have written you a letter today enclosing Elmira's letter to you and also read the Reflector[65] & put it back in the office and will try & have it go in the morning and taken up to you as I suppose you will get this about the time I got your letter tuesday night   I also send here-with my express package if found it at the Post Office today   it has been there in the safe for some time & I had been inquiring at the Rail Road office   I have been playing Cassino Seven up   Euchre with Dr Ruger   he beat me bad at Cas. & I him at Eu.   hoping you are having good times   love & kisses darling from your Husband J. M. DeWolf

Sunday Morning. all right had a nice evening last   the road is expected to be open to Fargo by tomorrow then they will go to work on the Bismarck end—Breakfast is nearly ready   give my kindest regards to Mrs. H. & the Genl Dr. & Mrs F and all enquiring   from your loving Husband

J. M. DeWolf

Letter, March 27, 1876

Fort Seward D.T.
March 27th 1876

Tuesday evening

Darling wife
I received your big letter and shirt & collar   the first I have been looking for all this afternoon   it finds me well &c. to pass time we all go down town to the telegraph office after breakfast 9 or 10 and

stay till about noon then after dinner which is at 3 1/2   we all go down again & go through the usual questions to the operator as to where the train is & when they will get through to Fargo. I think the train that left here sunday morning will reach Fargo tonight then they will have to come back & open this end again. we are not going to wait any longer but will march through saturday sunday & monday next if the weather permits and our team comes from Totten   I have just received my orders from Dept. Headquarters directing me to report to Custer & Dr. Kimball.[66] but last night we read the what was said to be the press dispatches which said Genl Terry[67] will take the field, and leave Lincoln the first of May; and that the Cavalry on the Rio Grande are to be increased & commanded by Custer. also that Lt. Col Grant & Babcock are to be investigated[68]   that Genl Crook[69] has been compelled to retire   these dispatches I do not know whether they are genuine or not   I have some reason to think they are, I at least hope so   there are other rumors that will not interest & are no doubt untrue.

Darling   *Privately*[70]
I am glad you are beginning to like Mrs. H and hope you will try to yourself as happy as possible under the circumstances. I caution you to be careful what you say or think of others and no doubt what was told you of the St. Paul talk was true for I think Mrs. H told me nearly the same but that Dr M. had only been expected previous to Mrs. H's   I shall try & do my duty while I stay & not beg for favors but do beg to be left in peace   do not dear be made a go between   hear all but say nothing to cause ill feeling; I have this day recd a letter from mother & the bond that I sent them has been kept & they want another   I am a mind to tell them something. if I was sure of my money I would not sign it. darling I hope I do not annoy you by the advice above for mothers letter annoys me   I will send it to you next mail as I want time to consider what to do.[71] I will write you once more before I leave here   it may storm so as to detain us but hope not   I like the people here at Seward much though I have called but a few times and my associates are men. I have had one glass of beer this week and have gained two pounds

177.⁷² I shall send you some funds from Lincoln   I have no Idea how much my mess will be here & washing &c   good night darling.

J.M.D.

8 A.M. Wednesday
It is a lovely morning   I have got shaved dressed & attended to my sick and will now finish my letter   I am going to remove four toes from one of the men that froze coming down which I thought would not require removal   I shall take this down to the office after breakfast then go to the hospital   I like Smith who has taken command much   he is married & says you had ought to come down to Lincoln & staid the summer   I hope I shall return to T next fall   give my regards to all Genl & Mrs H. Dr Mrs F   particularly you should fasten your doors at night if not for safety for fashion.⁷³ Love & kisses from your loving husband

J. M. DeWolf

Direct the next fort A Lincoln D.T.

LETTER, MARCH 30, 1876

Fort Seward D.T.
March 30th 1876

Darling wife
I recd your letter from Capt. Mc   they arrived last night about 9. I will answer some of your questions   I meant I would like part of my shirts to be made of Irish linen in place of muslin but never mind the shirts now. I will write you more by and bye. I sent you a box of stationary 75¢   I have made one another bond to mother and will send you a copy of it to keep   I also send you the latest on signatures   some come out very curiously   I operated on those toes yesterday removed four.⁷⁴

31st as I have a few minutes to breakfast I will improve it   I commenced yesterday to mess with Dr. Ruger as they reassigned

> Fort Seward D.T.
> March 31st 1876
>
> To the
> Medical Director
> Department of Dakota
>
> Sir:
>
> I have the honor to report that at the beginning of the past quarter there were no cases of "Wounded" under my charge. During the quarter there has been one case of Surgical Operation, a civilian George Zimmerman who was discharged from Troop L. 7th Cavalry for expiration of term of enlistment March 24th 1876. This man was Frostbitten March 10th 1876 which necessitated the removal of the Ungual Phalanges of the first, second, third and fourth toes and half of first Phalanx of the first toe and half of the second Phalanx of the second toe and the second Phalanx of the third and fourth toes of the right foot. The operation was performed March 29th 1876 and is now apparently doing well.
>
> Very Respectfully,
> Your Obedient Servant
> James M. DeWolf
> Acty. Ast. Surgeon U.S.A.

DEWOLF'S MEDICAL REPORT, MARCH 31, 1876
This letter relates his amputation of Sergeant George Zimmerman's frostbitten toes. *Courtesy of National Archives (also available at National Park Service, Little Bighorn Battlefield National Monument, LIBI_0007_04899, "Dr. DeWolf's Medical Report, 03/31/1876").*

everybody I like them very much I am just beginning to get aquainted with Dr. R there was no letter mail for us yesterday the train is through to Fargo. I spent the evening at Mrs. Forbe's Mrs Patterson[75] & Mrs. Mc was there had a nice chat we are having nice weather hope we will have some sent next week. Shall not leave here before Monday. Craycroft has read some orders directing him to remain till after action is taken on his application for sick leave, which he has not yet applied for

Monday April 3—76
Craycroft goes to St. P and then will apply for the retired list[76] the work train is expected from fargo tomorrow to open the west end of the road. We have orders to remain here until further orders so please have my zinc trunk put in repair and send my felt & straw hat[77] my coat pants vests &c as you think I will need. (I have the dictionary.) send it the trunk by Lunis first mail.

Evening. Well I have got all of my reports off and have written to Dr. Ferguson have just been down town no news. I asked Dr to ask Lt Reynolds[78] to let his carpenter fix my trunk you can have it fixed as you think best. I just learned that the mail or a team will leave here tomorrow for Tot so I will finish this & give you one more day to fit up my trunk Dr will not get his Receipts tell him until the mail as I have mailed them tonight I have also mailed the bond to mother and send you a copy to keep I hope you will have a nice time as soon as the mud dries up it is very muddy here now except some places where it is drying up. You ask about the folks here I like them very much. Of course I don't call often but I guess sufficient for ordinary civility there is some slight talk about the expedition being abandoned. But nothing to indicate it except Genl Crooks reports that the number of Indians off the reservation has been greatly exaggerated Gen Sherman has gone to Washington & it is supposed Army H. qrs will be removed to Washington[79] a Capt Harmon or Harman[80] (once of the army) has been appointed post trader at Lincoln. This post has been repairing all of their transportation some is destined for the expedition the news I wrote about Custer &c Promotion was all a hoax and I was only one of several of the victims it has become quite common to have bogus telegrams here and some one is hoaxed nearly every day but nobody was april fooled very seriously   Craycraft would have made several victims but he told to much   he said Custer was promoted to the 10th and then so much about officers retiring   that is killed the first time & I now mess with Dr. Ruger   Mrs Ruger I like very much for a southern woman   you will know that people from the south are not much like those from the north   Saturday evening Mrs McD & myself Played a Miss Forbs & Calhoun Whist 8 games   won two & one Whitewash making 3 games from 8   had a nice time but the folks don't begin with the Tottenites for entertainers but dont say this where it will come back to me   don't say it any where! Give my kindest wishes to Capt & Mrs Fletcher Dr & Mrs F[erguson] & Genl & Mrs. Hunt and Compliments to the Pedro Club[81] through Cap Harbach[82] I heard a lady remark that she liked Cap H very much   this last is private   well darling it is getting dark   hoping you are well & happy darling   love & kisses from your loving husband J. M. DeWolf

I think darling you had better if you can get some one to sleep in the house with you nights as you will not feel like being alone many nights you may be able to get Stewarts daughter or some one else. From your loving husband J.M.D.

I am so sick of seeing dogs lying around & could see them all in—we *have* only sixteen, or so JMD your husb.

LETTER, APRIL 4, 1876

Fort Seward D.T.
April 4th 76

Darling wife
I recd your letter   am very sorry you have such a sick spell this time   I have written you nearly all of the news in another letter that I expected to send by a team but it stormed & the team did

not go   well the train did not leave Fargo today and will not until the storm ends   it has stopped storming & perhaps the train will come out here in a few days but no doubt it shall be for 10 days or two weeks   you may send my trunk as I have directed   I will now tell you as near as I can what I have done with my money. My striker coming down here $2   mess $8 this mess was not charged but paid to the servant on intimation   Ex package 85 cts   wash $2.50   paper $1.50   Total $14.85   Postage stamps about $1.50   office & all matches 10 cts   telegrams 25 cts. I have now

   14.75
   14.75
Some postage stamps $4 due me
   4.00
I had when I left some
   <u>6.50</u>

   35.25
30 odd dollars   I have not wasted much so far   I send you herewith Erastuses[83] letter   I shall send him my amount this or next mail   I see Capt & Mrs M every day & Cray. Am having very nice time   Mrs. Forbes & some of the off go riding nearly every fair day   Cray Capt Smith or Capt McD. I like Lt Calhoun & Capt Smith very much and no doubt will enjoy their company this summer but of course they are not like Capt McD & Cray   I will tell you more when I see you   I would come up but I could have but one weeks leave I would be near all of that time on the road going & returning and then the Ex may be abandoned yet but do not hope so too much   please put my amount of postage to my trunk the little book I kept this amount in. we did not get the press dispatches today   I have tonight got my first shirt that has to be done up decent   The French lessons are still going on occasionally   Dr. & Mrs. R are quite proficient from all accounts. Give my regards to all enquiring friends   Cray & Cap McD wishes to be remembered

Darling it seems hard that we must be separated but perhaps it will come all right in time   I cannot very well try for the Arsonal, the pay of course would keep us but the position is not very apt to be permanent or of any long duration. But however I will write to Col Laidly[84] in a week or two but shall not ask for the place before fall if I could get it. From your loving Husband JM DeWolf   love & kisses to my darling wife   I have just been able to get two elegant neck ties from Dr. DuBray. So I have two nice ties & will send for me some shirts before long

from your Hub
JM DeWolf

LETTER, APRIL 5, 1876

Fort Seward D.T.
April 5th 76
Wednesday Eve 10

Darling wife
I just learned that the wagons are going to Totten tomorrow morning. the train has arrive here. they came in about six this afternoon   a scout also just arrive from Lincoln with some letters   one for Custer   I have been in Mrs Forbes a few minutes this evening. I am now in hopes we shall not get off to Lincoln until my trunk comes and think there is not much danger   in case I should I will leave directions here what to do with it. Mrs. McD Miss Forbes Capt McD Smith Patterson & Maize were down to see the train folks   they brought through three passengers in a caboose car   start west tomorrow morning. DuBray has come in & is going to be so bye bye darling   love & kisses (Give my regards to all) from your loving husband James M. DeWolf.

Fort Seward, D.T.

Letter, April 9, 1876

Fort Seward D.T.
April 9th 1876

After dinner

Darling wife.
It is nearly one month since I have seen you and it has seemed an age. well since my last letter it has been nice weather and our daily visits to town have been the rule. I have since at Dr. Rugers had breakfast at 9 and dinner at four   one hour each meal is about all I am there   I have been at Mrs. Forbes once and had a nice visit once since   Mr. McLaughlin is in town and is up nearly every day   he only calls on Patterson & Mrs. Forbes. the train is working its way to Bismarck, the three Companies of the 7th Cavalry in the South are ordered up to Lincoln immediately. McD & Cray.s Company is among them they expect orders to remain here until they come up   well it thundered & rained last night and has been raining some here today   the wind has blown very hard all day and some of the time it has snowed but the Thermometer has been about 40° all day so it is not cold. Mr DuBray has been out today and killed six (6) ducks so we expect to have ducks for dinner tomorrow   wont they be good   I wish we could have dinner together   Capt Maizes cook has been sick for two days   Ella[85] is now filling her place   General Emory[86] has retired so it gives one promotion   I see in the Bismarck Tribune that Custer has been caning Genl Rice of Washington. I have received another card of death in the South which I have sent   you will receive the receipted card some time   Please send me by the first mail three cakes of Boquet and three of the Elder flower turtle oil soaps   direct it In care of A. W. DuBray and if I should have left he will send it to me

Now What I wish to say is Private   I should like to stay at T the coming winter so you may not tell Mrs. H that I don't want to, but do not want you to say that I have spoken to you on that point of course   I shall try and work things as well as I can for our mutual benefit   I have paid Erastus my 125 or sent him my pay for march

ERNEST BRENNER
Brenner, a former enlisted man, was a colorful character at Fort Totten. As the post sutler, he was notorious for making a rather potent beer that he was eventually mandated to brew at a location several miles away from the fort. *Courtesy of State Historical Society of North Dakota, 00105-00567.*

and will get my pay as early for April as I can and will send you fifty dollars of it. I don't want you to pay B[87] anything yet so in case I am ordered away from there I may pay him in part with *stuff* you must keep your mess bill and I will try & have it there before the end of the month.

We expect now to get away from here some time this week but may not until the three Companies come up from the south or until the expedition was ready to start   I will have a small operation on toes again tomorrow and am some in hopes of having some more important work to do this summer   hope Dr. Kimbal will be up soon   Genl Custer out to be back next week[88]   I don't hear any more about Crooks report and guess it will have no effect on the expedition   well I want to go but do not much like to leave you but know you will have a nice time with the people at Totten for I assure you that I look back with pleasure to the past winter. give my kindest regards to Mrs Hunt Mrs Fletcher Mrs Ferguson & the Baby. tell the Pedroists that I hear they have vipers, or Pokerites at Lincoln.

Fort Seward, D.T. 65

Frank you asked me if I liked Calhoun. Yes and you would for he is a Gentleman and a Ladies man and does not talk for effect. A E Smith[89] is also an excellent man they compare well with any two officers you can mention DuBray is off again this evening after ducks I have been dreaming of you for several nights I hope you are well darling and am waiting very patiently for Tuesday evening the mail comes in here from the East and West on Tuesday and Thursday nights our mail ought to leave here Friday morning then you would get all of the latest news &c I believe Capt Harbach gets the telegrams that we get here daily. well bye bye darling love and kisses from your loving Husband J M DeWolf

P.S. suppose my darling is now writing to me or packing my trunk I will finish this up Tues night

Tuesday noon Darling since Sunday well Monday I went & took a ride in the ambulance with Capt. Patterson & Maize who went hunting ducks got home for dinner 3 ducks the Eastern mail came in read Harpers & sent it to you Played whist last evening Mr. (Lieut) Van Reily & myself against Maize and Lt Harrington[90] we made 44 to their 7 points have been down town this morning. got my Courier Journal. It is getting monotonous I hope you have sent my trunk & that it will arrive this evening in case it comes the bridge is impassable so I will have to have it brought across the RR bridge as the other is several feet under water it is snowing very hard here since about 10 A.M. the mail this time came up on a Hand Car & expects to go back the same way. General Crooks has had a fight without doubt but no particulars or at least I have not heard them that I could rely on.[91] Tuesday eve I just recd your letter & suppose there are some clothes down town for me send my trunk next mail if Tunis can bring it. Darling I fear I have did wrong to give you any expectation of our returning but there has been quite serious talk but of a non official nature of the expedition failing, though it is very probably that we may go out. you cannot miss me more than I do you darling so do not get impatient I hope all will come around in course of time. I hope it will not be so dreary after spring comes and it will not be long before we have nice weather   we expect now to get off to Lincoln the latter part of this week but the road may not be open & I am in no hurry & would rather remain so near than to go down to Lincoln for we are here very comfortable   I like the Drs very much Cray & McDs are here still   suppose they will get away the last of the week unless they get orders to remain for the arrival of their companies—it has been snowing all day   I attend to my sick as usual   I removed some bones of two toes yesterday which I think I mentioned are all doing nicely   Dr Ruger has had one case of Pericarditis[92] (look in Dictionary)   we shall very probably remain here or at Lincoln for a month   I have not talked to Mrs McD about you and do not talk to her or any of the ladies except as civility demands & suppose some think scarcely enough for that   I stay at my quarters most of the time go down town to find out the news. A. T. Steward[93] is dead of New York   spend an hour at Rugers for Breakfast & an hour for dinner   I have not had any striker here, but shall have one as soon as I move. I believe it would be nice to move down to L. soon if we must go for it is getting dull staying here. do you get on pleasantly   I really hope you do and hope to send you some funds as soon as I can put in my pay acts for April   If B. does not want me to pay up till I return it will accommodate me perhaps but I shall try & pay them up at the end of April and leave a little for you   I suppose there is some goods at the office for you from Ingersols & will see before the mail leaves & if I can pay the charges but if I have not enough I will let it go through to you to pay there darling I think of you every hour in the day and do so hope you are comfortable and as near happy as you can be apart   I have been in want of clothes & so have you. I do not care for myself but for you I will try & provide soon. I will try & have my coat braided over & then I am all right again   my regards to all and darling I will never leave you again for a field expedition unless you think best   I should like very much to see the Tottenites   give them all my regards & my love to my darling wife   how is your bird you had in the Dining room   love & kisses darling from your loving husband

James M DeWolf

Fort Seward, D.T.

I opened your letter & put in Postal Card

Tuesday evening
Dearest Darling I am so sorry you are so lonely up there I am as much mortified as you at this d—— fool move this spring but cannot help it I believe you feel our separation much the most for I am constantly occupied with some strange person and do not have to be alone, though I stay some day nearly all day in my quarters or DuBrays he goes to the office at 9 & returns at 3. we get on nicely I find him a nice room mate he wishes to be remembered to you. well I have been down town & got my bundle find coat pants vest & shirt & Duster hat all right & Postage book saw Brenner. well darling I want to tell you something that I have learned of late that I did not know which I believe to be true Cushman[94] I hear was warned in writing by B before B. reported him if so I think B was right now darling I hope you have not make yourself obnoxious to BK. And I do not regret C.s not calling & hope he will not if all is true for it would only make talk about you and I don't want any of that for your sake I know you are in a delicate place between two fires Dr. Fs are friends of M & necessarily enemies of B and the party here are bitter against B. I do not care to express my opinion here except to neutrals. I will see Brenner before he leaves here about paying him. and the soldiers wife you spoke of you may give her your wash & work after speaking to the Genl. & Mrs H. about it and perhaps you can get her if I return this fall which I hope I may of course we may possibly be ordered somewhere else the army bill I think will not interfere with us and I want to pay up this summer for the farm then we will be more independent I will finish this up tomorrow good night darling I should be most happy to chat with you if only for an hour but 80 miles of snow & slush divides us love & kisses dearest JMD

Wednesday after dinner darling I am going down town & will mail this you may send my trunk and I will have it sent up to Lincoln where I will leave my things in it when I go out & have it there when I come back do the key up in cloth & send it in a letter to me direct it as heretofore or Lincoln I recd your letter directed to Lincoln the P.M. look through all of the mails for me   I have retained the Journal this week and you may send me the last number of the republic and the last one that I forgot to bring. Capt McD expects to get away tomorrow but no certainty. we expect to get to Lincoln the last of this week and no doubt we shall succeed in getting through   I will make all arrangements about my trunk being forwarded from there. Just have my name on the card & cross of Fort Totten, D.T. on the card   I am lonesome without you and it seems hard to be separated but darling I am doing as well as you could wish morally. give my regards to all & love & kisses to my darling wife J.M.D.

Send the soap in a separate bundle & not in the trunk for it is for D.B *or do not send it and I will send him some from Lincoln*   well dear I will have to close   I have torn half sheet to finish up on but have not been able to close but now I must so bye darling from your ever true & loving husband

James M DeWolf

Letter, April 13, 1876

April 13th 1876

Before Breakfast

Darling wife. last evening every body was invited to Capt. Pattersons. some of the Band played during the evening in the dining room   Dr Ruger & myself Played Miss Forbes & Lt. Calhoun whist & Mrs. R. & Cray   Mrs. McD. & Maize I think had a nice time   refreshments at 10. then dancing until after twelve. altogether we had a splendid time   my coat & Pants came just in time   there was 6 Cavalry 7th 2 Infty, the Drs. 4 Ladies   it seemed something like Totten. the train that left Fargo yesterday and was to have taken the McDs went Back last night   cause unknown   suppose train will be through to Bismarck soon   we may stay here another week now. there may be some news this morning   our forage is exhausted and the horses will be entirely out of food in a day or two. —I have read up the reports & conclude that the expedition is very like to go out   I have seen Brenner   he will wait until I come in but don't ask him for much money   I will send you half of my pay for April the last of the month   I will try & have it reach you before the last. Put my rubbers in the trunk the numbers of the Republic, my black covered book on Pathology, Bilroths Surgical Pathology English Grammer, Huxleys Psysiology & such others as you may think I will need   I am not sure but I have Huxleys P.[95] I see there is another Doctor ordered for the field from Dept. Head Quarters   I have a case of Pleurisy now under treatment which is a very serious affair   my toe cases are doing well the first case operated on two weeks ago is nearly well   Three of the four toes are healed   McLaughlin[96] is down town yet   Brenner I expect will return today or tomorrow   In case Lunis cannot bring trunk this time and I am away from Seward so you cannot get a reply you need not send it except he can bring it this time but he has promised to bring it and suppose you will not have long to get it ready in as he will not leave here until tomorrow or was told so last night   I guess you will find these letters repetition but hope you are well & happy   we will soon have spring & nice out door sports &c &c   I miss you very much   you cannot miss me more but such is Army. it wont be forever. Love & kisses from your loving husband James M DeWolf

April 13th 6 P.M.
Well dear the mail & trains are in from Bismarck & the road is open through I believe there is some trussle work down between here & Fargo but the train will be in tonight and I think your things from Ingersolls will be along   I have told Lunis to enquire after the train comes in & take it to you   five officers are expected on the train from the East   well darling I suppose we shall leave here Saturday possibly tomorrow & possibly not so soon   give my regards to all enquiring and love & kisses to my darling wife from your loving husband James M DeWolf

Will you please send me some sample in gray goods plaid and plain in 2 or three shades darker than the sample I send and like of the same material

Diary Entry, April 14, 1876

14th Remaining at Seward at Mr. DuBrays quarters.

Diary Entry, April 15, 1876

15th Remaining at Seward, D.T.

Remained at Seward until April 14

CHAPTER 2

Fort Abraham Lincoln, D.T.
APRIL 16 TO MAY 14, 1876

"I AM QUITE COSY FOR THE FIELD"
[BUT]
"I HAD RATHER COME BACK TO TOTTEN."
Doctor James DeWolf,
letters of April 22 and May 14

DIARY ENTRY, APRIL 16, 1876

April 14th '76 Left Seward & arrived at Bismarck[1] at 4 P.M. Camped just below Camp Hancock until the 17th was very kindly rec'd & entertained to Dinner at Capt Howes[2] on the 16th. board at the Capitol met Dr Porter[3] & Col Lounsberry[4] Col Brown,[5] Wilson & Thompson[6] the latter returned from the 7th

LETTER, APRIL 16, 1876

Bismark D.T.
Sunday morning April 16th 76

Darling wife
I will give you an account of affairs since Friday morning   well we all got off with the train at 9 1/2 A.M. arrived here at 3 1/2 P.M. without any accident. went into camp about 1/4 mile from Bismarck and along side of Camp Hancock.[7] Bismark is a squalid dunghill

71

BISMARCK, DAKOTA TERRITORY, C. 1873
This view of Bismarck in its infancy shows what DeWolf described in his letter of April 16, 1876, to his wife as a "squalid dunghill sort of a place."
Courtesy of State Historical Society of North Dakota, C0529-1.

sort of a place   all wooden buildings   Broken board walks on the front street   it is on Prairie ground on the margin of a Bluff. the flats of the Missouri [River] extend back about one mile to this bluff   Hancock is on this bluff and we are camped immediately under this bluff on the Missouri flats   it is all dry & nice the first night the Prairie was on fire and presented a nice sight in the distance   we sleep in the tent and Board up town at the Capitol and about such board as at Fargo nothing nice but just tolerable but we are having on the whole very nice times. Mr Harrington & Van Reiley Lieuts 7 Cav are invited to dinner by Capt. Howe and Commander of Camp Hancock at 3 today. the night after our

Fort Abraham Lincoln, D.T.

arrival I got my sick admitted to Hospital had our tent pitched went & had dinner took a walk up main street (there is only one side to it)   Called on Capt. Howe & Lt. Chubb[8] 17th Infty called on Dr. Porter who attends Camp Hancock as Browman did the Arsenal only the govt furnish medicine   they have a steward,[9] Paymaster William Smith,[10] Capt or Lt. Burns[11] from Abercrombie[12] Dr. E. J. Clark,[13] who is also a candidate for the field (he also has failed before the Army Board)   Dr Kimbal[14] will not go out he has been relieved the Department. a steward also came up   Lincoln is down the river about five miles we shall march down & be crossed over on the Boat.[15] the Boat also leaves from the terminus of the R R about two miles from here and runs down to opposite Lincoln & lands goods &c   the Boat has been broken and has not commenced to run yet but expects to start every moment since we have been here, but no more prospect of starting than when we arrived here   it is somewhat doubtful about our getting over today   Smith & Calhoun are just going down to the landing to see about our prospect but we will have to go into camp when we get across it   now all the difference is that we will not have to board at the Hotel but may perhaps start a mess.

Evening. well darling we have had a nice time at Captain Howes. he went down to our quarters after dinner and paid us a long visit. we expect to get over to Lincoln tomorrow. well I am at Lt Chubbs qrs and as all the space around was occupied I wrote with a pencil until now one has finished Capt. White. I hope we shall get into our permanent camp tomorrow and mess where our meals are a little better or costs less. well darling I learn the mail closes tonight at nine & it is near nine   give my kindest regards to all enquiring   I hope darling you are well and having a nice time and hope the snow is all off and things looking lovely   darling I think of you and my only anxiety is for you   I think we are going to have a nice time this summer. well so much noise & chaffing I will have to say by bye darling   love & kisses from your loving husband James M. DeWolf

DIARY ENTRY, APRIL 17, 1876

Crossed over to Lincoln   Capt Smith[16] took me to dinner and was very kind   was called on by Lt. Porter[17] & Smith, Dr. Redd[18]   Dr R. asked me to Breakfast once while there   Capt Smith asked me to come at will & Mr. S. was tolerable kind   Middleton[19] offered very kindly to provide for me. Went into Camp No. 1. 2 1/2 miles below Lincoln April of 76

LETTER, APRIL 19, 1876

Fort A Lincoln D.T.
April 19th 1876

Afternoon

Darling Wife
I have arrived here at last   we came across the river on an old ferry boat on the 17th. I have got a wall tent up and am quite comfortable considering. I mess at Capt Smiths until I can find where I am assigned. I attend the sick of E. & L 7 Cav and the battery of artillery (that is going out) at the Dispensary at sick call, all that are seriously sick are sent to the Hospital[20]   Dr. Middleton attends the hospital and two companies of Infantry which are all up on the hill in a separate camp.[21] Dr. Redd attends the 5 companies of 7 Cavalry stationed in Fort A Lincoln at the Dispensary and sends his sick up to Dr. Middleton when he has any for hospital there is no hospital down in the cavalry camp[22] every body is very nice & kind in fact to kind. You I suppose what this post is noted for. well it is followed closely   I have seen none of the ladies except Mrs. Smith who I like and she is very pleasant and has made it very pleasant for Mr. Reily & myself. the Infantry officers who commands the battery are camped near me Lt Lowe[23] & McKinnie [Kinzie][24] who are very kind gentlemen   Capt Sanford[25] & Lt Chance[26] up on the hill I also like very much   the Cavalrys reputations of course are already made. I think if I had a choice of stations I should take

Camp Hancock officers' quarters, 2013
This building has been preserved on the site of Camp Hancock in downtown Bismarck and houses a small museum. Doctors Porter and DeWolf both stayed here. *Author's collection.*

STEAMBOAT *DENVER*, FORT ABRAHAM LINCOLN

The *Denver* and the *Union* were two smaller boats used for transporting supplies and people on short excursions between Bismarck and the fort, since they were not in good shape. The *Far West* and *Josephine* were used for longer excursions up and down the Missouri, as they were larger. Ferry Landing Fort Abraham Lincoln, c. 1877, Haynes Stereo. *Courtesy of State Historical Society of North Dakota, A5821.*

Totten. The wind has blown so for the last few days that *our* tent nearly blows down. not our now for Mr. (Lt) Reily has left me this morning   he was assigned to Co F 7 Cav and has gone on the sick report   a scouting party went out last night to ascertain if there was Indians in the vicinity as there has been a report that Bloody Knife[27] had come down to follow us out & pick up stragglers   it is not expected that we shall be out more than 3 months   Col Weir,[28] I like very much. this will be my last expedition   it is to much for the money   not that I don't like it or cant stand it but this dirt & waiting is disgusting   I hope darling you are having nice times now as spring has come   give my regards to Mrs Ferguson & Dr. tell Dr. I have had one interesting case (Pleuritic effusion)[29]   how is Metzdorf & OKeef?[30]   remember me to Mrs Hunt & the General & Capt & Mrs. Fletcher[31] in particular & the Pedroists   love & kisses darling from your loving Husband. J.M.D.

Letter, April 21, 1876

Ft. A. Lincoln D.T.
April 21st 76

Darling wife
I send you a check for $50.00   you must endorse it. Pay to —— and sign your name and any one will take it   Dr Ferguson will take it for you   I will send you more as soon as I can. I called on Dr Middleton last evening & saw Mrs M who is very sociable   I intend to call on Capt Smith & Moylan[32] tonight if I can get a clean shirt from the wash   my trunk is at Jamestown yet but will be down the first train   I have got a floor in my tent & am getting today a bedstead & mattress so I am very cosy   I have a box of Pistols in my tent so I am armed well.[33] I like Lincoln more as I become aquainted better but can see no comparison to Totten for Hospitality. Capt Smith & Dr Middleton are all that can claim to have extended ordinary hospitality. it is reported by the press dispatches this morning that the President had received authority

to send troops to Texas. the 7th may possibly go. My love to my darling wife. I will write often & will mail this so you will be sure & get it in time   I don't know how the mails leave here so I had better put this in the office[34] so it will be sure & get to you in time   bye bye darling

J. M. DeWolf

since finishing my pencil scriblings I have been down to the store & around the post generally. darling I some expect to get my pay for May & June before I leave here but in case I do not I will manage some way so you are provided for   It will take me more than I expected   I must have two flannel shirts a pair of boots or shoes a rubber coat a valise   my basin was crushed coming to Seward & looking glass   I have now $40. & credit at the store for $25. and also credit for my rations for april I am messing here at $5 per week which was the best I could do   I hope we will be able to get up a mess of our own soon here. Dr Ashton[35] who is going out with us has arrived   he will mess with me and has gone into a tent they managed to give him one meal & a sleep one night   you will not mention this to any one there but gambling is the mania here and there is not time for anything else.

A Band[36] are stationed at this post and have dress parade every evening and last evening Batallion drill and today again Battalion Drill   the band came out to guard mounting so there are some amusements. I had about 14 at sick call this morning. perhaps part of them on account of drill   Col Reno is in command of the Post[37] and lives up to reputations at least in making the soldier drill & turn out to parades   well darling it is very warm here today to warm for a coat. I am having new braid put on my coat today and am going to get me a pair of pants made of dark blue cloth while I remain here. now darling I hope you are well and you will have a nice time   I have a letter from Dr Bryan[38] will send it to you next time   love & kisses from your loving Husband

J M DeWolf

Major Marcus A. Reno
Courtesy of the National Park Service, Little Bighorn Battlefield National Monument, LIBI_00011_07109. D. F. Barry, photographer, "Major Marcus Reno in Small Oval View," n.d.

LETTER, APRIL 22, 1876

Ft A Lincoln D.T.
April 22 1876
Saturday

Dearest darling wife
It is now 7 P.M. raining dreadfully and I have just come up from Col Weirs & Dr Redds as they quarter together. have tied my tent up tight & turned into bed I am quite cosy for the field   I have a floor in my tent an Iron bedstead mattress my blankets & Robe and darling what I appreciate more than all is the Pillow you insisted on my bringing darling I remember you every time my eyes rests on it. my boots were loaded when I came in but I have got them cleaned up and my pants. I got some blue cloth from the Q.M.D. today & am getting me a pair of blue shirts made so I will have a pair that I can wear under a coat.[39] the worst here now will be getting to my meals it will be so dreadful muddy   I have today

sent you something which I think is nice & you ought to receive it at the same time as this letter   do write to mother kindly and if you get tired staying to Totten you may go home but if you can possibly stand it till I return perhaps it would be as well   Dr Clark who is going out says Dr Sloan[40] the Med Dir at St Paul said he intended that we should all return to our posts on the return of the expedition   Genl Custer is on his way back from Washington and ought to be here by the time this reaches you if he comes direct   the Infantry company from Wadsworth arrived today[41] 200 mules arrived yesterday. I have been about the store near all day seeing the usual game. Dr Ashton seems to be quite an expert, and is ahead of the dashing 7th Cavalry so far. he is quite young and thinks of entering the army. well I have Just lit my candle, and have told you all except Dr Redd Ashton & myself were directed today to examine a wounded soldier for or with view to his being discharged   the ball passed through the natis and much of the coxyecx   now go to your dictionary before you tell any one of it *ha ha*[42]   every boddy has been buying rubber coats today but me   I had picked out one but told him to sell it I will take my chances of getting one by & bye. the trader here keeps a nice assortment or at least has a store that shows everything to advantage. Col Reno came in to sick call this morning. I suppose he wanted to see what was the matter with so many   Dr Redd showed him some of his doubtful cases & asked him if he would excuse them   he said yes & was quite satisfied. he did not trouble my desk as I have my desk at one side of the room & Dr Redd at the other & have sick call at the same time

8 P.M. raining hard & pelting the tent   wind blows hard. happy dreams

love & kisses to my darling wife J.M.D.

Sunday morning
Darling I have been down to sick call & will occupy my time till breakfast with my one pleasure   writing to & reading your letters. it still rains hard[43] I slept splendid last night & everything

dry this morning but my overcoat which I had worn out in the rain. I have not met any of the ladies here except Mrs Smith & Mrs Middleton and civility seems to be the exception to a casual observer but I have no doubt it would be pleasant here after further aquaintenance   well I have one pleasant thought that I am giving no one any inconvenience. I am not complaining for all that have arrived here have felt the same want of direction. the rain is getting finer so I must go & get some Breakfast   you should get this one short letter & one with a $50. check and a pair of slipper all in this mail   the mail leaves here tonight I get your tomorrows letter about Thursday   we get mail three times a week   love & kisses darling wife from your loving Husband

J. M. DeWolf

I will get Ink next letter [*This letter was in pencil.*]

LETTER, APRIL 25, 1876

Fort A. Lincoln D.T.
April 25th 1876

Tuesday 7 P.M.

Darling wife
I have received my trunk today   I found the little note in it telling me to make myself agreeable to the ladies. well I have not here nor do I intend to for the simple reason that no one has called on me, nor shall I call on them. I am not complaining for I have been invited by Moylan Porter & Yates who are married. I go in to see Col Weir & Redd frequently. I no doubt would [*letter torn—several words missing*] nice station. but now there [*several words missing*] that all cannot be entertained and I am treated as well and better than some captains   two companies of Infantry arrived from Ft Ripley today[44] a Steamer arrived yesterday from below and has a company of Infantry going to Fort Buford.[45] I had the pleasure of seeing a nice game of seven up today for $20. per game   the officers of this

post are all fine Gamblers (don't mention this at Totten)[46] well darling I have a place to keep my things at last my trunk is in very good condition If I only had a chair & table I would be happy, but I cushion my Pannier with a pillow which does very well. I expect Capt McDougall will be along from the south with his company soon, then it will seem something like home again we have had a big hailstorm this afternoon and a nice shower of rain the grass begins to start. They are plowing the gardins at this post[47] Co L is going to make a garden here this summer that (Wednesday morning) looks some as though I would not return but it may Genl Custer I learned last evening that he had been ordered back to Washington and it is supposed here privately that he will get court martialed he & [*two or three words missing*] are the principals of course [*one or two words missing*] rumors are by telegraph and are not public yet there is also some rumor now of Genl Sykes or Genl

Fort Abraham Lincoln, c. 1875
Courtesy of the National Park Service, Little Bighorn Battlefield National Monument, LIBI_00019_00214. Unknown photographer, "Panorama of Fort Lincoln in Full View," c. 1875.

Terry or Crittenden taking command   I wish the d—m concern would bust up for I feel that it is a pure waste of money to send out such extravagant expeditions[48]   I called on Capt Smith last evening with Capt Maize & Lt Reily had a nice chat & looked through their album which was very nice. there is an artist here who takes excellent Photographs. I am reading your note in the trunk this evening   I find the sentence "I think I can not survive until you return I am hardly able to sit up." darling I hope you are well before this and hope your nerves are all sound again. It is now tattoo and I am in my little tent writing on my case of Instruments[49] across my knees and don't you think me extravagant   I have three candles lighted I have been down to the store seeing the usual game   I have just got my coat with new Braid so it looks all right again and am having two shirts made. I will tell you all about the Lincolnites when I come home or the male portion. Co E & L have got their

Campaign hats today they are heavy broad brim hats costing $1.68.[50] would cost here about 3 or four dollars   I hope darling you are well tonight and happy. If you really want to go home you must let me know and I will make provisions I have $25, & about $25 credit   my mess paid to next Friday   paid out for cloth for shirts $5.40 Buttons 25 Board $5. Ex coming here more than I had money $3. loans $2. trunk 75 cts collars 80 cts. striker $3.00. Braid for coat $1.25 the balance which would be about $5. I have squandered or spent it at the store which I feel I should not have done but could not have been decently avoided except I stay away from there which is not fashionable will your $50. pay up your expenses for April. my head aches tonight so good night darling wife. J.M.D.

Sunday morning   Darling I am just through my sick call we are going to have muster and a grand review if it don't rain but is sprinkles & looks very much like it   oh I will tell you that I tried to tell you that A. T. Stewart was dead not that he was at Rugers as you seem to have read it. well I hope you will be able to make out this   I should not send you this letter but it embraces the most of the current news here   I called on Lt. Porter & like him much & met Mr Edgerly[51] for the first time yesterday. Your letter was a balm to me you seem content & happy which I hope you are then my trip will be bearable   we of course are not having nice times but I sleep warm & have enough to eat & that is about all I can say & keep clean. You I hope will be able to take more exercise as it gets warmer   My Rubbers came just in time for the mud was awful for a few days. I suppose *all* will go into camp this week then I will have you some views taken if I can & send you   it is not known who will command the ex. yet but rather expected Custer will be back & I hope he will. the mail closes tomorrow & will write some in the morning again   love & kisses from your H J.M.D.

Letter, May 8, 1876

May 8th Monday evening

Darling wife
I have sent you today a letter and the studs & sleeve buttons hoping you will receive them all right. I have been around camp calling first into one tent then another   I get nearly all around every day   the wind has been blowing this afternoon & the dust is all over everything but it (the wind) has gone down tonight & the band have just been playing some hymns which dear makes me feel so lonely. I hear tonight that Custer will Command his regiment but he has not come yet & I don't believe it though I would prefer it not on account of my desire for an easy trip but that I believe he is the man and he has been out & knows better than them that have not been over the ground. I am expressing the opinions of the cavalry of course & I am assigned to the Cav so I must be a Cavalier. now darling I will tell you about my horse. well we had to come down here in the Ambulance[52] & two days after there was three—what the Q.M. called horses came down for the Med Offs   well Clark had first choice me second Ashton third   Clark asked my advise which of course I freely gave and got him to omit my choice so I got my second choice as if it had been first. Ashtons horse can barely get up a gallop mine is tolerable but poor Clarks is a stumbler. but they got the best saddles but I think I will get Clark to trade our mess. It is a dutch mess or the caterer & cook are. three (3) of us are Yankees. I have not yet been able to find your letter of April 30 & you do not say whether you have recd the check or not or the slippers though the slippers I should not hear from till next mail as the Ambulance left them tuesday   did you send a letter in mondays mail   you speak of some ones coming in last night after you had finished your letter so I take it for sure you wrote   it seems mean that the letter is here and I cannot find it. it makes me mad & I will make feel the miserable excuse we have for a post office. Cus damn them & every body else till I get my letter[53]   taps is going. I have just commenced to read the Republics[54] and expect to get settled in the field so I will feel at home as well as one can. darling I should so

like to be there to go with you for walks this summer to go out to the old Abbis & Glen Alin to Glencrofts slide[55]   wouldnt we have nice times but its no use talking darling   I hope you are content & happy   if you like you can send & have a servant sent up & keep house as soon as you like   I saw Ella[56] at Seward and asked her if she would like to go back to Totten next winter   she said she would to live with Mrs DeWolf   I asked her to send you her address and that I thought you would send for her. There is a Nigger man here that wants to go there with me when I come back so if you don't want or cannot get Ella or some other good girl then let me know in time & when I come back I will bring one man or woman as you choose from Lincoln   Mrs Hughes Sister may want to go up if L Co goes back there this fall   now you must let me know all about it in time & if it would be more pleasant get one any time   If Mrs Hunt goes east in the fall &c   I expect about the time I close this letter I will be leaving the old Missouri behind and hope we shall be successful in finding some of the cussed Indians that have been the cause of the expedition   I learn by the N.Y. Herald that there are to be a combined expedition Crooks from Ft Fetterman[57] Gibbon[58] from Buford Terry or Custer from Ft. Lincoln   the Prairie are all on fire north of us & Lincoln today & suppose the Indians will have the grass all burned up ahead of us. two horse are reported stolen two days ago from near the post   the man that owned them went out 15 miles & seen a party of fifteen mount at a distance & leave in haste   they got a pipe & some other stuff I do not know just what   The Black hillers[59] stole two muskets from Capt Howes Barrack room at Camp Hancock at Bismark a few night ago and Capt yates I believe had some revolvers stolen from his squad room a short time ago. supposed to be by men bound for the Black hills. well darling I have had a visit from the Vetinary Surgeon[60] & Guide [Charley Reynolds] the guide is a very nice fellow but the Vet. Not so very nice but tolerable   he imagines he knows something about medicine it seems so ridiculous to hear him talk mixed Latin German & English it would make you laugh. Charley Reynolds[61] is the most modest man I have known for some time   I hear Capt Weston[62] is coming up to go out with us as commissary officer. I

CAPTAIN FREDERICK W.
BENTEEN
U.S. Army Heritage and Education Center, Carlisle, Pennsylvania.

wish McDougall would get along too. I was up to the Infantry tonight and had a nice time before I commenced this letter   we had a long argument on the winds affecting a ball fired against, in the same direction and diametrically or across (I am not sure that diametrically is the right word). I hear the horses racing about some that have got loosed.[63] darling I must retire to my robe & blankets it is near 11. I hope darling you are in happy dream land and may your dreams be sweet for you have all of my love & soul for darling its you that hope to spend many happy days and think this will make you doubly dear to me   love & kisses darling wife from your ever loving husband

J M DeWolf

Tuesday evening. darling I have remained in camp all day today   read most of the time   was down to the lower end of the camp & called on Col. Benteen[64] 7 Cav from Ft Rice[65]   he reminds me of Capt McDougall in his regular fun & style of wearing his hair   he has silver gray hair & very easy spoken. I find the officers

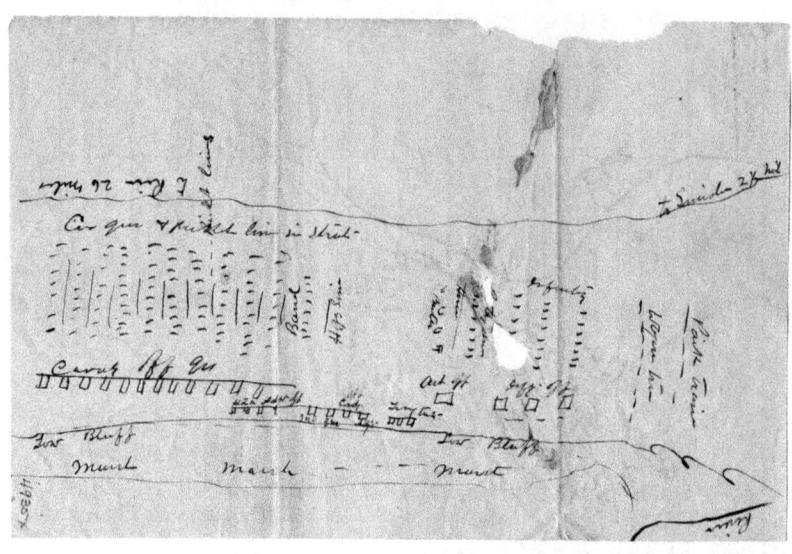

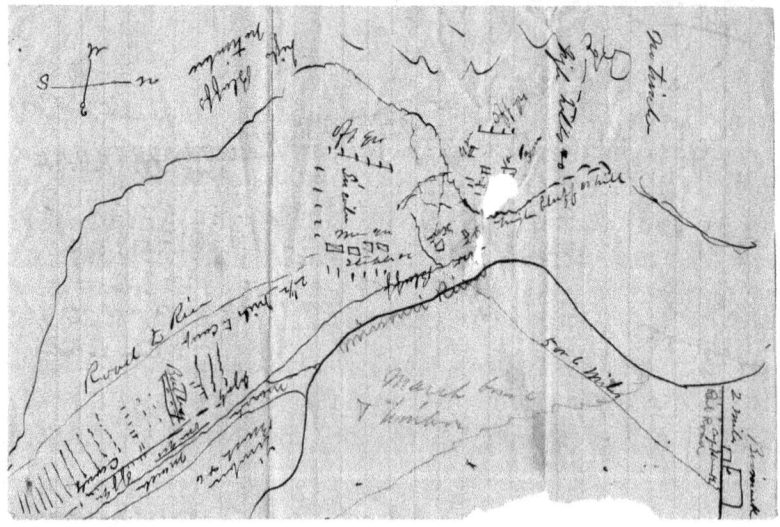

DEWOLF SKETCH OF CAMP AT FORT LINCOLN
AND ITS RELATION TO BISMARCK

This is included in his May 8 letter. *Courtesy of the National Park Service, Little Bighorn Battlefield National Monument, LIBI_00007_04935, "Dr. DeWolf's sketch of Fort Lincoln, 5/08/1876."*

of the 7 Cav very good fellows except the spirit for gambling here at Lincoln it is looked upon as not the thing by the majority well we expect Terry & Custer tomorrow night. I have examined 22 Indian Scouts today not a very nice Job we have a sentry in front of our tent night and day and let no one in except he be an officer or inmate or asking to see an inmate of one of the four tents. Col Reno Comdg. Col Cooke[66] Adjutant, Lt Nolan A.A.Q.M.[67] & myself are the respective occupants   Mrs. Edgerly[68] is still in camp it has been very warm today & yesterday the mosquitoes are getting quite plentiful it is talked of our leaving saturday or sunday but cannot tell yet   I hope so that we may get back soon to my darling wife   night   love & happy dreams   J M D.

Wednesday evening taps. Darling one more day has gone by this morning I got a box and made a wash stand &c and a table of the cover by driving some sticks in the ground which makes my tent much more habitable   It has been dreadful hot today. this afternoon we had a hard blow & nearly upset the tent and tonight it blows very hard   the Battery went up to the post this evening to fire a salute on Genl Terrys arrival at eight   the salute was fired so I suppose Genl Terry & Custer has arrived and now expect we shall move soon   Dr Clark has been in & spent the evening with me. I have this afternoon made a sketch to you how we are located on the River and relative to Lincoln & Bismark. the Battery have just returned & I hear the sentry challenge frequently so I suppose Reno & Col Cooke Adjutant & Nolan Q.M. who tent next to me are getting home. dearest darling I hope you are comfortable and happy tonight. I have got under my blankets & robe and am quite comfortable   I have two long pieces of wood placed on the ground hay filled in between my rubber over then 4 Blankets then two Blankets & Robe over me so I am quite comfortably fixed   Dr. Ashton has come down to stay he has been quite successful at the 7th Game so far   shant I try. no darling I am invited quite frequently, but have no desire to participate   I sent you last mail the studs & sleeve buttons & hope I am not mentioning the same fact in this letter twice. I hear Reno just answer the challenge of the sentry   the voice sounds queer—

Well darling love & kisses   happy dreams   wont we be happy when I get back   this for hoping it wont be long   *good night*

Thursday morning   S call & breakfast over. well Genl Terry & Custer arrived   Dr Williams who is to be chief Med Officer & the Paymaster. I have not got your letter of April 30 and fear you may have neither received the check or slippers   why don't you them or don't they fit or what is the matter   I will give you this week as I have c—— as it will no doubt be our last week in camp   next week no doubt we will be on the road & you may not get letters regular   it will be uncertain if I get any of yours again until we arrive at the stockade 20 or 30 days.[69] I should [have] thought you would have mentioned the check in connection with your mess bill   I hope it has not been lost.

Thursday evening. Darling wife last night I had just gone to bed when a scratch came at my tent door & the steward brought your letter of the 7th. of course I should be happy to be woke up every night with a letter from my darling. In reply to Mrs Hunt query Mrs Custer is at Lincoln and has been here since the Genls first arrival in March. Capt McDougall has arrived   Mrs. McD has gone south. Capt O. E. Mihaelis[70] has also arrived   Lt Gibbs Genl Crittenden   Lt Crittenden who lost an eye at Ft Abercrombie last fall is also up at Lincoln. Capt Bradley tells me that they heard from Mrs Fletcher &c Capt McD is as jolly as ever. in case the check has not arrived write to R. C. Seip[71] & Co Post Trader Fort A. Lincoln, D.T. and they will send you a duplicate of the draft which was for $50. I expect to get my pay tomorrow for May & June write immediately as above if the draft has not arrived. you say you received my letter on Friday & one from Mother   that's all the letter mail I recd   got my papers   you ought to have recd a pair of slipper and last friday you ought to recd studs &c. it is supposed we shall leave here Sunday or Monday so this may be the last letter for two or three weeks but I suppose we shall have a chance to send letters back once a week. Dr Williams has gone to Rice to leave his little son who came with him   he did not know he was going on the Ex till he arrived at St Paul   he I think I shall like is a little man middle aged & pleasant   the Band mounted & went up to the post to serenade Terry tonight. I rode my steed to the store today & got me a gum coat for fear of a rain storm   I have two dollars left of my April pay   of course darling I waste some but can not well avoid it except I be sort of a miser but you need not caution me about cards for I am not so forgetful for really darling I dispise gambling. if it was not for you dearest it might be different. I am reading Physiology and am now getting so I can read in camp. I have a chair now & box so I have my tent furnished. well it is long after taps & I hear the I raise I two dollars in a tent close by. I will close for tonight   happy dreams darling. good night

Friday evening   well darling taps have gone   I have been up to the post today & drew my pay for May & June[72]   I send Erastus $125. which will leave only $125. more to pay   I have paid $25. for my mess which it seems to me is pretty dear for the amount received but however time will tell when we see how long the things lasts   well darling I was just washing & was going up to Terrys qrs when a man came down from the store and brought you my letter from you dated April 30 or 29 acknowledging the receipt of check & slippers   so all the fuss I have made about it is all for nothing but the letter has laid here some where 8 or 9 days   is it not enough to make one swear. well darling the latest Dr Red sends me word tonight that he is ordered to Totten on temporary duty   what does that mean   has Dr Ferguson applied for leave or what is it all about[73]   I will try & find out tomorrow more about it he will no doubt arrive with this & perhaps bring it to you   he is a fine fellow &c he made excuses the second morning I had been at the post while we were walking from sick call for not entertaining me &c as he was quartered with Col Weir   of course it was all right. he asked me to breakfast once & called on me and I suppose he done what he thought sufficient. Dr Middleton and him do not hitch very well as Dr Red Dr M thinks is to[o] easy with soldiers & Dr M I think is the opposite &c &c[74]   I will try what I can learn tomorrow   Michais [Michaelis] is going to let me have a revolver on the trip then I am fitted out   good night darling—

Saturday morning. darling I had to attend the whole command this morning at Sick Call   Clark & Ashton went to Bismark & could not get across the river. I have seen Dr Redd this morning & have sent the check by him for $50.00   I kept 75 for use on the ex   I will send a letter of Introduction by him to Dr F   he is in a great stirr where to mess &c when he gets to Totten. I suppose he thinks folks at Totten are like the Folks at Lincoln about their treatment of arrivals   I tell him he can no doubt mess with Renolds or perhaps with you & Mrs F while the Dr is away   you will find him a good fellow though I am not much aquainted with him   I will write you another letter before the mail leaves   from your loving Husband

JMD

Letter, May 14, 1876

Camp near Lincoln D.T.
May 14th 1876

Dearest darling

I suppose this will be the last letter you will receive from this post   I will send this by Dr Redd I also send you a check for $50. fifty dollars by him   I am assigned to the right wing of the 7 Cav under command of Major Reno[75] we shall leave here tomorrow morning   march 10 miles I believe is all that is intended the first day. Dr Williams[76] has come he is splendid so far. well darling I suppose I could change off & not go but I want very much to go and expect we shall have a good time or as good as can be had in the field   I think I am doing well under the dirt treatment   I don't get fat but I feel well & strong & hope you will have a nice time   I have told Dr R[edd] he must make himself agreeable to the ladies and hope you will enjoy the summer. I cant write now dear for there is so much to be done   Dr Williams has gone to the post & left me to see to buis. love and kisses darling hoping to hear from you again soon   I shall write to you every oportunity. from your loving husband

James M DeWolf

Fort Abraham Lincoln, D.T. 93

Second Letter, May 14, 1876

Camp near Ft A Lincoln D.T.
May 14th 1876

Evening

Darling wife
As this may be the last night in camp here I will write you again well since giving Dr Redd a letter for you, I have & so have all the cavalry moved camp or changed around to get into shape and will pull out in the morning at 4 unless it rains too much and it just pours now. and such lightening & thunder I have not seen & heard for a long time   I only had my tent moved a few hundred yards and therefore have all my furniture along two boxes a little table a chair & tonight the steward has put a Pannier in here to have it ready for early morning   don't it blow & rain   my tent fly rattles so I cant think   Dr Clarke has got a Dr Porter to go in his place. Dr Porter was attending the company at Camp Hancock at Bismark but now the company is over at Lincoln[77]   he wants to go out. he of course wants to keep up pay and he only gets $60. for that & will not get $125. *now I will tell you something privately.* I perhaps could have made a change with Redd, but he has been so easy, or had so large a sick report here the past winter that they would not perhaps let me changed if he was willing   I never have spoken to him on the subject   Dr Middleton has sent one or two letters on the subject   he was of course under Dr Middleton & Col Reno came to sick call one morning to see why he excused so many men   well Dr Williams wanted to have Dr Ashton assigned to the Cavalry but Genl Custer said no he did not want him he wanted some one of experience. Dr Sloan the Med Dir asked Dr Williams to help Dr Ashton &c as Dr A. was a Gentleman   Dr W. says he told the M.D. dam the Gentlemen   he wanted men that could do their work.[78]   I learned the above from Dr Williams our chief medical officer   he has been very good to me has had me assigned to the right wing &c. Dr Middleton came down tonight to bid us good bye   he corresponds with the Med. Dir. I asked him to mention me if convenient & ask to have me ordered to a post as soon as we

return and that my family was at Totten &c   he promised me he would. I have been & think not from any talk but other things that he would like me in place of R. & I should like it but I fear the quarters would be deficient here & I had rather come back to Totten as I like Dr Ferguson and think we can have a nice time there   it rains hard yet & I must go out & fix up my tent or it will be down. well darling I have been out & got things so I think my house will stand till morning   I will finish this tomorrow before daylight if we move which I now think is doubtful   night darling from your Hub J.M.D.

Morning darling   the mail leaves in a few minutes so I will finish. it rained so much we shall not start this morning   I don't know whether we shall get off today or not   three mules were stolen last night   they are having a great time finding them this morning but found them tied to a tree some where. well darling I will have a chance to send you in one more letter next mail then you may miss getting one for two or three mails but I hope we will have a chance to send back letters all the time   it is a nasty wet foggy day today   love & kisses to my darling wife from your loving Hub. J.M.D.

CHAPTER 3

Misjudgment and the Trail to Disaster

MAY 17 TO JUNE 24, 1876

"I THINK IT IS VERY CLEAR THAT
WE SHALL NOT SEE AN INDIAN THIS SUMMER."
*Doctor James DeWolf,
letter of June 21*

DIARY ENTRIES, MAY 17, 1876

Genl Terry Staff Custer & Williams arrived May 10th and came to camp the 11th & ordered a move on the 15th but it rained & delayed until the 17th

Moved at 5 A.M. get in camp   Camp No 2[1] at 2 P.M. 12 miles on the little [Big] Heart River   Marched   Genl Custer went ahead & Scouts & Yates[2] Comp 7 Cav Genl Terry Reno Band 3 Co Cav & Batty in front   train in centre   3 Co Cav on each wing with flankers   Infantry behind train & 1 Co Cavalry rear guard & 1 Co—as flankers   quite a march   the teams stuck in the mud frequently some did not get in til 5 P.M. A nice camp on the south of the Heart river   the troops are paid at evening   Mrs Custer came this far

Letter, May 17, 1876

Camp on Hart or Heart River D.T.[3]
May 17th 1876

Darling wife
In my tent again and after the first days march we moved out 12 miles to this River[4]   had from 5 A.M. to 2 P.M. 9 hours waiting & laying in the sun for the wagons to pull out of the mud for the ground is soft for heavy teams yet. the Paymaster came out here to pay off here and is paying off this evening   I expect we shall made a short march tomorrow cross the river & perhaps camp on the other shore (Just beyond this river)   well darling the hardest of it is that the trains cannot get along fast & make the marching dreary   to much laying in the sun waiting for the trains   the trains consist of about 75 wagons. I have not went to much trouble to make the estimate so it may not be very near correct. my nose is pretty well sunburned. Dr. Red will arrive there tomorrow then you will get my last weeks letter   hoping it will find you well (as we go marching on)   I am glad to get out for now every day counts   I am not sure that I can send you another letter I hope to get yours tomorrow of last Sunday. I am enjoying the march first rate & expect we shall have a nice time as can be had in the field   I have my tent put up & taken down my bed made horse saddled &c and have a quart of nice whiskey in my valise in case of need   the ground is getting warm & dry to lie on   I have my coat & rubber leggings in case of rain   a tolerable saddle & horse. Capt McDougall wishes to be remembered to you. Mrs H & the General & all   specially to the Genl and Mrs Hunt   he is the same Jolly & good as ever & Capt Banteen is a perfect mate for him. & Capt or Lieut McGuire of the Engineers & Lt. Thompson of the 6th Infty who is our Commissary   I find different from the cavalry as a whole I think the Cav. are but there are many exceptions   Col Keho[5] & Cap French[6] are coming to Totten next winter. Reno who commands my wing I cannot like but suppose acquaintance will improve perhaps when we understand each other.[7] the adjutant of our wing Lt Hodgson[8] is a nice fellow   well darling my letters may be far between after this

but I shall write every oportunity and will try & keep a memoranda of the incidents. love & kisses darling. from your loving Husband.

J. M. DeWolf

Diary Entry, May 18, 1876

took 3 hours to cross the Heart R. marched 10 or 12 miles   Camped on Sweet Briar Riv or Creek[9] a broken country no timber no wood at Camp No. 3. Antelope for supper 5 A.M. to 3 P.M. making the march   showers in afternoon & evening

Diary Entry, May 19, 1876

Went with Custers advance   found an impassable stream flanked it   found the ground very soft for the train   Marched about 12 miles went in to camp about 12   6 P.M.[10] train not all in yet   sent back 20; 6 mule to help in wagons   rec'd letter from Frank [Charley] Reynolds[11] killed an antelope   had a dreadful shower while putting up tents—with some hail   tent full of mud tonight[12] bedding moist

Letter, May 19, 1876

Camp No 4   3 days out
May 19th 76

Darling: I recd your of the 13th today   it came in this morning but the mail was not distributed till evening as we have reveille at 3 & start at 4 1/2 to 5 A.M. I will answer your questions first. I Recd the Blanks & have returned them. I wrote to Dr about Col Weir & Received the Republic[13] so I have something to read many thanks. darling I think you had better make out a power of Attorney (I am sure if it has two to or one) and send to some lawyer to act for you or write to Mr Lovni[14] & ask him if he will do so for Mr Lovni if he will (or Mr Pease) can act just as well as you could if you was there. Mr. Brenner can make the paper for you and you had better attend to it at once   I think darling I will remain till next fall (1877) if U.S. is satisfied with me & then we will leave the army   Co G. 17th Infty. Co C. 17th & Cap Bakers Co of the 6th Infty I don't know the letter of Company.[15] Lt Low & Kensi of the 20th Infty command the Battery Lt. Crittenden[16] of the 20 Infty goes along with Lt. Calhoun 7 Cav Capt Hughes,[17] Smith,[18] Michailis & Gibbes[19] are on Terrys staff. McGuire[20] of the Engineers & Dr. Williams   about letters darling it will be uncertain after this & this I suppose will lay at Seward near a week as the mail for here will not get to Lincoln in time to reach you with my others or with the one of day before yesterday   yesterday we crossed Heart River & marched 10 miles   had a hard shower while having our tents put up & tonight as today noon & just poured & hailed Just as they were commencing to put up my tent so they had to wait till the shower was over. The Steward[21] had his up so I stood in there but I have Rubbers so I can stand the storm & keep dry   I am so glad I got them as it rained some today marching & I would have been soaken if I had not had them. if you see the Bushmark (Bismark) Tribune you can see what a bungle some reporter made Who is Woolsey. of course it meant *myself* your Hub   perhaps it was because I don't take his trash.[22] I expect we shall be up & moving at 5. Are only going about 5 miles tomorrow & am not sure if we can get that far   the roads or hills & vallies for there are no road will be dreadful soft for teams   well darling you must not worry for I am perfectly safe as we shall not see an Indian this summer and if they do I shall keep safe & s—— & I carry a carbine & revolver so I will be armed in case of need but I think it is nonsense to carry it but I do so want to be sure & get back that I take every precaution to be on the safe side. McDougall wishes to be remembered to all   I had a nice march today & think I shall like Genl Custer. Genl Terry of course every body likes   the Tribune describes Genl Custer very well   he likes to go ahead & Buckskin suits are very Fashionable & Nobby in the

7th Cav[23] I have not seen the mates for Mr Craycrofts ties yet in the 7 Cav. I am writing this on the Republic on my knee so you may have to study it some to read it. Dr Porter came in for thread & needles[24] and had a talk on the days trip & tells me we are to start at 8. tomorrow so wont we have a nice sleep. it will be better than at 5. and it is pretty cool tonight   I dont expect you will receive another letter until after we get up on the Yellowstone by boat   I think we can stand the expedition as well as Genl Terry he don't enjoy it much I think   I should like if you could see us all after we get in camp   the tents & wagons & animals all lariated out completely cover the ground for about 1/2 mile square   the horses are all hobbled to prevent a stampede. the wagons in the center the horses & mules around then comes the mens tents then the company officers then the staff officers then the march change of Guard then the Pickets & outside on high hills the mounted pickets so we cannot be surprised very easily. the Indian Scouts[25] are all camped tonight outside us   well darling I will write you again as soon as I have a possible chance to send it to you. I have been thinking of collecting you some stones &c if I find anything worth while but I wont promice you much for I dont like much to dismount to pick up stones &c   it is getting too dark to write so darling good bye for tonight   love & kisses from your loving husband

J M DeWolf

Diary Entry, May 20, 1876

Moved at 8 a.m. Marched about 7 miles   Camped at 2 p.m.[26] train delayed with stream beds soft & soft ground   bridged one stream   camped on high ground   saw mounted men in evening supposed to be Indians   showers at evening very cool during the day   No wood

Diary Entry, May 21, 1876

6 A.M. moved across a small coolie[27]   very drizzly and rainy cold & uncomfortable   Marched 14 miles reached camp 4 P.M.[28] no wood

Diary Entry and Letter, May 22, 1876

5 A.M. lovely morning   Marched 15 miles reached camp 1 P.M.[29] fair marching one creek to cross   wood & nice camp

Camp No 7 7 1/2 PM
May 22nd 76

Darling wife
I do not know when you will get this but I will write & mail it to you when oportunity presents itself   we are now about 73 miles from Lincoln   we have march very slow time for the ground has been soft & the trains cannot keep up with us so we wait & lay on the ground & sleep while the orderlies graze our horses   we have been in camp at four P.M. every day & not that late but once   from one to two P.M. is about the average   well darling it would no doubt be a treat for you to see the command & train in motion from front to rear of the command proper it always about one mile formed as on next page   this darling will give you some Idea of one form of marching   I am with Reno nearly all the time as I belong on his staff   he commands the right wing but Terry and Custer go about one mile or more in the advance he has command of all most of the time   the right wing is supposed to be on the right of train & left on left   they all march as shown as near as the country will admit   in crossing bridge of course all come in to one column   you can see the train is the largest part of the expedition   on starting form camp when it is nice the band play & this evening they play are playing while I am in tent writing to you   one man accidentally shot himself through the heel yesterday while mounting   flesh wound[30] not much sickness though it has been wet & dreary except

the first & today my nose & ears are nearly burned off we live on Antelope meat it is nice out in fair weather there is some fun occasionally in seeing a team stick & the teamster swear or see a mans horse get away & buck his saddle off a wagon upset & in the creek &c the second day a horse had the saddle turn going up a bank out of Heart River the horse bucked &c jumped into the river went out of sight twice the man of course fell off when the saddle turned tonight a horse ran away through the camp the man fell off & nearly busted him but not seriously hurt I have not been tired yet the horses get loose at night some times & make fun. I had a nice sponge bath tonight and changed all my clothes & feel nice & took a nasty pill.[31] Well darling as I have to get up at 2 1/2 or 3 A.M. tomorrow I must retire & it is getting chilly as I have taken off my flannel for the night remember me to all & love & kisses to my darling wife from your loving husband

J. M. D.

Diary Entry, May 23, 1876

Marched 8 miles 5 1/2 to 9 1/2 passed Young Mens buttes the grave of a Sargeant[32] Camped on high ground near a butte[33] timber & water in a ravine north of camp passed a place in the distance resembling an abandoned post put on summer coat lovely weather good grass water good but hard

Letter, May 23, 1876

Camp No. 8 7 P.M.
May 23rd 76

Dearest darling wife
I have had since 9 A.M. in camp only marched 8 miles today nice ground no mud yesterday we had a nice road but had a stream to cross camped early today we just took things easy had roasted

rib of Antelope for dinner & soup & meat for dinner   don't we live though & don't my appetite surprise every body   I ought to get fat   have slept all the afternoon   expect a mail tonight but of course will not get anything as it is now tuesday. The band has just struck up   dont you wish you was along   it is nice when the weather is fair and the marches short but my nose and ears are nearly burned off   I am trying Glycerine & alum[34]   I hope darling you are enjoying yourself as well as I am   I only had two sick in quarters & one Hospital   the Hospital is ambulance daytime & dog tents nights. When Drs don't care for the sick who will[35]   it has been lovely for two days and the marching good   plenty of Antelope. I gave my wash out today. Genl Terry I learn wishes to try first to bring the Indians into the Reservations & if they wont come to fight them   he I believe is not in favor of the treatment they have received for some time past. Darling I will try & find if there is another mail back & then finish this in time for next mail   no Indians yet or signs   love & kisses from your loving Husband JMD

Diary Entry, May 24, 1876

Left Young Mens Buttes at 5 A.M. went 8 miles & crossed stream nearly dry 8 miles or 9 miles   camped in a valley on Heart River passed a butte 3 miles from camp. no unusual incident   see the usual amount of chase of Antelope by the Hounds   band plays at every fish in the stream   camped at 3 P.M. had to bridge the coolie 8 miles back   Marched 18 miles

May 24 evening [*still part of May 23 letter*]

Darling it is with the greatest pleasure that I kneel to my board to write we have had a march of about 17 miles[36] splendid weather   the band plays & expect to move out at 3 A.M. hope to have an oportunity to send you this ere long   we are getting on near the little Missouri are camped on the head of Heart River tonight. Expect to reach Little Missouri in two days   have had a nice country today only one colie to cross or Bridge   love & kisses darling from your Hub J.M.D.

Diary Entry, May 25, 1876

Moved at 5 got in camp at 2 1/2 about 20 miles   camped on a Branch of heart River   nice country   one bridge to lay   stream to cross on starting   one mule nearly drowned   Dr A[shton] in ambulance   Porter sick   no unusual Incident

Evening 25 [*still part of May 23 letter*] Camp No 10—7 p.m.[37] Well darling I have marched 20 miles today   had a good supper & feel splendid   the sun has nearly burned my ears off but I guess they will get well soon. We crossed the heart river this morning or a branch of it had nice road & no dust much as yet   we expect to reach the Little Missouri day after tomorrow   Dr. Porter has been out from the command today & killed an antelope.[38] I should like to try but dear I am a little lazy & do not want to have my scalp lifted yet though I do not think there is any danger yet but I am going to be on the safe side and stay with the command.[39] I guess you will have some trouble reading this for I have wrote it in all shapes &c   the Band plays now & every evening & marching out of camp every morning. so we have something to cheer the dashing Cavalier.[40] Retreat is just going & I must retire to my sleep & rest for the morrow   darling I think of you often as I march along   I do not get tired   I can stand as much horseback riding as any of them   I guess General Terry gets about the most tired of anyone except Lt. Gibbs who is a poor rider & does not enjoy it much. The trip is not pleasant to some high in rank for several reasons which I will tell you when I come home   good night darling   happy hours to my darling wife.

J.M.D.

Diary Entry, May 26, 1876

Marched at 5 A.M. 10 miles Camped at 2 1/2 P.M. Crossed a branch of the Heart starting & the Heart 4 miles further   had two bridges to make   a very nice country rolling nice valley. very hot   mosquitos troublesome   have my first swim of the season in a pond hole   rec'd letter from Frank at mornings Camp.

May 26th 76 [*still part of May 23 letter*]

Darling I recd your letter with Mothers enclosed   yours dated the 21st 76   it was delivered just as we were mounting this morning   I heard that the mail was in but supposed it was thursday & did not expect it yet but the Steward came & brought it to me   I am very sorry darling that you are so sick but hope you will be well when this reaches you   I fear you have worked yourself sick   you told me in your last you were cleaning house   I do so hope you are well now and am so sorry for you that I cannot be with you. darling you must try & have a good time & if you want to, go in the Lake, but do not go when there is a wind.[41] Well darling we have had a very easy march today or at least only marched about 10 miles   had two bridges to lay & delayed about 2 1/2 hours at each   it takes a long time to get 100 wagons over a bridge when one or two runs off & has to be taken to pieces which nearly always occurs   the mosquitos have bit my hands badly   my face they cannot get at for hair & dirt & dear I had a compliment on my cleanly looks but I suspect the party was fishing for one himself (Dr. Porter)   the first Joke was tried on me yesterday but fell flat as I was not quite inquisitive enough. I suppose you have seen the Bismark tribune. Well I will give you the duties of the Surgeons of the Command. Dr J. W. Williams Chief M.O. Dr Porter attends H Qrs & Battery & one co of Infantry. Dr Ashton attends two Cos of Infantry (Maj. Surgeon commanding)   Dr Clark attends the Left Wing consisting of six companies of Cavalry, commanded by Capt. Benteen 7 Cav. I attend the Right wing, Col. Reno Comd consisting of six Companies of Cavalry & the Scouts come to my

Misjudgment and the Trail to Disaster

wing for attendance   of course darling there is not much to do, I could attend the whole command. but in case of an engagement then it would be too much for one   there has been a horse run just across the creek from my tent while I am writing this to you[42]   I had my first swim (in a pond hole about 20 feet square and up to my chin) this afternoon   have been & had my supper & I think we are going to have a shower tonight   shall I get a Pony for you when I come in   it has been very hot today. I find I am skipping from one thing to another so rapidly I guess you will not call this a real good letter   I don't know when I can send you this   it is now expected that we shall reach the Little Missouri Monday night   I don't see much of Terry. Custer they go in advance & of course I go with my wing commander. Good night darling wife   love & fond remembrance & hoping so much darling that you are well again.

JMD

Diary Entry, May 27, 1876

Marched 15 miles 5 A.M. to 3 P.M. got into the edge of the Missouri Badlands[43]   got an opinion of red Lava from a high mound back of tent in evening   no streams but some coulees to cross   fair day   Rain last evening on Davids [Davis] Creek at night   the badlands consist in Pyramids of Clay & red lava stair   mail lttr to F

Evening 27th [*still part of May 23 letter*] Darling we have arrived at the Badlands of Little Missouri and expect to reach the L Missouri tomorrow   I hear there will be an express back in a day or two so I will com this so it may be sure & go. darling we had a light shower & marched 10 miles this morning & had to turn back to find the trail to enter the bad lands. and came to the Davids [Davis] Creek about 3 P.M. the days are getting pretty hot & the horses get stuck up with wild cactus & then don't they bound and make it merry for their riders   it is sometimes fun to see a company march through a bed of it   My horse has not had the luck to get caught yet   well darling I do so hope you are well again   I am having nice times   my ears are nearly burned off   bye darling   love & kisses from your loving husband

James M DeWolf

Strength of Company	64	
Troop L. 7 Cavalry		parts frozen
Lieut W. T. Craycroft	1st Lieutnant Co. L.	nose + face
1 James Butler	Sergt nose	face + side
2 William Cashan	Sergt Mar 15th	nose face + fingers of right hand
3 Henry Bender	C Sergt	nose
4 William H. Harrison	Corpl	nose
5 Louis Lobering	Pvt Mar 15th	face + nose
6 Nathan T. Brown	"	toes of right foot
7 Louis Hankey [Hauggi]	"	face + chin severe
8 William Dye	"	Ears
9 Elmer Babcock	"	Nose + lips
10 Byron Tarbox	"	Nose
11 Thomas Tweed	"	Nose + Ears
12 James Galoon [Galvan]	"	fingers of both hands (tips)
13 Philip McCue [McHugh]	"	tips of toes of both feet
14 Weston Harrington	" 15 Mar	" fingers of right hand
15 George Zimmerman	Sergt Hospital	Toes of both feet
16 John Caldwell[44]	15 Mar Pvt Hospital	Toes of both feet
17 Peter E Rose	"	Great toe of right foot

Misjudgment and the Trail to Disaster   107

Strength of Company Troop E 7 Cavalry	59		parts frozen
Capt L McDougall		Capt of Comp B	nose + face
1 Robert [Owen] Boyle		Pvt	nose + lips tips fingers right hand
2 Henry Lange		Pvt	nose chin + toes of both feet
3 Thomas [Francis] Heagner		Corpl	chin + fingers tips of both hands
4 George A Moon [Moonie]		Trumpeter	chin + fingers of both hands
5 David Aikison		Pvt	nose chin + fingers of right hand
6 Henry Abbot		"	fingers of right hand
7 Owen Boyles		"	chin fingers both hands toes of both feet
8 John Heim		"	nose all left fingers + tips
9 William Reese		"	toes of left foot
10 Patrick OConnel [O'Connor]		"	Nose + fingers of both hands
11 John Davis		"	forehead + all of his fingers

12 Julius Gilbirt	"	nose
13 William A Lomy[45]	"	fingers of both hands toes of left foot
14 Henry Schele	"	ears + toes of right foot
15 Alexander Stella	"	Lips + nose
16 Henry S Mason	Corpl	tips of all of his fingers
17 Zach Henderson[46]	"	little finger of right hand
18 John S. Henley[47]	"	tips of all fingers Great toe of right foot
19 George C Brown	Corpl	all his fingers + nose
20 William B Jones[48]	Sergt	chin + nose
21 William H. Shields	Saddler	nose and all of his fingers
22 Patrick McAnn	Pvt	nose + cheek

Diary Entry, May 28, 1876

7 miles 4 1/2 A.M. to 12 M   Made Seven Crossings. 4 Companies went on below in afternoon to build crossing. Johnson Co I 7 Cav biten by a Rattlesnake   Cauterized wound & ligatured finger & gave Stimulant Whiskey. bit at 11 evening hand some swollen   had vomited from Whiskey perhaps[49]

Rain at evening camp on a Peninsula[50]

Diary Entry, May 29, 1876

5 miles 5 A.M. to 10 A.M. 4 Bridges   Camp on the little Missouri.[51] preparing for scout tomorrow. rough lands   pass down Canon of Davids [Davis] Creek

Letter, May 29, 1876

Camp on the Little Missouri (D.T.)
May 29th 76

Darling wife
I learn there is a mail to leave tomorrow night and as we are going to make a little detour tomorrow and will perhaps not be back until late I will write some now   we have been two days coming 13 miles and built 11 or 12 bridges   the bridges are just logs & brush put in the bed of the stream (there is little or no water) and dirt & sods piled on and the banks graded so the teams can drive in & out   yesterday we got in camp at 12 & today at 10 A.M. so you can imagine what hard times we are having   we arrived at the River today and are going out to look around & see if there are any signs of Indians but the scouts have been out 10 miles & found no signs so it is not very probable we shall find any. I am going to have my washing done tomorrow & must be up early. I hope dearest darling you are well again & hope to be able to get you a letter nearly every week   good night darling happy dreams   oh one man was bitten by a R. Snake   treated by Dr Williams & is now I think out of all danger[52]   my sick are nearly all from injuries   only one sick from other causes. love & kisses J.M.D.

Diary Entry, May 30, 1876

Left camp with General G A Custer & 4 Companies of 7th Cav and followed up the Little Missouri 23 miles or thereabouts   Crossed the river 13 times   went out on a Plateau & returned by way of going out   Crossing the River in all 26 times   Smelled gas at 22 miles down R   left at 5 A.M. & returned at 6 P.M. halted one hour for lunch & two short halts   animals tired   the crossings very quaky &c   mud terrible & soft sand. Mail letter to Mrs. D   Rained 7 P.M. to 9 P.M.

❧

30th Evening 6 P.M. [*still part of May 29 letter*] Darling have just got in   have had nearly 50 miles ride today with Genl Custer & 4 Co Cav   went up the Little Missouri 24 or 5 miles   crossed it 13 times each way 26 in all   had a great time   lots of fun seeing the horses mire & throw their riders   the Genls. nephew[53] got thrown over his horses head into a mud hole   My old steed made them all   saw no signs of Indians except those 2 or 3 years old   tomorrow we move forward towards the Yellowstone   I expect I will take 5 or 6 days   cannot send any more letters until I arrive there   well darling I hope you are well again   give my regards to all. I think of you every day & shall be careful of myself if need should be but do not expect there will be any occasion   love & kisses darling from your loving Husb.

J M DeWolf

Diary Entry, May 31, 1876

8 A.M. to 2 1/2 P.M. 8 miles through badlands after crossing the Little Missouri going west on Stanleys trail   Rained some in morning & evening   cloudy all day   no dust but hills & bad traveling. Smelled Gas & smoke at summit beyond the Buttes to be examined on returning[54]

Diary Entry, June 1, 1876

The rain continued through the night   Snowing in morning & continued all day. thawing   remain in camp[55] all day   do not move   it is hell & more. muddy.

Letter, June 1, 1876

8 Miles from Little Missouri
Camp No 15
June 1st 1876

Darling wife.
I got in camp yesterday at 2 P.M. it commenced raining at 6 and rained through the night   arose at 3 this morning found it snowing & the ground covered. reveille went and I went over for Breakfast but found no one up   came back & orders came that we would not break camp until further orders   went to bed with overcoat & all. went & got my breakfast at 10. & have just now 4 P.M. Just came from dinner   it has snowed hard all day & continues   I have got me a stretcher for a bedstead & have a fire built in the front of my tent and am nicely except for the ashes blowing in & also smoke but will make up for that by taking a hot toddy after a while. the men in their dog tents have it the worst   they have been standing around the fire most of the day. it is like a March or april day at home   snow & mud the ground has been nearly covered all day   now while I have it in mind the slippers cost $3.00 & 18 cts postage   good night darling

Diary Entry, June 2, 1876

Snow squalls every few minutes all day   mud & slush part of the train moved over the ravines beyond the Right Wing at 2 P.M.

Camp 16 June 2nd [*still part of June 1 letter*] 2 P.M. No move today   snow squalls all day   I laid in bed until 11 1/2   went & got some coffee mountain sheep hard bread & butter for lunch   we have had all the Deer Antelope Sheep &c we could eat since the first day out. It is snowing now and there are some of the wagons moving across on this side of a ravine to be ready for tomorrow and to get out of the mud so the animals can get better grass. I have a fire in front of my tent & it nearly smokes my eyes out. now darling

I occasionaly think how nice a home would be—"be it ever so humble." I think it hard & have a wall tent & all the conveniences possible.[56] how do those take it that have perhaps been reared more tenderly and are now mule driving or are in the dog tents   perhaps stationed on the highest hill in the vicinity and constantly to watch (or on Picket)   there are only a few of the men that have rubber coats they get wet & dry themselves by standing around the fires. I have two quite interesting cases now on hand   one Leeper the painter of E Troop an Abscess of the palm of the hand and one of solidified lung or portions of it[57]   I often think why live in such a life as this. but perhaps "the sun may be shining tomorrow." hope of the future is what keeps many heavy hearts in this world of hardships.[58] well darling I have until we get to the Yellowstone to finish this so I will wait until the sun shines in my soul as well as from the heavens   I do so hope you are well again darling   I can hardly wait till I get another letter

Diary Entry, June 3, 1876

Marched to Beaver Creek   Started 5 A.M. got in at 4 P.M. snow in the hill tops in the morning   quite cold   hot as hell in the afternoon   all headaches on our arriving in camp. Received news from Gibbon[59] who is short of rations & surrounded by Indians   has lost 1 Soldier & one or two citizens   nice country rolling Prairie today   boil on my cheek give me a severe headache

Letter, June 3, 1876

June 3rd 76 Camp No 16 Beaver Creek (Stanleys Trail)[60]

Darling wife we have march over 25 miles but took from 5 A.M. to 4 P.M. waiting for the wagons &c   it was dreadful cold this morning but hot enough this afternoon   we met a messenger from the stockade[61] which is about 30 miles stating that Genl Gibbin was up the Yellowstone opposite or on Rosebud Creek or river   you can find it on the map and we talk and expect to go directly up there from this point & not go to the stockade but it seems to be a hasty conclusion & we may not go but I will finish this so to send if we do not go to the stockade   if we do you will very probably get two when this is received   Gibbin has had one or two killed but they went out from the command to hunt & of course should have known better. they have had no fight & will not soon[62]   well we see enough to fire at but of course straglers may get killed   but I have not & do not intend to straggle so dear you can rest easy about me   my duties will not call me in any danger but I dont expect we will any of the command be exposed except perhaps some of the flankers may when we get up in the Powder river country   I hear Capt. Baker of B 6th Infty swing out 25 miles tomorrow so darling good night   love & kisses & hoping you are well. I suppose when you get this we will be near ready to turn back   hoping so   darling I expect we shall be in by Aug 15 or 20   night darling from your loving husband

J.M.D.

Diary Entry, June 4, 1876

18 miles up Beaver Creek 5 to 3 p.m. rolling several coollees to cross   go hunting find lots of Antelope   two young wildcats get nothing   nice cool day   some snow still remaining on the hills in patches from June 1st & 2nd   Cross the creek at tonights camp[63]

Diary Entry, June 5, 1876

Marched South 8 miles   passed over a divide between the Beaver C. & Cabin Creeks   bad sands for a mile after crossing the divide   went S.W. about 10 miles   Crossed Cabin Creek & west 2 miles 5 to 3 p.m. 18 to 21 miles[64]   1st Sergt of B Troop[65] reported an indian 2 miles from last night camp   see numerous signs of Buffalo   strike Stanleys trail at 9 a.m.

Diary Entry, June 6, 1876

Leave Stanleys Crossing. Cross a branch of O'Fallons Creek 10 miles and cross O'Fallons Creek   cross it 10 miles from Stanleys crossing above 5 A.M. to 4 P.M.[66] March 22 1/2 miles   hard days   some Indian signs   very high wind all day   one Buffalo killed. Man accidently shot through calf of leg coming out on back of right foot   pistol accidently went off while mounting[67]

Diary Entry, June 7, 1876

5 A.M. to 8 P.M. 32 miles about go direct across to Powder River[68] from O'Fallon Creek   keep up on the divides   a bad pass & several deep ravines about 4 miles from Powder river   steep banks & liable to wash   would be impassable in wet weather. Cloudy & cool all day   some fine misty rain   not enough to wet the ground   found several remnants of Buffalo carcases that Indians had killed   game getting scarce no doubt due to the presence of Indians in the vicinity found some wild Heilatrope[69] as found in Oregon   some sage brush and some Rolling Prairie & Badlands.

Diary Entry, June 8, 1876

Remain in camp on Powder River   Genl Terry & 2 Co Cav start for Boat at mouth of river fair

Letter, June 8, 1876

Camp on Powder River Montana
June 8th 1876

Darling wife
I have an oportunity to send a letter down to our base of supplies at the mouth of this River. well darling since I sent my last, we have traveled along over hills around muddy creeks through

badlands &c. Yesterday we started at 5 and marched & marched over hills   crossed some of the worst possible coolies for wagons to cross   got into Powder River where we remain today & tomorrow I suppose   arriving at 8 P.M. did we not have a day of it part of the way   we had a fine misty rain it was cool & high wind all day till 6 P.M. when we came down the divide into camp   it was fine & every one so glad to get into camp. well darling we are to start out for a scout for 8 or 10 days up this river.[70] (I cannot tell you much about it now as I have not been to it. It is over about 50 yards, the brush—) General Terry has not decided yet   he has gone down to the Boats at the mouth of the River to hear from Gibbon, when he will decide on what to do first   the wagons are going to be escorted down by the three companies of Infantry and the whole Regt of Cavalry & General Terry are to start from here after Wild Geese &c &c   we are thirty miles from the mouth of the Eastern shore the River is muddy like the Missouri   I am now somewhat inclined to think our stay up here will be short we have not seen an indian yet nor much signs & every one of the Command except a few think we will not find them on fighting terms. my nose & ears are nearly all off & lips burned   laughing is impossible. but don't we have delicious venison steaks & had Buffalo steaks two days past   today for dinner we had Beans, Bacon, Biscuit & Butter, Hard tack[71] Coffee & an apple Pudding & Peas and some of the most splendid venison steaks I ever eat. of course we had some ashes & dirt [sic, more humor] but things tasted good and my appetite has not failed me once and I have not been tired yet. my side has not pained me this summer   the Steward give me everything to stay at the base of supplies   they cannot furnish him a horse   he has given me his Cartridges & Rubber so I shall go out from here as well as the best   no tents are to be taken   wont that be Jolly. I suppose we shall have to ford this River as many times as the Little Missouri we have not heard from Crooks yet   our sick are sent down from here Dr Ashton goes with them. I have had my washing done today & had your blue necktie washed   it looks nice. I hope you are well and having a nice time   suppose Dr F is back before this   I will finish this before we leave here   love & kisses darling from your loving Hu J.M.D.

Diary Entry, June 9, 1876

Remain in Powder River camp all day   Rain afternoon Genl Terry returned at night late

June 10th [*still part of June 8 letter*] darling we have remained in this camp to date   we—our wing is going up Powder River on a scout   the balance of Comd & wagons are going down to Boats   then up the Yellowstone or that is the current report   we are going to take Pack Mules and expect to be able to travel rapidly but it has rained since yesterday   not very rapidly will we go I guess for a day or two at least   I am well and am glad to think we are about to turn the home corner for I expect after this scout we will know when to expect to return   all is in hurry today so bye bye darling love & kisses from your ever loving Husband

J.M.D.

Dr Porter goes with me.

Diary Entry, June 11, 1876

5 A.M. to 3 P.M. 26 miles   March 6 miles & cross the River ten more miles & cross a large Creek on west side 5 1/2 A.M. to 1 1/2 [P.M.]   March 26 miles   see a smoke in the distance when we went into camp the flats are very soft & very hard marching   cross the River without difficulty   Showering in afternoon.

Diary Entry, June 12, 1876

5 A.M. to 2 P.M. 24 miles   follow up west shore of River to the forks   pass mouth of creek 12 miles from starting point today and another 4 miles below tonights camp   both crossing in on the eastern side find where a large body of Indians had moved from about one week ago perhaps 30 families   find one Pony   see him

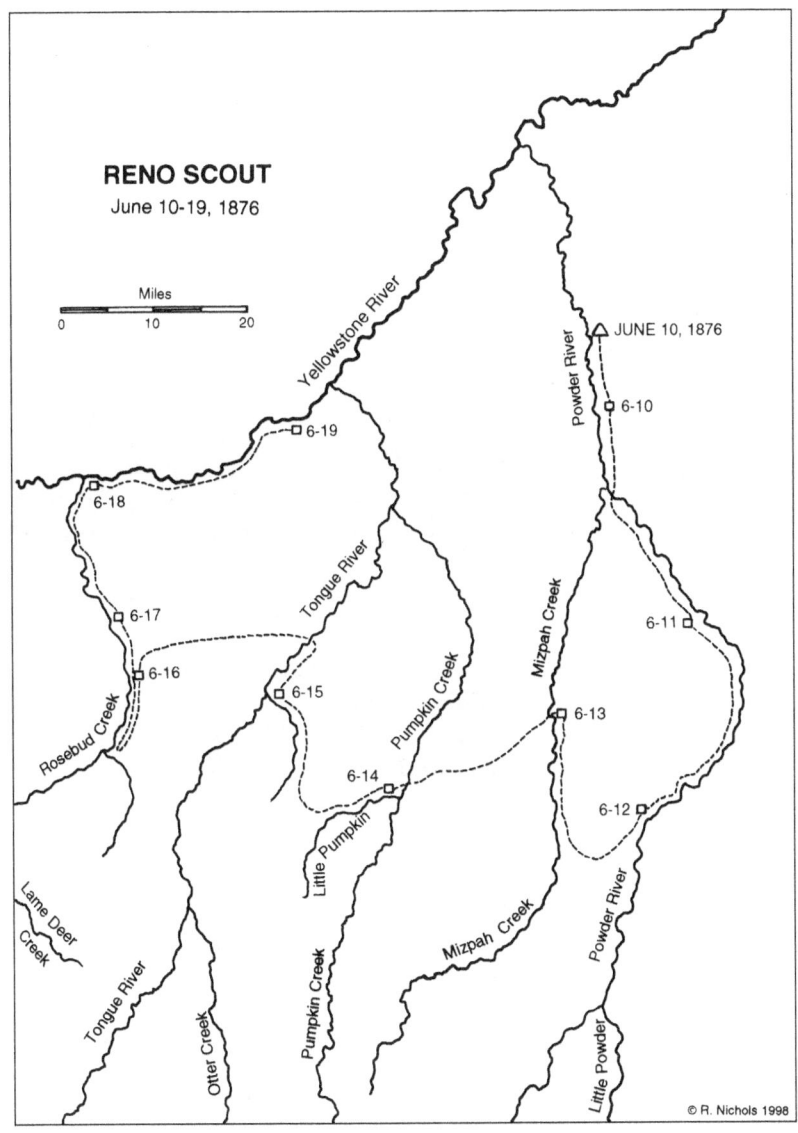

Map originally published in
Ronald H. Nichols, In Custer's Shadow: Major Marcus Reno
(Norman: University of Oklahoma Press, 2000).

DeWolf journal page, entries for June 12–14, 1876
*Courtesy of the National Park Service,
Little Bighorn Battlefield National Monument,
LIBI_00007_01992, "Dr. DeWolf's Diary, circa 1876."*

first 2 miles distant   fair day walked on high Buttes where Indian was on Picket   saw the two branches of the River   I[Indian] tells me + E fork & 50 or Sixty west of W fork

Diary Entry, June 13, 1876

5 a.m. to 1 p.m. 24 1/2 miles   Cross from Powder River to Mizpah Creek or dry creek   rough crossing   very crooked trail & hard & hot marching   saw one Buffalo   one running across a divide

& saw one in the distance   the branches of creek nearly all dry & very little where we camped   S of W

Diary Entry, June 14, 1876

5 a.m. to 1 p.m. 22 1/2 miles   Crossed from Mizpah Creek march up Pumpkin Creek from mile to about 1 mile above its forks on west. fork about 12 miles from M Creek to divide   fair road divide   some pine & ravines but not so bad as to Powder River from O'Fallon Creek   fair day   trails S of W

Diary Entry, June 15, 1876

5 a.m. to 1 p.m. 25 miles   Up a branch of the Pumpkin   broad valley   10 miles to divide   found & kill an Elk   see one more up mountain pass down ravine   Gatling gun upset[72]   march down a branch of Tongue River to Tongue River & camp on the Tongue   timber plentiful on the divides   fine cotton wood along the stream   the Tongue is not so muddy as the Powder perhaps due to no late rains.

Diary Entry, June 16, 1876

8
5 a.m. to 2 p.m. 27 miles marched 8 miles down the Tongue T then direct across to Rosebud Creek
   35
West   rough & sage brush but could be crossed by wagons by some work   plenty of old Buffalo signs   none new or of Indians   now boil water for camp & poor grass 8 1/2 to 11 1/2 p.m. 8 miles marched at evening 8 miles 4 1/2 to Rosebud and about 3 1/2 up the Rosebud Creek   find a large trail week old   trail lodge-pole &c

Diary Entry, June 17, 1876

8 A.M. to 10 A.M. 6 1/2 miles 4 P.M. 8 P.M. 14 miles   Marched up the Rosebud 7 1/2 miles & camped till afternoon then marched down the valley about 15 miles   the valley is broken by ravines but broad & not high bluffs   the land slopes gently back   Cotton wood & rose bushes no grass[73]   Very large trail passing up the valley all of todays march

Diary Entry, June 18, 1876

5 1/2 A.M. to 12 M. 20 miles march down the Rosebud to the Yellowstone river 18 3/4 miles march down to near opposite Gibbons camp[74] communicated with them   the valley of the Rosebud is quite Broad & could be passed up by wagons   some ravines &c to cross   fair & quite hot day   the Yellowstone seems navigable at this point   the remains of an old trading fort are at the junction of the Rosebud & Yellowstone E. Ent of R & S of Yellowstone.[75]

Diary Entry, June 19, 1876

4 1/2 A.M. to 4 P.M. 33 miles marched 9 3/4 miles back from the river on the bluffs 8 miles along river bottom then the balance on Bluffs   the last mile was dreadful badlands & almost impassable   found lots of Agates   some pretty

Diary Entry, June 20, 1876

4 P.M. to 8 1/2 P.M. 14 miles marched back up the Yellowstone after the Boat came up to us from 4 miles below the Tongue R. we were 6 miles above the mouth of the Tongue R   the left wing & Genl Custer Joined the latter & taken command   Genl Terry Hd Qrs remaining on the Boat Far West   Camped on the

Misjudgment and the Trail to Disaster

Y[ellowstone].R[iver]. Meet Genl Terry Custer & Williams and the Dept Staff on board   have hair cut & shave

DIARY ENTRY, JUNE 21, 1876

Marched 6 A.M. to 12. 19 miles to 1/2 mile below the mouth of the Rosebud Creek. Camp & get ready to fit out for our Expedition. Genl Gibbon command moves up opposite

LETTER, JUNE 21, 1876

Yellowstone, Mouth of Rosebud Creek
June 21st 76

Darling wife
Since my last from Powder River we went up to the forks of the powder river 58 miles   Crossed the country to Tongue River 72 miles down Tongue River 8 miles   Crossed to Rosebud Creek about 25 miles up Rosebud creek 12 miles then back and followed it to its mouth   from there down the Yellowstone 33 miles to near the mouth of Tongue River where we met Custer & the other Six Companies of Cavalry, General Terry & Staff   Genl Terry & are on the "Far West" Steamer. last night we marched 14 miles up the Yellowstone & today we came up here 19 miles to where we left three days ago the mouth of the Rosebud Creek and are fitting up for a scout under Genl Custer with 12 Companies of Cavalry up the rosebud across to the Big Horn River & down that to the Yellowstone or that is where we expect to go on our scout   we marched about 25 miles a day in all about 285 miles   I and Dr Porter messed together and had a nice time   have just been getting a supply for the next scout   the Commissary is a very good supply on the Boat. we found no Indians   not one   all old trails   they seem to be moving west and are driving the Buffalo   I think it is very clear that we shall not see an Indian this summer   the Post

Second Lieutenant Benjamin Hodgson
Courtesy of the National Park Service, Little Bighorn Battlefield National Monument, LIBI_00256_07822. Produced by Mason Aferon, "Studio Portrait of Lt. Benjamin Hodgson in 7th Cavalry Dress Uniform and Plumed Helmet," c. 1872 (produced in 1879).

Trader or John Smith has opened his Whisky &c & of course you all know what will follow for the time we remain here[76] General Gibbons Command are encamped opposite us   the Boat will take our Battery over to him this evening   it has hurt three men already (the Battery) by upsetting. Dr. Lord[77] has joined us and will take Dr Williams place as chief Medical Officer on this scout. there is lots of feeling among the Troops out this summer or the would be commanders   a Genl snubs somebody   somebody snubs one lower & so on down &c&c

Darling I did so hope I should hear from you on returning to the Boat and may before we start out though we shall start tomorrow or next day. we usually start at 5 A.M. and march until 1 or 2 P.M. which is not hard and is fun when there is any trail but I fear we shall not find even a sign that is new this time   it is believed that the Indians have scattered & gone back to their Reservations. Yesterday I went out with Dr Porter Lt Harrington & Hodgson

Misjudgment and the Trail to Disaster

pistol shooting and came out second best   Porter was best so you see some of the cavalry cannot shoot very well   Hodgson & I are harassing (Joking &c &c) each other & have some nice times   he is Adjutant of the Right Wing "6" Companies of Cavalry   I do so hope you are well again   I am very anxious to hear how you are getting along   I hope when we return from this scout we shall be nearly ready to return   then darling only think we will have 300 or 400 miles to march home again   these horseback rides are nice but there is to much in this to suit me but it cheers me up to see the Cavalry wild we had two cases of *slight* sunstrokes (it was before the Whisky was opened)[78]   It has been trying hard to rain this afternoon but not succeeded so far & guess or hope it will be some cooler after it. Rosebud Creek takes its name by being profusely bordered by the wild Roses like those of Warner. I send you one in this letter. we found one Buffalo and some Elk the last scout   have had Elk Buffalo Antelope Deer and nearly all games Bighorn sheep &c.[79] My nose & Ears have are nearly well   yesterday & today was very hot but now the air begins to feel quite comfortable. well darling I must close this as the Boat moves down the River some little distance & the mail closes tonight & I want to be sure this goes in this mail for it has been 11 days since I wrote or had a chance to write. you must remember darling that one feels pretty tired after getting into camp and then we have so much to do to fit up again for this   every thing goes on pack mules & dirt is plentiful. love & kisses darling   my regards to all. from your loving Hub

J M DeWolf[80]

Diary Entry, June 22, 1876

12 M to 4 [A.M.]. 12 miles   marched up the rosebud Creek on our trail of the 18th ult part of the way but keep on west side of creek

Diary Entry, June 23, 1876

5 A.M. to 3 P.M. 33 miles   continued up the Rosebud C find large deserted camps   the valley completely barren   has been an enormous number of horses passed about 10 to 20 days ago   11 miles above where Reno was the 17th ult   very hot

Diary Entry, June 24, 1876

5 A.M. to 7 P.M. 3 hour halt. marched 10 miles & found a large branch nearly as large as main stream   found another 7 miles beyond   marched within a few miles of the forks   found lots of new signs   old camps in profusion   they begin not to be so high
[*End of entries*]

CHAPTER 4

"If He Had Gotten a Few Feet Further..."
THE RETREAT TO RENO HILL

> "[W]HEN THE RETREAT WAS ORDERED,
> I WAS JUST BEHIND HIM AS WE CROSSED THE RIVER.
> I SAW HIM SAFE ACROSS AND THEN HE TURNED UP A RAVINE
> A LITTLE TO MY LEFT WHICH WAS THE LAST I SAW
> OF MY FRIEND AND COMPANION."
> *Doctor Henry R. Porter regarding*
> *Doctor James DeWolf during the Reno valley fight*

THAT DOCTOR DEWOLF was near his new friends Henry Porter, Benny Hodgson, and Charles Varnum when he died is no surprise. With little sleep following a long night ride, they probably had no idea of the magnitude of events they would encounter that day, despite knowing that the Indians had been found.

At mid-evening of June 24, information from the Crow scouts indicated that the Sioux village was nearby on the lower course of the Little Big Horn River. Upon receiving this report, Custer sent Second Lieutenant Varnum, in charge of the Indian scouts, ahead of the halted regiment with a scouting party to determine the location of the village. Varnum and his party, consisting of the interpreter Mitch Boyer, Charley Reynolds, and six Arikara and five Crow scouts, left about 9:20 P.M. and proceeded to a prominence called the Crow's Nest. This was a high ridge in the Wolf Mountains located above the divide between the Rosebud and Little Big Horn valleys, from which the Crows said they could see for miles toward the Little Big Horn.

They made their observations as dawn began to appear about 3:30 A.M. on June 25, and Varnum sent word to Custer to tell him what they thought they had seen. Reporting to Custer at their early morning meeting around 8 A.M., the Crow and Arikara scouts, along with Boyer, attempted to convince him that the village in the distance was huge. They described seeing smoke from the village and a huge dust cloud from a massive horse herd that "looked like worms squirming around" in the distance. The herd was estimated at about 20,000, which meant that the inhabitant account of the village would be extremely large; "immense," in the words of Varnum, although he later admitted he could not see it. Custer decided to go to the Crow's Nest to investigate for himself. For whatever reason, be it fatigue, poor eyesight, the distance, or simply the early morning haze—most likely it was a combination of all of these aspects—Custer said he could not see the village, even with his binoculars.[1]

Upon returning from the Crow's Nest, Custer's brother, Captain Tom Custer, told him that when one of the sergeants had been sent with a detail of soldiers to retrieve a box of hardtack, which had fallen from one of the pack mules, they came upon several Indians who were opening the box. The soldiers fired at the Indians, who fled on horseback. When told of this incident, Custer assumed that the Indians now knew of his presence.

The column then advanced another three miles to the divide between the Rosebud and Little Big Horn Rivers. There, about twelve miles from the mouth of the Little Big Horn River, Custer gave his last battalion orders just after noon.[2] He split his force, and each group was to go its own assigned way in search of the Indian camp. Of the three groups, Custer took Companies C, E, F, I, and L; Major Reno was assigned Companies A, G, and M; and Captain Benteen was given his own Company H, along with Companies D and K. Of the medical personnel, Doctors DeWolf and Porter were assigned to Reno's division, while Doctor Lord was to go with Custer's column. Lord, who had not been feeling well that day, declined Custer's offer to exchange with Porter (who was agreeable to doing so), a decision that saved Porter's life.[3] Why Custer did not assign a physician or any medical personnel to accompany Benteen's detachment remains a mystery, and neither DeWolf nor Porter commented on it.[4]

Benteen had been ordered to move southwest over a series of two or three bluffs and "sweep everything before him."[5] His assignment, at least in part, was to see whether there were other Indian camps in that direction that might present a counterattack, not just to prevent Indians from escaping in that direction. Benteen and his men disappeared over the bluffs, and Reno would not see him again until later that afternoon. The remainder of the command then moved several miles farther west down Reno Creek to the Little Big Horn valley, Reno's three companies on the left bank paralleling Custer's five companies on the right. They eventually came to a lone tepee, which contained the body of a dead warrior who had been killed at the Rosebud battle with Crook's troops on June 17. Custer called Reno over to join him on his side of the creek. As the columns approached, they saw several Indians fleeing from just beyond the lone tepee.[6]

The two columns then continued about four miles from the lone tepee to the flat, which was near the entrance to the valley and one of the fords of the Little Big Horn River. There Custer's Crow scouts saw additional Sioux.[7] These sightings, along with the earlier ones at the lone tepee and the hardtack box, convinced Custer to attack. Having been told by Adjutant Cooke that "the village was only two miles and a half ahead and running away," Reno also said Cooke relayed Custer's order to proceed as the initial engaging force and "to move forward at as rapid a gait as prudent, and to charge afterward, and that the whole outfit would support [him]."[8] Custer and his staff anticipated that there would be a village to attack, but they assumed that the Indians would flee from an attacking force. Not until Reno rode down the valley to a point where he could see tepees peeking over the trees by the river (or until Custer eventually

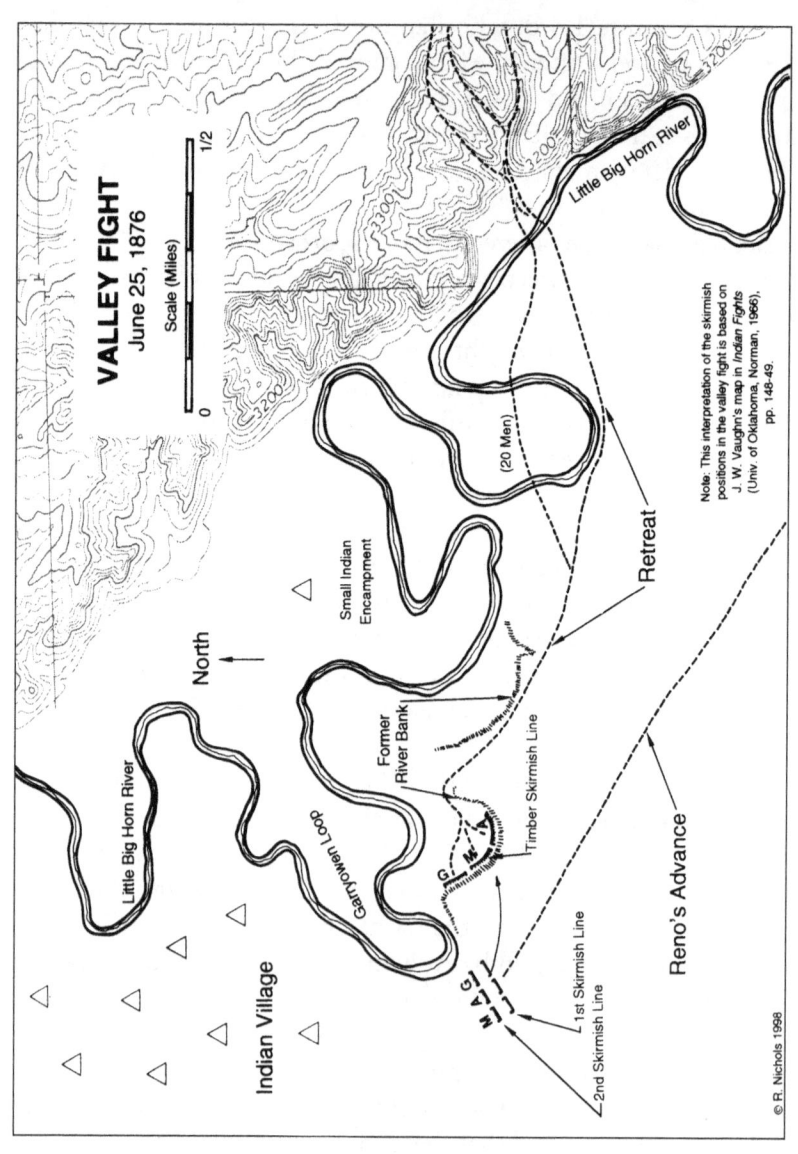

Valley and timber fight areas and Reno's retreat
Map originally published in Ronald H. Nichols, In Custer's Shadow: Major Marcus Reno

The Retreat to Reno Hill

got up onto the bluffs overlooking the river) did anyone know for sure there was a village on the Little Big Horn.

Reno and his companies proceeded slightly northwest over subsequent ridges, at a "trot which [he] thought a prudent gait," to that final ridge overlooking the vast valley.[9] Immediately below, the village came partly into view, although even then it was only a fraction of what was hidden beyond a grouping of trees in their line of sight from that vantage point. After crossing the river and waiting for perhaps ten minutes to "gather the battalion" and allow the horses to water, Reno ordered the battalion to charge the village. It was just after 3:00 P.M.[10] Describing the sequence of events in his own official report, Reno said,

> I deployed and, with the Ree [Arikara] scouts on my left, charged down the valley, driving the Indians with great ease for about two and a half miles. I, however, soon saw that I was being drawn into some trap, as they would certainly fight harder, and especially as we were nearing their village which was still standing, besides, I could not see Custer or any other support, and at the same time the very earth seemed to grow Indians, and they were running toward me in swarms, and from all directions. I saw I must defend myself and give up the attack mounted.[11]

After forming a skirmish line and continuing intense firing for just under half an hour, Reno could see that the Indians were attempting to outflank and surround his command.[12] Reno thus ordered his men to head for the timber, where they remained and fought for about twenty minutes more. There Bloody Knife, Custer's favorite scout and friend, was killed at Reno's side.[13] During this timber fight, DeWolf's whereabouts are not known, but it can be reasonably assumed that he was attending to wounded soldiers just as Porter did. During the desperate fighting, Porter had rendered medical assistance to a mortally wounded private just before the disintegration and retreat to the river.[14] Porter said that amid growing confusion, Major Reno decided to disengage and seek a better defensive position at high ground across the river.[15] As Reno explained in his official report (and at his court of inquiry three years later),

> It was plain to me that the Indians were using the woods as much as I was myself, in sheltering themselves and creeping up on me. I then rode

out on the plain. There was firing there that I could hear but not see. Lieutenant Hodgson came to me and said the Indians were passing to our left and rear, and I told him to bring the skirmishers in round the horses. After going down to the river there and seeing the facilities they had, I knew I could not stay there unless I stayed forever.[16]

During his retreat, several of Reno's command staff, including Hodgson and First Lieutenant Donald McIntosh, were killed. Some made valiant stands, among them Charlie Reynolds, the black interpreter Isaiah Dorman, and McIntosh.[17]

DeWolf was killed in the mad rush to cross the Little Big Horn and ascend the bluffs on the opposite side after Reno ordered the retreat from the timber. As Porter said, "Every man seemed to be looking out for himself, trying to get across as soon as possible."[18] Fleeing soldiers used two retreat routes after recrossing the river just north of where Reno's battalion initially crossed in commencing the attack. Some were forced farther north, or to the left of other retreating soldiers, because the Indians were flanking their left and rear to the west and southwest. The first escape route was the highest and steepest, described by survivors as having a nearly vertical climb. Many of the troopers hung on to their horses' necks while riding or in some instances even held onto their tails to be pulled up from behind. The second route, an easier and more gradual slope, was about thirty to forty yards farther on the soldiers' left. In the wild flight to the bluffs, some soldiers were forced to the left or went left because the climb was significantly easier. DeWolf was in this small group of four or five men. They apparently did not see that some Indians had already made it up across the top of the ridge and were bearing down on them directly as the soldiers ascended the route's more gradual slopes. Typical of later descriptions of this frantic dash to and up the bluffs were those of Private William A. Slaper and Sergeant John Ryan. Slaper related,

> After getting across the river, I had steep bluffs to climb. These were so abrupt that many of the already-wearied horses were unable to carry their riders to the top, and many of the men had to dismount and lead their exhausted animals, all the time being under a murderous fire from the Indians hidden in the brush along the river. On the way up, I passed

the body of Dr. De Wolf, one of our surgeons, who had been shot and killed while trying to gain the top. I arrived at the crest of the hill without even a scratch.[19]

Said Sergeant Ryan,

> In scaling the bluffs, Dr. DeWolf, a contract surgeon on the expedition, was killed. Also Sergeant Clair [actually this is Private Elihu F. Clear of Company K], William D. Myers [Meyer], a farrier of Co. M, and Henry Gordon of Co. M. Their bodies with a number of others laid under cover of our guns, so the Indians did not get a chance to scalp them. After we gained the bluffs, we could look back upon the plains, where the Indians were, and could see them stripping and scalping our men and mutilating their bodies in a horrible manner. The prairie was all afire.[20]

Several accounts note DeWolf's last moments that day, including that of Lieutenant Varnum, who supplied the most detailed description because he was closest to the doctor. To the Reno court of inquiry, he stated, "When I got across I started up a ridge to the left of the command and some of the men called to me to come back and I came back. Evidently they saw Indians I did not see because Dr. DeWolf started up that same ridge and was shot."[21] In another statement, Varnum said,

> I saw Dr. DeWolf with his orderly going up where I did. Men were calling him [to come back]. He turned and just then received a bullet which killed him when about halfway up the bluff. Our men had seen a few Indians laying for persons going that way, and that is why I was called back.
>
> When I got out of the river, I turned to the left, and some of the men called to me to come back. They could see Indians up there [on the bluffs] that I could not see. Dr. DeWolf was going in that direction, and I called to him to come back. He had just started to do so when he was shot.[22]

Another officer, Lieutenant Edgerly, corroborates Varnum's account with additional detail: "Dr. DeWolf seems to have been crowded to the left of the [retreat] ravine, and [while] climbing up the first spur he was all the time in full sight of the Indians who killed him when he was from 50 to 75 yards from the river."[23] Sergeant Edward Davern, a private at the time of the battle, testified, "I saw Lieutenant Wallace shoot across at some Indians who were

SECOND LIEUTENANT CHARLES VARNUM AND COMPANIONS
A rare albumen carte-de-visite (card photograph), c. 1873, of a group including *(left to right)* Varnum of the Seventh Cavalry; Lieutenant Nelson Bronson, Sixth Infantry; Captain Frederick Benteen, Seventh Cavalry; and Captain Thomas French, Seventh Cavalry. *Courtesy of the National Park Service, Little Bighorn Battlefield National Monument, LIBI_00015_00612. Unknown photographer, "Studio Portrait of Lieutenant Varnum, Lieutenant Bronson, Captain Benteen, and Captain French," c. 1873.*

killing a man three or four ridges from there. That hill was divided into ridges of water cuts. . . . I found out afterwards it was Dr. DeWolf."[24] Responding to a question of whether Indians were on the hilltop, Wallace said, "Yes, sir, it has always been my impression that Lieutenant Hodgson was killed from a shot fired from the bluffs. Dr. DeWolf was killed by the Indians on that side. . . . We had lost twenty-seven killed, seven wounded, and Dr. DeWolf and one scout, and an interpreter."[25] Said Sergeant Daniel Kanipe,

> Reaching the pack train, I gave Captain McDougall the orders sent him, and went on toward Captain Benteen as I had been told to take them to him, also. McDougall and his outfit rode on to the top of the hill and reinforced Major Reno as he retired from the bottom of the bluffs.
>
> The Indians were following close at their heels, shooting and yelling, and men were dropping here and there. They, the Indians, would hop on them and scalp them before we could rescue them. Dr. DeWolf was killed just as he reached the top of the hill. If he had gotten a few feet further he would have been saved.[26]

Some have questioned whether DeWolf's orderly was among that group of five scrambling up the left bluff and killed within several yards of each other. Lieutenant Godfrey later mistakenly identified DeWolf's orderly as being Private Elihu Clear. As previously noted, Edward Abbott was DeWolf's orderly. Abbott survived the retreat and rejoined the column after DeWolf's death. Clear, Lieutenant Hare's orderly, apparently was killed on the bluffs just after crossing the river during the retreat, although his burial marker has been placed near DeWolf's.[27]

Another possible reference to DeWolf, published years after the battle, relates,

> One officer of the fleeing [Reno] command aroused the highest admiration of the Indians. He emptied his revolvers in a most effective way and had crossed the river when a gunshot brought him down. There were three noted young warriors of three different [warrior] lodges vying with one another for bravery. They all happened to pursue this officer; each one was intent upon knocking him off with a war club before the others, but the officer dispatched every one of them. The Indians told me of finding peculiar instruments on his person, from which I thought it likely this brave man was Dr. DeWolf who was killed.[28]

SECOND LIEUTENANT
GEORGE D. WALLACE
Wallace witnessed DeWolf's death. He and Private Davern returned fire at the Indians who were shooting at DeWolf in an attempt to help save the doctor; however, the distance was too far. *U.S. Army Heritage and Education Center, Carlisle, Pennsylvania.*

While at first glance this would certainly suggest that the "officer" killed was DeWolf, since DeWolf had his revolvers with him, it is only speculation, as all the other eyewitness accounts describe DeWolf being shot by an Indian from above and not being chased.

Upon reaching the bluffs of what was later designated as "Reno Hill," the surviving members of Reno's battalion regrouped and dug in for an intense defense over the next day and a half. The Custer fight was nearing its conclusion, although the troops with Reno and Benteen had no idea what had happened to Custer and his command. Porter quickly set up an open field hospital in a natural depression near the center of the hill and heroically administered care to sixty-eight wounded soldiers as the fighting continued around him.[29] Benteen and his companies arrived about 4:20 P.M., with Benteen and Reno sharing command. Captain Thomas Weir made an unauthorized attempt to go to Custer's aid, but by then Custer's command had been wiped out some three miles in the distance. The massive "wave" of Indians coming back from that direction to attack the Reno Hill defenders was repulsed with

DeWolf's death site, 2013
National Park Service marker of Doctor DeWolf,
looking toward the timber fight area. *Author's collection.*

what Lieutenant Godfrey would describe as valiant actions by the defenders.[30]

In the next thirty-six hours, the soldiers fought off constant Indian sorties, sniping fire, water shortages, and the sickening stench of dead soldiers and horses. The extreme conditions of hot days and cold nights took their toll as well. Eventually, the Sioux and Cheyenne warriors gave up the siege and left with their families, abandoning the massive village upon the approach of Terry's and Gibbon's columns. Terry and Gibbon, who arrived on the morning of June 27, were greeted by the ghastly and horrifying scenes of carnage. As Godfrey described it, "[T]here was scarcely a dry eye; hardly a word was spoken, but quivering lips and hearty grasping of hand gave token of thankfulness for relief and grief for the dead."[31] Beneath the hot sun, the bloated and decomposing dead bodies on Last Stand Hill and Calhoun Ridge made a grim scene described as "white boulders scattered over the field."[32] Troopers cared for the wounded and began the grisly task of burying the dead.[33] For more than a week, the wounded soldiers were transferred to the steamer *Far West* and transported to Bismarck and then to Fort Abraham Lincoln from June 27 to July 5.

The bodies of the casualties on and around Reno Hill were in close proximity for protection by the surviving soldiers, so DeWolf's remains were protected from mutilation: "Upon the side of the bluff lay three or four bodies, among which was Dr. DeWolf," recalled Sergeant John Ryan. "They laid under cover of our guns so that the Indians would not get a chance to scalp them."[34]

By July 5, news of the Little Big Horn events had reached the East via the newspapers, and people across the nation learned of the death of Custer and 268 men of the Seventh Cavalry. Families received letters similar to the one that Porter eventually sent to the now-widowed Fannie DeWolf. Porter's compassion and desire to console are obvious in his July 28 letter to her:

Camp on the mouth of the Big Horn River Montana Ter.
July 28, 1876

Dear Madam

You have heard the sad sad news—the terrible disaster of the Custer fight and the saddest (to you) of all—the death of your husband Dr. DeWolf. He and myself were very good friends.—We tented and messed together—were riding side by side during the charge and when the retreat was ordered I was just behind him as we crossed the river. I saw him safe across and then he turned up a ravine a little to my left which was the last I saw of my friend and companion—alive. As soon as we reached the bluff, I found he was missing and soon found his body which I had buried the next day. I know it will be a great relief to you when I say that his body was not mutilated in the least—that he was not scalped or his clothes even taken. The Indians had stolen his revolver but not troubled him otherwise. I have collected all his things that I could find and hold them subject to your order as soon as I arrive in Bismarck D.T. where I have sent some of them and where I be at as soon as the campaign is over.

Please address me at Bismarck D.T. when your letters will be forwarded.

I have several letters—addressed to him which are evidently from you and which I will forward to you with the other articles.

You have my heartfelt sympathy in your terrible affliction—and if there is anything I can do please let me know.

Very Respectfully
Your obt Servt.
H. R. Porter
A.A. Surg. USA[35]

This letter is important for several reasons. First, Porter corroborates the previously mentioned eyewitness accounts of his friend's death and supports Sergeant Ryan's claim that his body was protected from desecration. Second, it provides important detail about DeWolf's location during the course of the Reno valley fight, including the fact that DeWolf and Porter rode together side by side at the beginning of the attack. Third, it provides evidence that DeWolf carried his revolver into the battle (a potential correlation with the account that DeWolf may have also been involved in the fighting), unlike Porter, who had refused Reno's offer of a pistol. Why Porter refused the revolver and chose not to carry a weapon into the battle remains a mystery, particularly in view of his experience in the army's Arizona Indian campaigns and his being an avid hunter and marksman.[36]

Some two months after his first correspondence with Fannie DeWolf, Porter sent a second letter. That he and DeWolf had become good friends is readily apparent in Porter's stated admiration for his late friend and his sensitivity and compassion in reply to what was obviously Fannie's request for further details of how her husband had been killed. Although details of the condition of DeWolf's body had been purposely concealed out of respect for

Fannie, Porter's description of DeWolf's body is kind and consoling. His letter reads as follows:

Bismarck, D.T.
Sept 14 1876

Mrs. Fanny DeWolf

Dear Madam
I returned a few days ago & found your letter waiting.

Yes he was killed instantly—he was shot in the left chest and four times in the face—probably the first shot in the breast caused instant death as it was in the region of the heart. The other 4 shots, I think, were fired from his own revolver after he was dead by the Indian who killed him and who stole his revolver.

The Dr. never said anything which indicated that he feared any harm would befall him yet sometimes I thought he appeared rather sad and once or twice it entered my mind that he had a presentiment of that kind.

Next spring there will probably be an effort to get the remains of the officers; if so, his body will of course be sent to you. I send you tomorrow by U.S. Express all of his things that I could find. You will find some of your unanswered letters which never reached him; also his watch—pocket book containing $10—pillow, overcoat, clothing, &c.

In regards to his pay I do not know—am under the impression that he drew pay in advance as quite a number of the officers did—perhaps you know all about it.

Please let me hear from you again on receipt of the things. I hope they will reach you safe & if there is anything I can do please let me know.

Very Respectfully Yours
H. R. Porter

If you have a photograph of the doctor to spare I should prize it very highly H.R.P.[37]

JAMES MADISON DEWOLF
Possibly the photo that Fannie DeWolf gave to Doctor Porter on his request for a photo of his late friend.
From Reverend Calbraith Perry's *Charles D'Wolf of Guadaloupe*, 1902.
Date and photographer unknown.
Courtesy of Firelands Historical Society, Norwalk, Ohio.

Aside from its condolences and compassion, this September 14 letter provides additional information Porter alluded to in his first letter. Mentioning in July that he had "collected all [DeWolf's] things that he could find," Porter lists those items specifically at the end of this second letter, including DeWolf's pocketbook (or diary) and overcoat. Perhaps the most important aspect is Porter's recovery of DeWolf's pocketbook/diary, which was subsequently given to the Little Bighorn Battlefield archives, providing rare historical insight into the campaign. During the Reno court of inquiry in 1879, Porter recounted the recovery of DeWolf's personal effects: "I was right there in the vicinity [when Captain Weir moved to go toward Custer;] I don't know where. I went into a ravine to see Dr. DeWolf and get his pocketbook and some things he had on his person. He was killed there. I was there a few minutes."[38] Porter's second letter to Fannie DeWolf also confirms what DeWolf was wearing during the battle when it references Porter's having "recovered [DeWolf's] overcoat."[39]

In reading through his diaries and letters, we can tell that DeWolf was not afraid and that he also deeply loved his wife. His ultimate goal and wish was to be reunited with her once the campaign was completed, particularly in his last letter of June 21, just four days prior to the battle. Perhaps this is the somber mood to which Porter referred.

One final observation regarding the September 14 letter pertains to the discrepancy in the reported number of DeWolf's fatal wounds. Among the official medical reports compiled by the chief medical officer, Doctor Williams, during the campaign, he indicated additional bullet wounds found on DeWolf's body. His report for June 1876 noted that DeWolf "had been shot once through the abdomen and Six times through the head and face."[40] The reason for this discrepancy between Porter's and Williams's reports is unknown. Doctor Porter may have intentionally softened the graphic details of the wounds to console Mrs. DeWolf, or perhaps he thought William's and Porter's "chest" and "abdomen" bullet wounds were one and the same. The latter seems less likely, coming from two experienced frontier surgeons. Nonetheless, whether Fannie DeWolf ever saw this "official" army report is unknown, although she did keep the personal correspondence on the matter with Porter.

After the initial burial of the bodies on June 28, the U.S. Army and the federal government began making arrangements to return the remains of officers to those families requesting hometown burial. This was a more complicated and daunting task than it would seem, partly because of the need to create a uniform procedure and also because of bureaucratic resistance and procrastination. There was also some initial resistance to providing funds to assist in that process. Lieutenant General Sheridan noted his initial efforts to implement the process in his letter to General Terry, dated March 26, 1877:

Chicago, March 26, 1877
Headquarters Military Division of the Missouri

Brig. Gen AH Terry.
Comdg Department of Dakota
St. Paul, Minn.

General,

I have been much pressed by the friends of the officers who fell with Custer on the 25th of last June in the Battle of the Little Bighorn to bring in their bodies. I have assured them that we would do all we could to accomplish this purpose, and I now feel like asking the authorities in Washington what they will be able to do in furnishing the necessary cases and coffins for the remains, and desire to consult you as to the probability of recovering their bodies or bones. There is an incidental fund in the War Department from which the outside expense of performing this work can be paid.

Will you please communicate with me on the subject and give me your views?

Yours truly,

P. H. Sheridan
Lieut. General[41]

This request was granted three weeks later by the secretary of war, though it was also requested "that the expenses may be *made as small as possible*." This expense was subsequently kept to a minimum, as only "$1,000 to accomplish this task" was authorized.[42] In addition, Lieutenant Colonel Michael V. Sheridan, Philip Sheridan's brother, was put in charge of the expedition for "bringing in and burying the body of General Custer and those of the fifteen officers who fell with him on the 25th of last June."[43]

While the authorization of funds was eventually approved, the War Department only paid to have the remains transported as far as Fort Lincoln in Dakota Territory and eventually to Fort

Leavenworth, Kansas, which had been "designated as the place of burial."[44] To take them to further destinations was the responsibility of the individual relatives and families. The War Department's decision was no doubt a disappointment to many of the families.[45]

General Custer's remains were to be buried at West Point in New York, and those of Lieutenant Crittenden were left where he fell on the field, at the request of his father. The remaining officers were to be buried at Fort Leavenworth, although Captain Keogh's final resting place was Fort Hill Cemetery in Auburn, New York.[46]

The base of operations for retrieval of remains at the Little Big Horn was on a high plateau overlooking the junction of the Little Big Horn and Big Horn Rivers, some twelve miles north of the battlefield. Terry and Sheridan had urged the need for a fort at this location as early as 1875, but not until a year after the battle was the request approved. Construction commenced that spring, in late April and May 1877. Initially called Big Horn Post, and also referred to as Post No. 2, it was renamed Fort Custer in November that year.[47] The sprawling fort was a cavalry post among several other forts to protect the region and would be in existence from 1877 to 1895, when it was decommissioned and torn down. During its day it was considered the finest cavalry post in the world.

From Fort Custer, Lieutenant Colonel Michael Sheridan sent the cavalry horses and wagons along the established road carrying the pine boxes in which to place the remains. Upon being returned to Fort Custer, they were stored until transported down the Yellowstone River to Fort Lincoln, where metal cases replaced the pine boxes for further shipment as designated by the slain officers' families. These operations, taking place in July 1877, were a daunting task, in part because a year had passed since the battle and the remains had deteriorated. Not surprisingly, some made accusations of misidentification and poor handling of some of the remains as well as erroneous location of the graves. In response to this, Lieutenant Colonel Sheridan took specific measures to refute these unfounded rumors once and for all. In a scathing (and deserved) letter to the editor of the *Chicago Tribune*, he wrote that "all these statements are lies" and asked for "a wholesale denial of these stories as will forever sit at rest the imaginations of such of your correspondents who desire to earn a few pennies by telegraphing to you sensational stuff on this subject."[48]

Fannie DeWolf and her brother-in-law, David Hall, made arrangements to have her husband's remains returned for final burial in their family plot in Norwalk. Contrary to Major Reno's later supposition that it would be difficult to locate DeWolf's grave in the future and unlike the remains of those who were buried on Custer Hill, DeWolf's initial interment at the battlefield was easily located and would not be disputed. Porter and other soldiers knew the exact location of the grave because of Porter's close attention and care in the initial burial.[49] Although DeWolf and Porter were contract surgeons, they were considered part of the battalion staff of the Dakota Column. As such, DeWolf's body was included among the group of officers whose remains were retrieved, including Lieutenants Cooke, Riley, Algernon Smith, Calhoun, and McIntosh, Captains Keogh and Yates, and George and Tom Custer.[50]

Lieutenant Colonel Sheridan wrote to Fannie DeWolf to assure her that her husband's remains had been found:

Headquarters Military Division of the Missouri
Chicago, IL July 16, 1877

My Dear Mrs. DeWolf,

I telegraphed you yesterday that your husband's remains had arrived at Fort Lincoln. I have sent from this city a metallic case to receive those and I think they will be ready for shipment to you by the 20th inst, even as they are shipped I will inform you by telegraph. If you have any other wishes, telegraph them on receipt of this.

I found your husband's grave without any difficulty, and wolves left a small lock of his hair and also a button from which I recovered. The grave had been somewhat touched by wolves but not so much as I expected. I have the satisfaction of assuring you that we have recovered all of his remains except what would have certainly perished by decomposition after this length of time.

Yours truly,
M. V. Sheridan

DAVID AND EMMA HALL'S HOUSE, NORWALK, OHIO
The home of Fannie DeWolf's sister and brother-in-law still stands on Seminary Street in Norwalk. This is where James DeWolf's funeral was held in 1877 when his remains were taken back to his wife's hometown. *Author's collection.*

P.S. I regret to say that the Secty of War has not authorized the shipment of the bodies east from Fort Lincoln to be done at public expense. All other expenses have been paid by the Govt.

Yours,
M.V. Sheridan[51]

Fannie DeWolf apparently chose to stay at Fort Totten for some six weeks after the Little Big Horn battle. Like Libbie Custer, who eventually chose to go back to her hometown in Monroe, Michigan, Fannie returned home to Norwalk on Friday, August

The Retreat to Reno Hill   145

GRAVES OF JAMES MADISON DEWOLF AND FANNIE DEWOLF
The original obelisk marks the graves of James and Fannie in the Hall-DeWolf family grave section at Woodlawn Cemetery, Norwalk, Ohio. In the foreground is the new U.S. government–issued military headstone placed through the efforts of Henry Timman, cemetery docent and former director of the Firelands Historical Society in Norwalk. *Author's collection.*

11, 1876, to live with her sister, Emma, and brother-in-law, David Hall.[52] The month following her return home, Fannie received a letter of comfort and resolution of tribute to her late husband from members of his Pequossette Masonic Lodge in Massachusetts. The letter clearly indicates that the doctor was well liked and held in high esteem by his former lodge brothers.[53] Fannie and Hall, a Civil War veteran and insurance agent, would make arrangements over the ensuing months to have DeWolf's remains shipped to Norwalk the following summer in 1877 after Lieutenant Colonel Sheridan had completed the retrieval.[54]

Both of Norwalk's newspapers noted the arrival of DeWolf's remains at the Norwalk train station on the morning of Wednesday,

August 1, at 9 o'clock, as well as the subsequent funeral held that day at the Halls' residence. As the *Norwalk Reflector* reported, "Mr. M. L. Chappell took charge of the remains and after carefully unpacking them at his rooms, conveyed them to the residence of Mr. D. T. Hall, 58 East Seminary Street, brother-in-law of the deceased, where appropriate funeral services were conducted by the Rev. Mr. Mills, of the Baptist church, at 4 o'clock in the afternoon. A number of our citizens and sympathizing friends assisted in the last sad rites for one who fell in the defense of his country, and now sleeps in our beautiful Woodlawn Cemetery."[55]

Epilogue

AFTER HER HUSBAND was buried in Woodlawn Cemetery, Fannie DeWolf decided to stay on in her hometown of Norwalk. She resided there for the next two years with her sister and brother-in-law, Emma and David Hall. In 1879, she married Elijah Dodd, a local area farmer and blacksmith and carriage shop owner in Waterville, although the union ended in divorce in 1912. They had one son, Verne Adams Dodd, born in 1881, who went on to become a respected physician and professor and was chief of staff at the Ohio State University Hospital from 1921 to 1948. He also served in the U.S. Naval Reserves during World War I in 1917–18 while on leave from the teaching staff at the medical school.[1] Fannie's previous military pension as the widow of James DeWolf had been discontinued when she remarried. It was reinstated after her divorce from Dodd and continued until her death at the age of sixty-five on May 19, 1918.[2] She was buried next to James in the family plot at Woodlawn Cemetery.

Although she remarried, Fannie cherished her memories of James DeWolf long after his death. While none of her letters to him are known to have survived, her feelings and past memories are reflected in her personal autograph book and diary, which remain with family descendants today.[3] Those interested in the Little Big Horn story owe a tremendous debt of gratitude to her son, Verne, for his preservation of his mother's letters from her first husband and the diary of the 1876 expedition. Verne Dodd began transcribing those writings in 1941 and eventually donated the collection to the National Park Service through Major Edward S. Luce, then superintendent at the battlefield. Luce and the State Historical Society of North Dakota reprinted them in the society's monthly historical journal in 1958, the only prior publication until this current expanded annotated and edited work. The original letters and diary remain in the Little Bighorn archives collections today.

By visiting several of the sites DeWolf wrote about in his diary, one can add a deeper perspective to the events he described that occurred at those locations. The buildings of Fort Totten have survived, the site of Fort Seward has been preserved, and Fort Abraham Lincoln has been partially reconstructed, all three under the auspices of the State Historical Society of North Dakota and supported by local historical organizations. At the Little Bighorn Battlefield National Monument, one can look down the steep ravine and bluffs near the Reno-Benteen defensive site and sense the confusion and fear that DeWolf must have experienced during his fateful attempt to reach safety during Reno's retreat.

Today, one can stroll down Seminary Street in Norwalk and pass by Emma and David Hall's former house, which still stands on that quaint street. Not far from there is beautiful Woodlawn Cemetery, where one can visit the Hall-DeWolf family plot in Section 20 among tree-shaded lanes.[4] An old and weathered obelisk marks the DeWolfs' graves, along with a newly placed U.S. Army headstone authorized through the diligent efforts of local historian Henry Timman. Viewing this peaceful scene, one has a sense of coming full circle after reading the DeWolf letters and diary.

APPENDIX A

Account Book Pages of DeWolf's Diary

T HIS FIRST PORTION of the postage account from March 31, 1876, to April 4, 1876, is contained in DeWolf's diary immediately before his April 17 entry.

Bill of lading no 667 To Fargo D.T.
Given St. Paul by Lt E. B. Gibbs   AAGM

    Postage Amount
    March 31stcts
    Asst Adjt Genl
    Hdqrs Dept Dakota Rept for SO n 27   3
    April 3   Med. Dir. Offc St. Paul
                 Report   21
    "   3   Surg. Genls Offc. Report   9
    "   3   "   "   " Recipt Supplies   6
    "   4   Surg Gen Off. Personal Report   3
    "   4   J. Bryan Receipt   12
    For Lading + file [*illegible*]

The remainder of the postage account constitutes the final pages at the end of DeWolf's diary.

Postage Amount Commencing
October 20th 1875   cts

Oct 20th	to S.G.O. Oath of office and Contract Acceptance of contract + department	6
" 28	to S.G.O. Personal Report	3
Nov 5th	S.G.O. arrival at St. Paul	
paid by M.D.O.	arrival + assignment to duty	
" 18th	S.G.O.	3
" 18th	M.D.O.	3
" 18th	S.G.O. Military Record	6
" 30th	S.G.O. M.D.O. Personal Report	6
" "	A.G.O. hospital Report	5
Dc 12th '75	AQ.M. St. Paul E [*illegible*]	3
" 31st '75	S.G.O. M.D.O. I.G.O. one each Personal Report for Dirs	9
Jan 16 '76	4 J. H. Baxter[1] Chief Med Pur as [*illegible*] A.DG	
	Reciep from Physicians [*illegible*]	3
" "	Major R Smith PM Gl[2]	3
" 22nd '76	Chief PM Dept Dakata Sent check for $1.37	3
Jan 31st '76	Med Dir Office Personal Report	3
	Surgeon Genrls O " "	3
	Brought Forward	56 cts
Jan 31st '76	To A.G.O. Personal Report	3
Feby 4th '76	Chief Paymaster Dept. of Dakota (Pay Ammounts)	3
" 29 '76	M.D.O. Personal Report	6
" "	S.G.O. " "	3
" "	S.G.O. " "	3
March 10	M.D.O. Report Expenses from Totten	3
" "	S.G. O. " " "	3
" "	A.G. O. " " "	3
" 31st	Dept Hd Qtrs Receipt of order no. 27	3

Appendix A 151

April 3	M.D.O. Reports	01
" "	S.G.O. Reports	9
" "	A.G.O. Reports	3
" "	S.G.O. Receipt for supplies	6
" "	J. B. Ferguson A.A.S. F. Totten Receipt for supplies	12
April 23	A.G.O. Report arrival at F.A.L. DT	3
" "	S.G.O. Reports to April 17th	6
" "	M.D.O. " " "	21
" "	M.D.O. Reports my arrival at F.A.L. DT	3 170
	Brought Forward	1 70
April 23	A.G.O. Report my arrival A Ft. AL DT	3
" "	M.D.O. Report Ex of liquire	6
" 26	W Matthews aply compounds in [*illegible*] to James Ryan	6
" 30	M D O Personal Report	3
" "	A G O " "	3
" "	S G O " "	3
May 4th	S.G.O. Ex of R[*illegible*] }	9
" 9	[*illegible*] of P [*illegible*] S.G.O.	3
" 13	Post Adjutant Totten acct Bills for Sundy expenses	6
" 14	S.G.O. Personal Reports	3
" "	M D O " "	3
" "	A G O " "	3
June 10	A G O S G O + M D O Personal Report for May	9

$80.00 on Lien on durabouls [durables]
Expences From March 10th

March 14th	Strickers	2.00
" "	Postage Stamps	0.75
" 20th	Mess. Ex Do	8.00
" "	Ex of Packages	0 95
April 4	Postage Stamps	0 58
" "	Package of *Tofess?*	0 75

"	"	"	"	" for Mrs. F		0 75
"	"	March bill				2 50
"	"	Matches + wisk broom				35
"	"	Relief Assc Of Mass				1 25
April 6th		"	"	"	"	1 25

The following was the final entry on last page of DeWolf's diary:

Memorandum Receipt

Received from J. M. DeWolf, A.A. Surg., U.S.A. one Medicine Pannier and one Field Case of Surgical Instruments. Asst. Surg. U.S. Army

Camp near mouth of Rosebud Creek Mont.

June 22nd 1876

APPENDIX B

DeWolf's Early Diary Entries
OCTOBER 1875

THESE ARE the first eight pages of Doctor DeWolf's diary, which he started in October 1875 while treating his first patients as a physician. My research has documented that most of these patients lived in DeWolf's hometown region of Forkston and Mehoopany, Pennsylvania, where he practiced while waiting for approval of his application and subsequent appointment as a contract physician for the army. These first diary entries were not included by Edward Luce in his printing of DeWolf's diary and letters in 1958.

My annotations are indicated with brackets: [ ]. In portions of DeWolf's entries, his writing was extremely difficult to decipher, and the following interpretations are the best that could be ascertained. Apothecary (pharmaceutical) and Latin symbols and definitions are as follows: *Div* = divide; + or ++ = drops; *gr* = grain; *m* or *M* = mix; ℥ = ounce; *pulv* = powder; ℞ = prescription; i = one or ii = two, etc.; *sph* = sphalerite, for zinc sulfide; *dub* = dubosine, for alkaloid of hyoscyamine, used as an antispasmodic, analgesic, and sedative; *nit* = nitromersol, a synthetic mercurial compound, used as an antiseptic for skin and mucous membranes. *Officinal* (abbreviated *Ofin*) denotes a chemical or pharmaceutical kept in stock, as distinguished from one prepared extemporaneously according to a physician's prescription; *magnesium sulfate* is epsom salt, the active ingredient of most of the natural laxative waters, which, when applied locally, has anti-inflammatory action; *linsum*, or *linum*,

153

denotes linseed, used as an infusion; lithium bromide is a white deliquescent powder, used as a sedative and hypnotic.

October 11th 9 P.M.   Mr. Brown Teacher   urethral irritation due to long retention of urine while in school room and fatigue and exposure to dampness—℞ lithium notusi ℨi   To Ofin [officinal] m ++ at night   12 A.M. improved

sph nit dub ℨii T Ofin ℨii A.M. Begin ℨii   M. S. [magnesium sulfate] ten drops three or four times daily and the evening dose to be m ++   14:15 relieved

Charges $1.25

Oct 16th   11 1/2 A.M.   Mrs Isaac Page delivered of a Boy 7 1/3 pds after 13 hours labor found her after 10 hours head against the Pubis and not engaged in the inferior straight. She was lying flat upon her back and the uterine severe pain was accomplishing nothing. Elevated head and shoulders and brought the uterus into position and labor progressed the infant rotated to the front from the right. Delivered the placenta in fifteen minutes the decidua was somewhat adherent   she had severe after pains took afterbirth by inserting hand into vagina and fingers 1 + 2 into uterus easily accomplished after one hour   the pains being severe while uterus was contracted give Li [Lithium] Ofin m + and leave [*illegible*] to be given in two hours if pain continues and + at bedtime if required and give directions what to do in case of hemorrhage or no apparent danger and do not make any examination   Pulse 90 in half hour after delivery

Oct 17th 4 P.M. Pulse 76 took Pulse Dir + last night and + at 2 P.M. today has had sharp labor pains at times quite severe. Oct 21st Mr. Page called said wife labor had stopped for two days and that she had severe pains headache &t. and Hydrate m + Div + and at bed times   Oct 22nd 1 P.M. Pulse 84 resp normal Temp now normal Lochia scanty   had been to examin thru 2nd day   Pains had been severe up to last night   feels pretty comfortable today   bowels moved freely this morning. Urine scanty and high colored

This case seems to have done extremely well for one with labor so protracted as then. Was apparently severe pressure upon the urethra + Bladder. There was no doubt some pelvic inflammation of a mild character

Charges 1st visit and after $5,

Third visit + medicine $2

Oct 19th 7 P.M.   Mrs. Alice Robinson sent asking me to send her something for her headache   did not want a visit   Send Chloral ++ to be dissolved in 1/2 thumbleful of water and take and lie down.

Charge nothing

October 21st 7 P.M.   Daniel Frazier called by C. Fanny found him tossing and lapping his tongue slight delirium easily made to recognize me   right tonsil swollen coated   Phayrnx coated same as in Diptheria

Pulse 108 full high temperature complains of severe pain in frontal and prickling sensation all over his lips and fingers particularly so Hyd [Hydrate] m + Div + at bedtime

(had been constipated) ʒs evy 4 hours to 4 doses and Div + at 11 if not better

Oct 22nd 8 A.M. Pulse 96 Resp 20 temperature almost 100 F. Sph nit dulo ʒiii every 2 hours   Mag sulph q.s. [a sufficient quantity] to mov bowls   Had to repeat later in the afternoon

2 P.M. Pulse 104. Fever high   give sph nit dulo ʒi [*illegible*] sph nit

9 P.M. Pulse 109   high Fever   giv Pulv Div + and Continue sph mit dulo while awake

Oct 23rd. 9 A.M. Pulse 84 fever off headache going off   rested some during the night

bowels moved twice yesterday afternoon and once during the night   urine high color

9 P.M. Pulse 84   feels comfortable has returning appetite—slight headache and some cough occasionally

Given pil [*illegible*] given [*illegible*] given ℥+++ Ofin 1/8 gr to be taken before meals and to [*illegible*] if he requires one more. Charges $2

Oct 23. 9 1/2 A.M.   Elder Mr. Couch complains of severe pain in region of right kidney and extending mid-penis and almost constant desire to urinate but passage of urine very scanty   Pulse 60 tempt cool and skin moist and clammy. Pulv Div ++ and repeat + at 11   if not easier use freely of infusion of Linum [linseed]

2 P.M. Vomited several times pain continues is somewhat drowsy   skin clammy and cool   Pulse 60 looks depressed   pulse fallen at times.

Oct 24th 9 A.M. Pulse 64   some pain in region of kidney   Continue treatment of M Linsum & Div at night

Oct 25th &. P.M. nearly free of pain Pulse 72 Constipated   Pulv Div + Hyd [*illegible*] give + at night.

APPENDIX C

Edward S. Luce's Introduction to DeWolf's Diary and Letters, 1958

THE DIARY AND LETTERS OF DR. JAMES M. DEWOLF, ACTING ASSISTANT SURGEON, U.S. ARMY; HIS RECORD OF THE SIOUX EXPEDITION OF 1876 AS KEPT UNTIL HIS DEATH

Transcribed and Editorial Notes by
EDWARD S. LUCE

IN THE EARLY STAGES of the Battle of the Little Bighorn River on the afternoon of June 25, 1876, Dr. James M. DeWolf retreated with Major Reno and his battalion. He had successfully forded the river, but in his haste to reach safety he evidently moved a little too far to the north of the other troopers and was soon cut off from them. Lieutenant Wallace and several others saw Indians overtake the doctor and fired in an attempt to protect him, but the distance was too great to render effective assistance.

After the Indians moved farther down stream to engage Custer, Dr. H. R. Porter, the surviving surgeon, went down to see Dr. DeWolf and found he had been killed. Dr. Porter removed "his pocket-book and some things he had on his person." The diary which DeWolf had faithfully kept during the campaign was recovered at that time.

In a letter to Mrs. DeWolf dated "Camp on the Mouth of the Big Horn River, Montana-Territory, July 28th, 1876," Dr. Porter wrote, ". . . I was just behind him as we crossed the river. I saw him safe across and then he turned up a ravine a little to my left which was the last I saw of my friend and companion alive. As soon as we reached the bluff, I found he was missing and soon found his body which I had buried the next day. I know it will be a great relief to you when I say that his body was not mutilated in the least—that he was not scalped or his clothes even taken. The Indians had stolen his revolver but not troubled him otherwise. . . ."

No mention was made of recovery of the physician's medicine case or instruments, but it is quite possible that they were carried away. In a letter dated August 1, 1876, Fort Peck, M.T., Indian agent Mitchell stated that an Indian there had brought in an army pistol and a surgeon's pocket case, but nearly all the instruments belonging to it were missing. This case could have been either from Dr. DeWolf or Dr. Lord, who was killed that same day with General Custer.

Dr. DeWolf's remains, along with the officers who were killed in the battle, were disinterred and shipped to Fort A. Lincoln, Dakota Territory, in June of 1877. At Fort Lincoln the body was placed in a metallic case for shipment to Norwalk, Ohio, where final interment was made. Capt. M. V. Sheridan, who was in charge of the party to recover the bodies, sent Mrs. DeWolf a lock of her husband's hair and a button from his vest as mementos.

At the age of 17, DeWolf had joined the Pennsylvania Light Artillery and was wounded on August 30, 1862. As a result of these wounds, he was discharged and pensioned as of October that year. In September 1864, he resigned his pension and reenlisted again in the same organization where he continued to serve until discharged June 14, 1865.

In October 1865, he enlisted in the Regular United States Army at which time he gave his occupation as laborer and his place of birth as Wyoming County, Pennsylvania. In less than a year he was promoted from private, 14th U.S. Infantry, to Hospital Steward, U.S. Army. His first assignment was to take charge of the Hospital Department at Camp Lyon, Idaho Territory. Three years later he was transferred to Camp Warner, Oregon.

By May 1872, he had fully decided upon his future career and wrote the Surgeon General, "I have prepared myself for the study of Medicine as far as practicable without the benefit of Medical Lectures and I desire, if possible to be stationed so that I may attend these lectures without interfering with my duties as Hospital Steward. I am willing to refund to the United States the cost of my transportation, should that be a barrier to the change of station."

In forwarding DeWolf's request, the Asst. Surgeon at Camp Warner recommend it with the following indorsement: "I have known Hosp. Steward James M. DeWolf since October 1868, and his character has been most excellent both officially and morally. He has ever been diligent and attentive, is *very* accurate in his accounts, and a thoroughly temperate man. One of his objects in making the request is to enable him to attend Medical lectures after office hours, for which I consider him thoroughly prepared."

It is interesting to note that DeWolf's term of service from October 5, 1868 to October 5, 1871 was under the name of DeWall. We find no reason for use of an alias and assume it could have been through error that the name was so entered on the army records.

As a result of this request and "in view of his long service in the army," in April 1873, Hospital Steward James M. DeWolf was ordered to the Department of the East, New York City, at his own expense. From there he was sent to Watertown Arsenal, Massachusetts for duty, from which point he entered Harvard Medical School, in addition to his duties as Hospital Steward. He was awarded the M.D. Degree from Harvard on June 26, 1875.

By the time he was prepared for examination by the Army Medical Board, he was over-age, but as a special concession and "in view of his long service in the army," on August 28, 1875, he was invited to appear for examination. He appeared but failed to pass the Board. Evidently at his request, by Special Order, he was discharged from the army on October 5, 1875.

That same year on the 23rd day of October, as a Private Physician, he signed a one year contract with the Army to serve in the Department of Dakota at $100 per month, except that while serving west of the Mississippi or with troops on marches, his pay would be advanced to $125 per month.

On November 18, 1875, he entered on duty at Fort Totten, D.T., as Acting Assistant Surgeon, U.S. Army. By Special Order, dated March 2, 1876, he was ordered to proceed with two companies "E" and "L" of the 7th Cavalry to Ft. A. Lincoln and report to Lt. Col. George A. Custer for duty with troops in the field. By the 10th of that month they were on their way and that evening he made an entry in a paper bound pocket sized notebook recording the first day of the ill-fated expedition.

It is interesting to compare the diary with letters sent to his wife during the period covered. Fannie J. Downing had married DeWolf the latter part of 1871, but after four years she had not become completely aware of the many pitfalls of an isolated army post, and in addition, she was sick with loneliness for home and civilization. The doctor being considerably older and having practically grown up in the army, never ceased to caution her and guard her from the Fort gossips. We believe these letters reveal the personal anxieties and financial frugalness typical of most military families. They should give an insight into the personal sacrifices made by those who manned our army.

The diary, contained in two pocket sized notebooks, is displayed in the museum at Custer Battlefield National Monument. With the letters and other personal papers, it was donated to the National Park Service by Dr. Verne A. Dodd, son of Mrs. DeWolf by her second marriage.

In transcribing the diary and letters, considerable difficulty was encountered in deciphering some of the words. The doctor was schooled in grammar and could write a beautiful hand, as shown in certain parts of some letters and in the addresses on the envelopes. However, as he mentions several times in his letters, the facilities for writing were quite inadequate in the field and haste in writing resulted many times in the elimination of most punctuation,

Appendix C

capitals, etc. In some cases, his spelling of words was not consistent. We must remember that the letters especially were written for his wife. However, they add considerably to the study of this particular phase of our history, and it is as history that they are presented, but with all personal deference for the doctor and his wife.

The Diary begins with an entry shortly after leaving Fort Totten.

Notes

Abbreviations

ACP	Appointment, Commission and Personal Branch file, 1875
AGO	Adjutant General's Office Records (RG 94)
FHS	Firelands Historical Society Museum, Norwalk, Ohio
G.O.	General Order
NARA	National Archives and Records Administration, Washington, D.C.
NPL	Norwalk Public Library, Norwalk, Ohio
O.R.	War Office, U.S. Army, *War of the Rebellion: A Compilation of the Official Records of the Union and Confederate Armies,* Series 1, 1881–1884, Washington, D.C.
PHMC	Pennsylvania Historic and Museum Commission State Archives
Revised U.S. Army Regulations	War Office, U.S. Army, *Revised United States Army Regulations 1861, with an Appendix Containing the Changes and Laws Affecting Army Regulation and Articles of War to June 25, 1863*
S.F.O.	Special Field Order
SGO	Surgeon General of the Army records, White Swan Library, Little Bighorn Battlefield National Monument
SHSND	State Historical Society of North Dakota
S.O.	Special Order
WFPL	Watertown Free Public Library, Watertown, Mass.
WHCS	Wyoming County Historical Society and Genealogical Museum, Tunkhannock, Pa.
WSL/LIBI	White Swan Library, Little Bighorn Battlefield National Monument

Preface

1. The third physician, the assistant surgeon First Lieutenant George Edwin Lord, was killed with Custer.
2. See Luce, "Diary and Letters."
3. Willert, *Terry Letters*; Barnard, *I Go with Custer*; Windolf, *I Fought with Custer*; Carroll, *Frank Anders* (also, Anders's notes can be found in O'Neil, *Critical Notes*); Chorne, *Following the Custer Trail*.
4. For a brief note regarding the continued controversy over the spelling of the historic name "Little Big Horn" versus "Little Bighorn," see Hutton, *Custer Reader*, 235–36n1.

Introduction: James Madison DeWolf of Mehoopany, Pennsylvania

1. Perry, *Charles D'Wolf of Guadaloupe*, genealogical tables, sec. 2, p. 138.
2. The small village of Forkston, a few miles southwest of Mehoopany, did not officially become established until about 1830. Jenningsville, a few miles west of Mehoopany, had its first settlers circa 1795, although it was not permanently settled until circa 1815. All three of these villages were in the larger Windham Township, established in 1830 from part of one of the original three townships (Braintrim). Forkston and Mehoopany Townships, taken from the eastern/southeastern portions of Windham Township, were established in 1844. All the farms and towns in these areas were in Wyoming County, formed from a portion of the original Luzerne County in 1842. Wyoming County Historical Society, *Lest We Forget*, Feb. 1982; see also F. W. Beers, map of Wyoming County and its townships and farms, 1869, original map at the Wyoming County Historical Society, Tunkhannock, Pa.
3. Perry, *Charles D'Wolf of Guadaloupe*, 83–85. See also Salisbury and Salisbury, *Family Histories*; *Notes on the DeWolf Family*, 124.
4. Perry, *Charles D'Wolf of Guadaloupe*, 86, 107; Salisbury and Salisbury, *Family Histories*, 126–27.
5. Browne, *Traces of the Trade*, independent film documentary, 2001; DeWolf, *Inheriting the Trade*. See also "The DeWolf Family Burden," *Providence (R.I.) Journal*, Feb. 3, 2008. In addition to providing rum, firearms, and supplies in the merchant trade business, this Rhode Island branch of the DeWolf family also owned a waterfront bank, an insurance company in Bristol, and plantations in Cuba and South Carolina.
6. Pennsylvania's General Assembly enacted a law abolishing slavery on March 1, 1780. However, this act resulted in the indentured servant system becoming more prominent in both rural and urban areas. See Harper, *Slavery in the North*, www.slavenorth.com/slavenorth.htm (accessed Sep. 12, 2012); author's personal communication with Gregory J. W. Urwin, professor of history at Temple University, Sep. 12, 2012. There is no evidence that the Mehoopany/Forkston/Windham Township DeWolf families ever had slaves or indentured servants. For a more in-depth overall evaluation of

slavery in Pennsylvania, see Nash and Soderlund, *Freedom by Degrees*; and Turner, *Negro in Pennsylvania*.

7. Moses Dolph (DeWolf), a Revolutionary War veteran and second cousin to Charles "The Hatter" DeWolf, has been traced to the other line of Pennsylvania DeWolfs living in that region of the state. Moses moved from Connecticut to Mountain Meadows in Wayne County, Pennsylvania, near the present city of Scranton, some thirty miles east of Mehoopany. Perry, *Charles D'Wolf of Guadaloupe*, 67.

8. Charles "The Hatter" DeWolf is not listed in the U.S. Census of 1810 for Braintrim Township (Mehoopany settlement), Luzerne County. However, he settled in Mehoopany near present-day Forkston circa 1780, and two of his sons had been given tracts of his land by 1795. He died on December 16, 1814, at the age of sixty-seven, and is buried in the Robinson Cemetery in Forkston. As of 2002, the broken pieces of his headstone had been placed in concrete and were still in the cemetery.

9. James Madison DeWolf's uncle, Amasa Robinson DeWolf (1830–59), did not inherit land from his father but instead purchased a farm from John Fassett in September 1865 in Windham Township west of his father's original lands. This farm, which is still in existence today, is located at the west end of present Town Line Road, south of Jenningsville, and is currently owned by Amasa's great-great-grandson Tim DeWolf and his wife, Sherri. The various DeWolf family members are buried in several small local cemeteries, some of which are family cemeteries, in the three township areas west of Mehoopany.

10. Charles "The Hatter" DeWolf (spelled "Deaulph") had given portions of his land to his first and second sons, Amasa (1778–1859) and Wyllys (also spelled "Willis" or "Wyllis," 1780–?), by 1798. Both farms are noted on the survey of that year, just north of present-day Forkston and south of present-day Jenningsville on Big Mehoopany Creek. Aside from farming, Wyllys had also established a sawmill there and had married Waity Brown from Mehoopany. Land Records, Copied Surveys, D-27-1458 and Warrant Register, no. 233, D, Wyllys Deaulph, PHMC (documents available online).

Although neither Charles nor his sons are listed in the 1800 and 1810 U.S. Census of Luzerne County despite having permanent residence there, Wyllys and the fourth son, Elisha (1784–1869), are listed in the U.S. Census of 1820 for Exeter and Braintrim Townships, respectively, which were two of the original three townships of Luzerne County (the other being Tunkhannock) surveyed by Connecticut settlers between 1771 and 1778. Wyllys appears to have died circa 1824, as Luzerne County Orphan's Court records (dated April 5, 1824) indicate a request for a guardian for his son Erastus DeWolf, who was then a minor at the age of seventeen and had no guardian appointed to take care of his person and estate (Asa Stephens was appointed as his guardian). Wyllys's widow, Waity, and the children later moved to Bristol, Connecticut, where they resided with the family of Henry DeWolf; Erastus, who became an Episcopal clergyman, died in battle during the Civil War while serving as a chaplain (Perry, *Charles D'Wolf of Guadaloupe*, 3–4). Amasa is listed in the U.S.

Census of 1830 for Windham Township. This Amasa is the grandfather of James Madison DeWolf. U.S. Census of Luzerne Co., Pa., 1810, 1820, and 1830, WCHS; Wyoming County Historical Society, *Lest We Forget*, Feb. 15, 1982 (regarding the establishment of Wyoming County and its townships), and Sep. 15, 1984, 35 (regarding Charles and Wyllys DeWolf). See also Perry, *Charles D'Wolf of Guadaloupe*, genealogical tables, sec. 2, pp. 123, 128, 138.

11. Although records and deeds are preserved in the Wyoming County Historical Society's collections, not all land transactions in Mehoopany, Forkston, and Windham Townships were recorded during the nineteenth century. Nonetheless, Wyoming County records suggest that James DeWolf's parents' farm was near the Forkston and Mehoopany Township lines and not in Forkston proper. As mentioned, James's grandfather Amasa had large tracts of land west, northwest, and southwest of Mehoopany Village within the original larger Windham Township, and some of these tracts were located in the later Forkston and Mehoopany Townships, formed in 1844. Amasa eventually deeded several tracts to his sons; a large portion went to his oldest son, Mark Anthony DeWolf (father of James), most likely circa 1843. Records show that Mark Anthony and Achsah Clapp DeWolf sold a small portion of their farmland to William Robinson of Forkston Township in 1856. This tract of land is immediately across the road from the small preserved Forkston Creek/Pearson (or Pierson) Cemetery on State Road 87 at the Forkston Township/Mehoopany Township border, where members of the DeWolf and Robinson families are buried, including Amasa DeWolf, Amasa Robinson DeWolf and his wife (Diantha) and their children, and Mark Anthony DeWolf. *Index of Deeds*, Mark A[nthony] and Achsa[h] DeWolf (grantors) to William Robinson (grantee), Aug. 25, 1856, WC 7:275, microfilm, WCHS; author's personal telephone conversation with Mrs. Jean Brewer Robinson, a Robinson family genealogical historian (formerly of Wyoming Co., Pa., now residing in The Villages, Fla.), Nov. 6, 2012.

12. Wyoming County Historical Society, *Historical Development*, 26; *U.S. Census Bureau Agricultural Source, 1850–1966, for Wyoming County, Pennsylvania*, WCHS; see also 1850 Wyoming Co. Census, Federal Census Film no. 836, WCHS. The U.S. Census records indicate that the 1860 population of Wyoming County had grown to 12,540 and by 1880 had increased to 15,590 persons, and the U.S. Census Bureau agricultural records note that the number of farms had increased to 1,647 by 1880 (161,479 farming acres total). The population was 28,080 as recorded by the 2000 U.S. Census of Wyoming County. Consistent with the national trend in the past several decades, the county saw a decrease in farms by 1960 to 746 farms (118,443 farming acres total), although it remains a primarily rural and agricultural region. 1860, 1880, 2000, and 2010 U.S. Census of Wyoming Co., Pa., available at WCHS; see also U.S. Census Bureau, *American FactFinder*, available at http://factfinder.census.gov/ (accessed July 23, 2016).

13. DeWolf, "Synopsis of Services Performed," 1 (personal summary of his military service by James M. DeWolf), photocopy, FHS, Norwalk, Ohio (first quotation);

Wyoming Republican (Tunkhannock, Pa.), Apr. 24, 1861 (second quotation), in Radwanski, *Civil War*, 1:4.

14. *Wyoming Republican*, May 15, 1861, in Radwanski, *Civil War*, 1:6. This article lists the names of the thirty-eight men in the company, including DeWolf, who went on to Harrisburg, as two men had dropped out from the original group. In addition, Captain Campbell is documented as the enlistment officer for DeWolf on his later disability certificate (see n. 31, this chapter), although the enlistment date is noted as May 28 as recorded in AGO, certificate of disability, Mar. 21, 1863, WSL/LIBI.

15. Dept. of Interior, Bureau of Pensions, July 16, 1912, U.S. Army certificate of disability, Oct. 26, 1862, and U.S. Army record of discharge/reenlistment, Oct. 5, 1868, Camp Lyon, Idaho Terr., AGO, DeWolf Collection, WSL/LIBI.

16. Bates, *Pennsylvania Volunteers*, 2:944. Bates's history includes a chapter on the First Artillery/Forty-Third Regiment, complete with muster rolls (from the National Archives), a list of officers, and detailed accounts of the engagements in which each battery was involved, including Battery A. DeWolf is noted in the muster rolls, and although his name is initially listed as "J. M. DeWoll," this is clearly a transcription error, as the service dates are identical to DeWolf's. Dryer's *Compendium of the War of the Rebellion: Compiled and Arranged from Official Records of the Federal and Confederate Armies, Reports of the Adjutant Generals of the Several States, the Army Registers, and Other Reliable Documents and Sources* includes a brief yet detailed chronological history of Battery A. See also Howard-Smith and Scott, *History of Battery A*, although this narrative focuses more on the later years of the regiment's history (the Spanish-American War and World War I). Until her death in 2015, author/historian Alice P. Gayley also maintained an excellent website, "Pennsylvania in the Civil War" (www.pa-roots.com/pacw, accessed Sep. 22, 2008), which utilized official records, including Bates's *History of the Pennsylvania Volunteers* and Dryer's *Compendium of the War of the Rebellion*, and contains information on Battery A; author's personal e-mail communication with Mrs. Gayley, Nov. 15, 2012.

17. Bates, *Pennsylvania Volunteers*, 2:944.

18. Muster rolls show that Edwin A. DeWolf enlisted in the Fifty-First Pennsylvania Volunteer Infantry, Company B, of Wyoming County, as a private on October 11, 1861, was promoted to corporal on November 6, 1864, and mustered out with the company on July 12, 1865; Amasa Robinson DeWolf enlisted in the Fifty-First Pennsylvania Volunteer Infantry, Company H, of Luzerne County, on November 4, 1861, was promoted to corporal on June 14, 1864, and mustered out with the company on November 5, 1864. Bates, *Pennsylvania Volunteers*, 3:47–91.

19. Radwanski, *Civil War*, 2:78.

20. DeWolf, "Synopsis of Services Performed," FHS, 1; Bates, *Pennsylvania Volunteers*, 2:945–47 (regarding the involvement of Battery A in the Battles of Dranesville, Mechanicsville, and Gaines's Mill). For a comprehensive overall narrative of the Seven Days Battles, see Sears, *To the Gates*. Gallagher's *Richmond Campaign* offers essays on various aspects of the campaign. Baumgarten's "A Splendid Little Affair:

The Battle of Dranesville" provides a detailed account of this smaller yet important early engagement of the war (Civil War Trust, www.civilwar.org/battlefields/dranesville/a-splendid-little-affair.html, accessed July 16, 2016). Hennessy's *Return to Bull Run* provides an in-depth narrative on the Second Battle of Manassas.

21. *O.R.*, 5:475 (both quotations); see also Bates, *Pennsylvania Volunteers*, 2:945.

22. Thomas L. Kane to E.O.C. Ord, *O.R.*, 5:482; see also Thornson and Rauch, *History of the Bucktails*, 78.

23. Sears, *To the Gates*, 383.

24. *O.R.*, 5:384–86 (McCall's Report); see also Lt. John G. Simpson to Gen. Fitz John Porter, July 5, 1862, *O.R.*, vol. 3, pt. 2, pp. 407–9; Bates, *Pennsylvania Volunteers*, 2:945. This position and setting is also described in Sears, *To the Gates*, 201–2, but the specific batteries are not named.

25. Simpson to Porter, July 5, 1862. Simpson commended his entire battery for their brave actions and singled out several wounded noncommissioned officers, although DeWolf and other enlisted men are not mentioned by name in his report.

26. Ibid.; Bates, *Pennsylvania Volunteers*, vol. 2, Muster Roll for Batt. A, 1st Pa. Artillery; certificate of disability for discharge, Oct. 26, 1862, James M. DeWolf, cpl., in Lt. John G. Simpson, comm., Co. A, 1st Pa. Artillery, AGO, DeWolf Collection, WSL/LIBI.

27. Hennessy, *Return to Bull Run*, 556; *O.R.*, 12:585.

28. Hennessy, *Return to Bull Run*, 381–84, 537n1.

29. Invalid army pension for James M. DeWolf, cpl., Co. A, 1st Pa. Artillery, Mar. 11, 1863, AGO, DeWolf Collection, WSL/LIBI.

30. Finley Hospital was a U.S. general hospital in Washington, D.C., from June 1862 to August 1865. During the Civil War there were over fifty-six hospitals in the capital city, housed in various churches, warehouses, private homes, and formal barracks. Initially a regimental camp of the First Rhode Island Cavalry known as Camp Sprague, Finley was located on Bladensburg Road near Kendal Green, north of Boundary Street. See Lawrence et al., *Civil War Washington*, http://civilwardc.org/data/places/view/152 (last modified Dec. 8, 2011); and Buckley, "War Hospitals." See also Leech, *Reveille in Washington*; and "Washington and Georgetown, D.C.," in Indexes to Field Records of Hospitals, 1821–1912, RG 94, AGO, NARA.

31. Certificate of disability for discharge for James M. DeWolf, cpl., Co. A, 1st Pa. Artillery, Oct. 28, 1862; U.S. Army assistant surgeon Dr. William Bradley to C. H. Barrett, commissioner of pensions, Dec. 5, 1863, AGO, DeWolf Collection, WSL/LIBI.

32. DeWolf, "Synopsis of Services Performed," FHS, 1; U.S. Civil War Pension Index, *General Index to Pension Files, 1861–1934*, RG 15, microfilm publication T-288, NARA, available at www.ancestry.com (accessed Mar 20, 2015). See also invalid army pension for James DeWolf, Mar. 11, 1863, AGO, DeWolf Collection, WSL/LIBI.

33. DeWolf, "Synopsis of Services Performed," FHS, 1.

34. Ibid.; Bates, *Pennsylvania Volunteers*, 2:947–48.

35. For a similar injury, documented with a photograph of the patient and a woodcut (fig. 683), see Barnes, *Medical and Surgical History*, vol. 2, *Surgical History*, Case 1891, p. 937. Barnes's huge five-volume publication documents multiple examples of forearm injuries and the associated treatment during the Civil War.

36. Muster rolls for Batt. A, 1st Pa. Artillery in Bates, *Pennsylvania Volunteers*, 2:972.

37. For the marriage of Jonathan D. Fisk to Achsah DeWolf, see *Wyoming Republican*, Aug. 28, 1872, WCHS.

38. One 1870 transaction in Wyoming County's deed records notes that Achsah DeWolf sold a portion of land to Carlisle E. Burgess, whose family lived in Forkston and owned surrounding tracts of land. *Index of Deeds*, Achsa[h] DeWolf (grantor) to Carlisle E. Burgess (grantee), 1870, WCHS, microfilm, WC 15:733.

39. *Tunkhannock Republican*, Aug. 10, 1882, WCHS. The newspaper article relates that Jonathan Fisk and his wife, Achsah, had returned to the area to visit relatives and were willing to help arrange for family members who were thinking about moving to Iowa to reside near them. Also, the 1880 U.S. Census of Jones County, Iowa lists Achsah and Jonathan as residents of the county (available at www.ancestry.com, accessed Jan. 15, 2015).

40. Declaration of Achsah Fisk, dependent mother of James M. DeWolf, late cpl. of Co. A, 1st Pa. Artillery in the Rebellion, Oct. 7, 1890, to Arthur A. Vaughn, notary public for Jones Co., Wyoming, Iowa, witnessed by James A. Ashcraft and Jonathan Fisk, endorsed by the U.S. Pension Office, Oct. 10, 1890, DeWolf Collection, WSL/LIBI. This declaration was an official request to the U.S. Army Department of Pensions for the granting of her son James M. DeWolf's Civil War army pension to her for subsistence, as his widow had since remarried and therefore the original pension had lawfully ceased. According to Achsah, who was then seventy-three years old, her current husband (Jonathan Fisk) was seventy-five and "physically disabled" so as to not be able to provide sufficient support and "that notwithstanding the Marriage of her Said Son, She was Dependent on him for her support made under an agreement made by him during his lifetime and during his marriage to Said widow Lady and that by his death She became diverted of Said support . . . and that she was still Dependent." The pension request was denied. The pension was eventually restored to Fannie when her second husband died in 1917, and it continued until her death in 1918. James DeWolf only occasionally mentioned his mother in his later letters to his wife, and it is not known how close he and his mother were. Some of his letters (and potentially this 1890 declaration) suggest that their relationship was limited to financial aspects.

41. Achsah died at age ninety on August 25, 1907. Her tombstone in Wyoming Cemetery also lists Jonathan's name and birth/death dates. Iowa Cemetery Records, 1662–1999, Iowa Select Deaths and Burials, 1850–1990, and Pennsylvania Death Certificates, 1906–1963, available at www.ancestry.com (accessed Jan. 6, 2015); www.findagrave.com, Memorial no. 121366056 (accessed Jan. 5, 2015).

42. DeWolf, "Synopsis of Services Performed," 1. See also Register of Enlistments in the U.S. Army, 1798–1914, RG 94, microfilm M233, Vol. 58 (1864–65, A–I), p. 333,

AGO, NARA available at www.familysearch.org (accessed July 16, 2016); also quoted in Nichols, *Men with Custer*, 85.

43. For a meticulously researched and comprehensive history of the Snake War, see Michno, *Deadliest Indian War*. See also Magid, *Gray Fox*, 3–50.

44. The Fort Vancouver where DeWolf served during the Northwest Indian wars was actually the later U.S. Army fort built on the site in 1866 after a fire destroyed both the original former British Hudson's Bay Company fort and the 1849 Columbia Barracks (later renamed Vancouver Barracks) built by the U.S. Army at the same site. Fort Vancouver was first built in 1824–25 on the Columbia River in Oregon country (in present-day Vancouver, near Portland, Oregon) by the Hudson's Bay Company to oversee British fur-trading interests in the Pacific Northwest. The National Park Service has reconstructed the fur trade–era fort, which, along with the Vancouver Barracks, constitutes the current Fort Vancouver National Historic Site. See www.nps.gov/fova/historyculture/index.htm; see also www.nwcouncil.org/history/fortvancouver.asp (both accessed Jan. 28, 2013); and Ferris, "Fort Vancouver National Historic Site," 101–3.

45. Register of Enlistments in the U.S. Army, 1798–1914, RG 94, microfilm M233, AGO, NARA, U.S. Hospital Stewards List, roll 74, vol. 161 (1859–1899), p. 64, available at www.familysearch.org (accessed July 16, 2016).

46. DeWolf, "Synopsis of Services Performed," 1.

47. Ibid. DeWolf does not indicate the specific expedition he accompanied. However, a review of Michno's narrative of the actions against the Indians during DeWolf's three months at Boise (July–September) suggests two possible candidates involving his regiment. The most likely choice is the expedition under Major Louis H. Marshall that left Fort Boise on July 16 with most of the fort's garrison of the Fourteenth Infantry to build a new post on the Bruneau River near its junction with the Snake River. The other, albeit less likely, possibility is the scouting expedition in August under Captain Richard F. O'Beirne with Company E of the Fourteenth Infantry (DeWolf's actual company). However, this latter expedition did not originate at Fort Boise, although it continued on from that post to scout other areas in the region. The other engagements during these three months either involved civilian volunteer troops or had troops of the Fourteenth Infantry originating from other forts. See Michno, *Deadliest Indian War*, 158–62, 165–75.

48. Camp Lyon Post Returns, Oct. 1866, NARA.

49. Camp Lyon (1865–69) was a crude fort consisting of log structures built near the Oregon/Idaho border. It was garrisoned by troops involved with Lieutenant Colonel George Crook's offensive against the Snake Indians in 1867–68 during the last part of the Snake War. Nothing remains of the original fort, the site of which is on private property, although a small cabin that remains on a hill overlooking the fort area is believed to be constructed of lumber from the original fort. The site is marked with a sign and is in Owyhee County, Idaho. See Ferris, National Park Service (NPS), *Soldier and Brave: Survey of Historic Sites and Buildings*, 12 (1971), 120; see also Idaho State

Notes to Pages 15–16

Historical Society Reference Series, Camp Lyon, No. 357, July 16, 1965, http://history.idaho.gov/sites/default/files/uploads/reference-series/0357.pdf (accessed Sep. 7, 2012, and Aug 16, 2016); and Michno, *Deadliest Indian War*, 115.

50. S.O. No. 33, Camp Lyon, Idaho Terr., Oct. 21, 1866, to James De Wall [DeWolf], hospital steward, from Capt. James C. Hunt, post commandant, AGO, DeWolf Collection, WSL/LIBI. Normally, a hospital steward would not have been allowed total oversight of a post hospital. However, a review of Camp Lyon post returns confirms Captain Hunt's statement, as there was no surgeon assigned there at the time of DeWolf's arrival and Acting Assistant Surgeon William Bryant did not arrive until December 1866. Camp Lyon Post Returns, Oct. 1866, NARA.

51. DeWolf, "Synopsis of Services Performed," 1; Register of Enlistments in the U.S. Army, 1798–1914, RG 94, microfilm M233, roll 35, vol. 68 (1868), p. 63, AGO, NARA. These latter records show that DeWolf was enlisted under the name of DeWall. The reason for this discrepancy is not known. Men commonly enlisted under aliases in the army during this period, but in DeWolf's case, it was most likely a clerical transcription error rather than a deliberate alias, given his character and personality. Although this was the second time his name was misspelled during army enlistment, subsequent reenlistments and other official records in later years list his correct last name, DeWolf.

52. S.O. No. 55, May 9, 1969, Dept. of the Columbia, Portland, Ore., by Capt. A. H. Nickerson, 23rd Infantry, ADC and AAAG, and letters of May 22 and 25, 1869, Capt. John P. Coppinger (bvt. col.), 23rd Infantry, commandant of Camp Three Forks, Owyhee, Idaho Terr., AGO, DeWolf Collection, WSL/LIBI; see also Register of Enlistments in the U.S. Army, 1798–1914, RG 94, microfilm M233, U.S. Hospital Stewards List, roll 74, vol. 161 (1859–1899), p. 64, AGO, NARA; Camp Warner Post Returns, May 1869–June 1873, NARA; and DeWolf, "Synopsis of Services Performed," FHS.

53. New Camp Warner (1867–74) was located along Honey Creek in south-central present-day Lake County, Oregon. Bach, "Camp Warner Moved."

54. S.O. No. 87, HQ: Military Division of the Pacific, San Francisco, Calif., May 8, 1871, Maj. Gen. Schofield via John C. Kelton, asst. adj. gen., AGO, DeWolf Collection, WSL/LIBI.

55. Hospital Steward James DeWall [DeWolf] to Lt. F. L. Dodge, 23rd Infantry, post adjutant, May 8, 1871, Camp Warner, Oregon, AGO, DeWolf Collection, WSL/LIBI.

56. Hospital stewards and acting hospital stewards were under the direction of the commanding medical officer. They were appointed from the ranks of enlisted men and could reenlist at the time of their discharge due to expiration of service. Only one steward was allowed per post. Their duties included management and distribution of hospital stores and supplies, administering medicines, supervising the preparation of food, cleaning and oversight of the hospital quarters, and preparing hospital reports and returns for the commanding medical officer, as well as providing assistance in the

tending of wounds. During and after the Civil War, hospital stewards were essentially trained "on the job" to render first aid to the sick and wounded and assist the medical officers and physicians, much like the apprentice surgeon system of the eighteenth century. By the late 1880s, stricter standards had been implemented, as soldiers aspiring to be hospital stewards were required to serve at least one year as an assistant hospital steward as well as pass a general proficiency examination. The army regulations in effect in 1876 were the same as those of 1863. *Revised U.S. Army Regulations*, Art. XLIV/no. 1323–27, pp. 316–17; Agnew, *Medicine in the Old West*, 33; War Office, *Regulations for the Army of the United States, 1889*, Art. LXXXI/no. 1555–59, p. 174.

57. Thomas Jefferson Downing is listed as originally being from Connecticut (b. 1814) and with the initial occupation of farmer, *U.S. Census (June 1, 1860), Norwalk Village, Ohio, Huron County*, 4, NPL, Norwalk, Ohio. He died in Wakeshma, Kalamazoo County, Michigan, on October 25, 1875, where he was living with his third wife, Phebe Jane Allison, and their son Frank (b. 1867); author's personal communication with Norwalk historian Henry R. Timman, Apr. 23, 2009.

58. *Norwalk City Directory, Norwalk, Ohio*, 1885–1900. See also *U.S. Census, Norwalk Village, Ohio, County of Huron (June 6, 1869)* and *U.S. Census, Norwalk Village, Ohio, County of Huron (June 10, 1870)*, NPL, both of which list David Hall as originally from New York and his initial occupation as machinist.

59. Early published histories of Norwalk Village make only a vague reference to Elvira Downing's death. However, her death date and her obituary are noted in the October 21, 1858, issue of the *Norwalk Reflector*. For the remarriage of Fannie's father, Thomas, to Nancy Wadsworth, see cert. no. 1312, Marriage Certificates, 1859, Notary Public Records, Norwalk Village, Ohio, Huron Co., Oct. 4, 1859, NPL, Norwalk, Ohio. Also, the *U.S. Census of Norwalk Village, Ohio, Huron County (June 1, 1860)*, NPL, lists Nancy (Wadsworth) Downing as being originally from New York or Kentucky and as forty years old, while Thomas Downing's age is listed as fifty-one. Downing was married for a third time on September 26, 1861, to Phebe Jane Allison; cert. no. 1895, Marriage Certificates, 1861, Notary Public Records, Norwalk Village, Ohio, Huron Co., NPL.

60. *1860 U.S. Census, Norwalk Village*, NPL.

61. *1870 U.S. Census, Norwalk Village*, NPL. There is no record of Fannie obtaining a formal teaching degree (which would not have been possible, as she was only seventeen years old at the time). Most likely her knowledge base was a result of her local schooling, her own natural ability, and perhaps some practical experience as a nanny.

62. Erb and Erb, *Voices in Our Souls*, 22. Although a historical novel, the Erbs's book is based on the lives, diaries, and letters of James and Fannie DeWolf. Mrs. Erb is a distant cousin of DeWolf's. Per oral family history from Mrs. Carolyn Dodd, widow of Verne A. Dodd Jr. (Frances J. DeWolf Dodd's grandson and part of the DeWolf lineage via Fannie's later marriage to Elijah Dodd), Fannie took a stagecoach on her own out to Oregon for this job. While oral family history is naturally subject to attrition over years, it should never be completely discounted, and Carolyn Dodd's

documentation of this fact came directly from Fannie, her son, and her grandson (the latter being Mrs. Dodd's husband). Author's telephone conversation and personal visit with Gene and Ann Erb, Mar. 21 and June 24, 2013, respectively.

63. Declaration for original pension of a widow, Sep. 8, 1876, for Fannie J. DeWolf, age 25, widow of the late James M. DeWolf, acting assistant surgeon, U.S. Army, deceased June 25, 1876, while on active duty; made and signed to D. H. Fox, judge of the Probate Court of Huron County, Ohio, at Norwalk, Ohio, U.S. Dept. of Interior, Pensions Office, DeWolf Collection, WSL/LIBI. This declaration contains confirmation of James and Fannie's wedding at Camp Warner and the chaplain who married them.

64. James M. DeWolf to surgeon general, War Dept., May 13, 1872, DeWolf Collection, WSL/LIBI (endorsements on request of James M. DeWolf, hospital steward, for change of station, post hospital, Camp Warner).

65. C. W. Knight to surgeon general, War Department, May 13, 1872, quoted in Luce, "Diary and Letters," 2. C. W. Knight was appointed as acting assistant surgeon at Camp Warner by the Medical Department per S.O. No. 41 in April 1871, serving there until August 1871; Camp Warner Post Returns, Apr.–Aug. 1871, NARA.

66. C. H. Crane, asst. surg. gen., to Hospital Steward Jas. M. DeWolf, Camp Warner, Ore., Mar. 14, 1873, SGO, WSL/LIBI; also quoted in Luce, "Diary and Letters," 2.

67. The U.S. Arsenal at Watertown was established in 1816 to manufacture cannonballs and for the storage of ordnance. For a more extensive history, see Dobbs, *History*; and Earls, *Watertown Arsenal*. For a short overview of the recent environmental and commercial renovations of the arsenal site, see Lenny Siegel's report at www.cpeo.org/pubs/watertown.pdf (accessed Feb. 8, 2013).

68. Green, *A Broad Foundation*, chap. 3, para. 4; https://legacy.countway.harvard.edu/chm/rarebooks/exhibits/broad_foundation/index.html.htm or https://collections.countway.harvard.edu/onview/exhibits.

69. Ibid., chap. 4, paras. 1–8.

70. Ibid., chap 3, para. 9.

71. There are no remaining academic records of medical students (including DeWolf) of that era in the archives at Harvard Medical School Library. DeWolf is listed as an enrolled student and as having graduated from the medical school in 1875; author's personal communication with Mr. Jack Eckert, public services librarian, Center for the History of Medicine, Francis A. Countway Library of Medicine, Harvard Medical School, July 6, 2009.

72. Petersen, "Surgeons," 42–43 (three quotations). DeWolf also noted that he passed the Harvard Medical School examination on February 9, 1875; DeWolf, "Synopsis of Services Performed," remarks section.

73. The Pequossette Lodge of Free Masons was founded in 1858, chartered by the Grand Lodge of Masons. The name was derived from the Indian name for Watertown, Pegsguesset, meaning a "well-watered place"; *Watertown City Directory*,

1869–1870, WFPL, 107. At the time of DeWolf's membership, meetings were held on the third Thursday every month at the Old Masonic Hall in the Noyes block on Church Street in Watertown; *Watertown City Directory, 1874–1875*, 173. Both the Pequossette Lodge and the Bethesda Lodge remain as members of the Third District of Grand Lodge of Masons in Massachusetts.

74. For a detailed discussion regarding this letter, see chap. 4, n. 53.

75. War Office, *Revised U.S. Army Regulations*, Art. XLIV/no. 1317, p. 315.

76. Surgeon General's Office to Mr. James M. DeWolf, hospital steward, U.S. Army, U.S. Arsenal, Watertown, Mass., Mar. 13, 1875, SGO, DeWolf Collection, WSL/LIBI.

77. C. H. Crane, asst. surg. gen., U.S. Army to Jas. M. DeWolf, M.D., Forkston, Pa., Aug. 28, 1875, SGO, DeWolf Collection, WSL/LIBI.

78. Certificate of Discharge from the U.S. Army (citing S.O. No. 189), Sep. 18, 1875, signed by T. T. J. Landley, commanding, colonel of ordnance, AGO, DeWolf Collection, WSL/LIBI; also Watertown Arsenal Post Returns, Oct. 1875, NARA.

79. Petersen, "Surgeons," 3 (examinations at Harvard); Green, *Broad Foundation*, chap. 4, paras. 6–8 (medical school educational curriculum and examination reforms), www.countway.harvard.edu/chm/rarebooks/exhibits/broad_foundation/index.html.htm (accessed July 28, 2009, and July 16, 2016).

80. Petersen, "Surgeons," 2; also quoted in Noyes, "Custer's Surgeon," 17; Surgeon Joseph B. Brown, President, Army Medical Board, to the Surgeon General, January 9, 1875, ACP, AGO, Letters Received, File 3231, NARA (details regarding Lord's examination).

81. The Army Medical Department during the Victorian era was an elite fraternity and held to the highest standards in both medical and classical training. As such, examinations in languages, mathematics, social sciences, and history were considered essential and equal with that of basic medical training. Nonetheless, there existed some controversy among professionals in the medical and academic communities, just as there is today, with regard to this premise, as well as disagreements about the specific treatments of various afflictions. There are examples of candidates who were passed by the boards solely based on their ability to answer the minutiae of the strict examinations and were incompetent with regard to their medical ability, although the Army Medical Department sought to weed out all but the most qualified and highly educated physicians. There were some candidates, such as Dr. DeWolf, who were not passed by the army medical board, and other competent civilian physicians such as Dr. Henry Porter never even applied to the army medical board. For additional perspective and opinions regarding the Army Medical Department and its examination process in the 1860s–80s, see Kimball, *Soldier-Doctor of Our Army*. See also Hedren, "Sioux War Adventures"; Cunningham, *Doctors in Gray*, 32–35; Adams, *Doctors in Blue*, 9–13; Lowry and Welsh, *Tarnished Scalpels*; Gillett, *Army Medical Department*; and Ashburn, *History*.

82. Adams, *Doctors in Blue*, 10.

83. C. H. Crane, asst. surg. gen., U.S. Army, to Dr. James M. DeWolf, Forkston, Wyoming Co., Pa., Oct. 16, 1875, SGO, DeWolf Collection, WSL/LIBI.

84. In the early 1870s, the U.S. Army employed 175 contract surgeons to help alleviate the shortage of medical officers; there had previously been only 161 surgeons/assistant surgeons as medical officers for the entire military. To cover the numerous posts scattered in the South and West (217 posts in 1870 and 239 by 1874), the army employed 264 acting assistant (contract) surgeons in 1866, and that number climbed to 282 by 1868. To cut down on expenses, by 1874 the government had limited this to 75 contract surgeons, but the restriction was lifted that year. Agnew, *Medicine in the Old West*, 32; Gillett, *Army Medical Department*, 16; Ashburn, *History*, 89.

85. "Contract with a Private Physician (Form 24)," Oct. 23, 1875, between the surgeon general (C. H. Crane) of the U.S. Army and James M. DeWolf at Forkston, Pa., AGO, DeWolf Collection, WSL/LIBI; War Office, *Revised U.S. Army Regulations*, Art. XLIV/no. 1305, p. 314 and appx. B, Medical Department, no. 71, p. 518.

86. Understandably, Edward S. Luce did not mention these initial entries of DeWolf's diary, because of their lack of relevance to the Little Big Horn story; see Luce, "Diary and Letters." DeWolf's entries are dated October 11, 16–22, 19, 21, and 23, and records in the Wyoming County Historical Society indicate that at least two of these five patients lived in the Forkston/Mehoopany area. The October 19 entry relates that Mrs. Alice Robinson (wife of Alvin) was provided advice for a headache of "chloral ++ [drops] to be dissolved in 1/3 teaspoon of water and take and lie down" (chloral being a sedative [see Miller, *Domestic Medical Practice*, 1090]). The detailed entry for October 16–22 was for a Mrs. Isaac Page, for whom DeWolf successfully delivered a healthy boy weighing seven and one-third pounds after thirteen difficult hours of labor. DeWolf's total charges for the delivery and follow-up visits totaled seven dollars—a seemingly unrealistic and inadequate amount even when compared to today's medical expenses. DeWolf, personal notebook and diary, entries for Oct. 16–23, 1875, original diary in LIBI collections.

87. S.O. No. 219, HQ, Dept. of Dakota, St. Paul, Minn., Nov. 5, 1875, to Acting Assistant Surgeon J. M. DeWolf, from Alfred H. Terry (brig. gen., commanding) and O. D. Okeene (asst. adj. gen.), AGO, DeWolf Collection, WSL/LIBI. For a brief history and description of Fort Totten, see chap. 1, n. 25.

88. Fort Totten Medical History Log, entries for Nov. 1875–Mar. 1876, Microfilm Roll 4277, p. 242, entry for Nov. 15, 1875, by Fort Totten post surgeon Dr. James Ferguson, SHSND. For a brief biography of Ferguson, see chap. 1, n. 41.

89. Fort Totten Medical History Log, entries for Jan. 31 and Feb. 29, 1876, pp. 249, 255.

90. Ferguson noted that about two days before Christmas in 1875, two cavalry privates, George Miller and Michael Currau of Company E of the Seventh Cavalry, were found frozen to death two days after leaving the post to buy whiskey at a nearby ranch. He inscribed that "near the body of Miller were found five canteens

of liquor . . . and although frozen, there can be no doubt whatever that had they been sober these men would have returned to their quarters in perfect safety." Fort Totten Medical History Log, entry for Dec. 31, 1875, p. 246.

Chapter 1.
Fort Seward, D.T.

1. For a brief synopsis of the Fort Laramie Treaty, see Utley, "Little Big Horn," 239–41; see also Ostler, *Lakotas*, 58–79; Hedren, *Fort Laramie*, 2–6; and McChristian, *Fort Laramie*, 304–11. A full transcript of the 1868 treaty is in Lazarus, *Black Hills/White Justice*, 435–49. A detailed history of Red Cloud's War can be found in McDermott, *Red Cloud's War*.

2. Ostler, *Lakotas*, 71–74; Gray, *Centennial Campaign*, 308–20. Gray's chapter provides an analysis of the various Sioux bands and the agencies serving them during the Indian wars period.

3. Lazarus, *Black Hills/White Justice*, 440; Utley, "Little Big Horn," 241.

4. Lubetkin, *Jay Cooke's Gamble*, 286.

5. Many historians consider Grafe and Horsted's *Exploring with Custer: The 1874 Black Hills Expedition* to be the definitive study of the expedition.

6. The published literature on Custer is extensive. Among this voluminous list, those providing a good overview include Utley's *Cavalier in Buckskin*, considered by most historians as the definitive biography; Custer's *My Life on the Plains* and (his wife) Elizabeth Custer's *Boots and Saddles*, both of which provide their personal perspectives on his Indian fighting years; Merington's *Custer Story: The Life and Letters of General George A. Custer and His Wife Elizabeth*; Hutton's *Custer Reader*, a collection of personal narratives, published scholarly essays, and research; and Urwin's *Custer Victorious* and Hatch's *Glorious War*, both in-depth studies of his Civil War career. Stiles's *Custer's Trials* provides a perspective on Custer's complex personality and personal life.

7. Ostler, *Lakotas*, 91.

8. Ibid., 92; Hutton, *Phil Sheridan*, 297–98.

9. Several historians have provided excellent reviews of this secret meeting; chapter 3 of Gray's *Centennial Campaign* is the most in-depth analysis.

10. Hutton, *Phil Sheridan*, 300–305; Gray, *Centennial Campaign*, 31–58.

11. Hedren, *Great Sioux War*, 41; Hutton, *Phil Sheridan*, 302.

12. S.O. No. 27, HQ, Dept. of Dakota, Alfred H. Terry (brig. gen., commanding) via George D. Ruggles (asst. adj. gen.), St. Paul, Minn., Mar. 2, 1876, assignments of Drs. Kimball, Comfort, Clark, and DeWolf, DeWolf Collection, WSL/LIBI; see also Fort Totten Medical Log, entry for Nov. 15, 1875, by post surgeon Dr. James Ferguson, Microfilm Roll 4277, p. 258, SHSND.

13. Gray, *Centennial Campaign*, 47. Crook's first column numbered 662 enlisted men and 32 officers, over eighty wagons with some 84 civilians, five ambulances, a fifty-mule pack train overseen by 62 packers, and forty-five head of beef cattle.

14. While there are several good secondary sources on this fight, Hedren's *Powder River: Disastrous Opening to the Great Sioux War* is considered the definitive study.

15. Kappler, *Indian Affairs*, 2:985; Hoig, *Battle of the Washita*, 30–36; Gray, *Custer's Last Campaign*, 81.

16. For a more extensive analysis of the Clymer-Belknap Hearings and their ramifications for Custer, see Utley, *Cavalier in Buckskin*, 148–64; Hutton, *Phil Sheridan*, 305–11; Smith, *Grant*, 593–95; Gray, *Centennial Campaign*, 59–71; Stewart, *Custer's Luck*, chap. 6; Hatch, *Last Days*, 4–6; and Prickett, "Malfeasance." See also U.S. House of Representatives, *Report on Management of the War Department*.

17. Utley, *Cavalier in Buckskin*, 160–63; Hutton, *Phil Sheridan*, 310–11; Overfield, *Little Big Horn*, 17 (Sherman's reply telegram). While Terry and Sheridan were more overt in their efforts to assist Custer, Sherman simply endorsed and forwarded Custer's humbling telegram to Grant, which asked the president to "spare him the humiliation of not being with his regiment to share in its dangers."

18. Hedren, *Great Sioux War*, 96–97; Overfield, *Little Big Horn*, 109–12.

19. Seventh Cavalry Regimental Return, May 1876; James Calhoun, dispatch to *New York World*, June 3, 1876; C. Lee Noyes, personal correspondence with the author.

20. S.F.O. No. 5, Brig. Gen. Alfred H. Terry, camp near Fort Abraham Lincoln, May 14, 1876, War Department Records, AGO, NARA.

21. Walker, *Dr. Henry R. Porter*, 39; Stevenson, *Deliverance*, 31.

22. Gray, *Centennial Campaign*, 73–74; Stewart, *March of the Montana Column*, 50. This column numbered 409 enlisted men and 27 officers (Lieutenant Bradley's account lists 426 men total), 25 Crow scouts and 4 quartermaster scouts, 12 civilian teamsters and packers (for twelve contract wagons), twenty-four government wagons, two Gatling guns, and a 12-pound Napoleon gun. Although referred to as the Montana Column by some historians, it was never officially designated as such.

23. Stevenson, *Deliverance*, 33. This column numbered 51 officers, 1,000 enlisted men, a pack train of 250 mules driven by 81 men, and 106 wagons overseen by 116 men. Hedren, *Great Sioux War*, 100.

24. For an in-depth review of the onset of the 1876 campaign, see Hedren, *Great Sioux War*, pt. 1, 41–54 (organization, objectives, and results), and pt. 2 (officer rosters/troop organization, objectives). Overfield's *Little Big Horn* also provides company muster rolls for officers and troops; Gray's *Custer's Last Campaign*, 134–80, provides an extensive account of the column formations and movement; and Gray's *Centennial Campaign* is a comprehensive volume on the Sioux War of 1876. Chapters 1–4 of Sarf's *Little Bighorn Campaign* provide a good general overview of the onset of the campaign.

25. Fort Totten (1867–90) was built to protect the U.S. border in North Dakota (then Dakota Territory) with British Canada. It was named for General Joseph G. Totten, former chief of the Army Engineer Corps, who built forts during and after the War of 1812. Located on the south shore of Devil's Lake in current Benson County, the fort was a major garrison post during the U.S. Indian wars of the 1870s–80s. Much of the Seventh Cavalry regiment that was lost with Custer at the Little Big Horn was

stationed at Fort Totten just prior to the conflict. Barnes, *Forts of the Northern Plains*, 126–29; Frazer, *Forts of the West*. See also Davison, *Fort Totten Military Post*; Fort Totten Medical History Log, 1875–1876, SHSND; and Wertenberger, "Fort Totten."

26. The Davis Ranch/Brenner crossing was one of three main crossings of the Sheyenne River on the trail from Fort Seward (Jamestown, Dakota Territory) to Fort Totten, the latter of which was located 81 miles north of Fort Seward. Of Mr. Davis, the original overseer/homesteader of the crossing, no information has been discovered to date other than that he apparently ran the station prior to it being taken over by Ernest Brenner, a former soldier and sutler from Fort Totten in the early 1870s. Dana M. Wright Papers, SHSND, Series II, Box 5, no. 15, "Trails—Fort Totten to Fort Seward" and Box 7, no. 24, "Trail between Fort Totten and Fort Seward." The actual site today is unmarked and located several miles from the state-maintained Brenner's Crossing State Historical Site northeast of New Rockford, North Dakota.

27. Beland was a stage station on the Fort Totten–Fort Seward Trail at present-day Lake Juanita. Wright Papers, SHSND, Box 5, no. 15, "Trails—Fort Totten to Fort Seward."

28. Private Nathan T. Brown (b. 1844), Company K, Seventh Cavalry. Nine men with the last name of Brown are listed for the Seventh Cavalry at this time (two sergeants, a corporal, and six privates). DeWolf identifies this Brown in his journal sick call list of March 10 with frostbite of the tips of toes of both feet. Nathan Brown survived the hilltop fight at the Little Big Horn with Reno and Benteen; he later fought in the Snake Creek fight in 1877 and was discharged from service in 1880 at Fort Abraham Lincoln. Nichols, *Men with Custer*, 39.

29. Although DeWolf gives his name as "Carpiti" in the March 12 letter to Fannie, this is most likely Sergeant William Cashan (1845–76). Cashan was in Company L of the Seventh Cavalry and is listed among the first four men who sustained frostbite of their feet. See Nichols, *Men with Custer*, 53.

30. Private John R. Colwell (b. 1845), Company L, Seventh Cavalry. DeWolf misspelled Colwell's last name; there is no record of any John Caldwell enlisted in the Seventh Cavalry for 1876 in the army register of enlistments. Private William M. Caldwell of Company B (1857–1913) was on detached service at the time of the Battle of the Little Big Horn and was not present in the Dakotas on March 10. See Register of Enlistments in the U.S. Army, 1798–1914 (1876), RG 94, microfilm M233, vol. 72 (1871–1877), p. 321, AGO, NARA. John R. Colwell enlisted in the Seventh Cavalry on September 17, 1875, at Cincinnati, Ohio. Register of Enlistments in the U.S. Army, 1798–1914, RG 94, microfilm M233, vol. 72 (1871–1877), p. 311, AGO, NARA. See also Nichols, *Men with Custer*, 60. DeWolf noted that Coldwell suffered from frostbite to the nose and face and also conjunctivitis (eyelid infection); see DeWolf diary, sick call entry, Mar. 10, 1876, DeWolf Collection, WSL/LIBI.

31. Sergeant George Zimmerman, Company L, Seventh Cavalry (b. 1844). A native of Ohio, he enlisted on March 24, 1871, in Cincinnati. DeWolf noted in his journal entry sick call list of March 10 and in a subsequent monthly report to the medical

director of the Department of Dakota that Zimmerman had sustained frostbite of the entire toes of both feet during the journey from Fort Totten to Fort Seward. Zimmerman was discharged from his company on March 24, 1876, while at Fort Seward, "for expiration of term of enlistment." DeWolf also related that he had to perform amputation of several phalanges (toe bones) of both feet of then-civilian Zimmerman on March 29 but that the patient was "apparently doing well." DeWolf, journal entry of Mar. 10 and letter to medical director, Dept. of Dakota, Mar. 31, 1876, DeWolf Collection, WSL/LIBI; Register of Enlistments in the U.S. Army, 1798–1914, RG 94, microfilm M233, roll 40, vol. 76 (1871–1877), p. 330, AGO, NARA.

32. Fort Seward (1872–77) "was located near Jamestown, Dakota Territory [in present-day Stutsman County], which is 80 miles directly south of Fort Totten and slightly more than 100 miles east of Bismarck (Luce, "Diary and Letters," 4). Fort Seward was built to protect railroad workers as the Northern Pacific Railway was constructed across the northern plains. Originally called Camp Sykes and then Fort Cross, both short-lived designations during its first five months, it was soon renamed in honor of William H. Seward, President Abraham Lincoln's secretary of state. A sprawling post on a terraced hill with buildings of wood construction, it was garrisoned by the Twentieth Infantry and served multiple purposes for support of the military and civilians, including telegraph services and protecting cattle herds and the railroad. The fort was decommissioned and dismantled in 1877. For a more detailed history, see Brown, *Fort Seward*. See also Barnes, *Forts of the Northern Plains*, 119–22; and Frazer, *Forts of the West*, 113.

33. Iron Springs are on the east slope of Grasshopper Hills, which are in northern Stubman County, east of Jim Lake. Grasshopper Hills was a landmark elevation—200 feet above the level of Jim Lake. Wright Papers, SHSND, Box 7, no. 24, "Trail between Fort Totten and Fort Seward," 1.

34. New York native Captain John Henry Patterson (1843–1920) of the Twentieth Infantry was the second and last commanding officer of Fort Seward, from 1873 to 1877. See Brown, *Fort Seward*, 59–60; Heitman, *Historical Register . . . to March 2, 1903*, vol. 1, pt. 2 (hereafter cited as Heitman, *Historical Register* [1903]), 775; and Josef W. Rokus, "John H. Patterson, Hero of the Civil and Spanish-American Wars" (2009), www.civilwar.org/battlefields/wilderness/wilderness-history-articles/john-h-patterson.pdf (accessed Dec. 20, 2013).

35. Arthur William duBray (1847–1928), whose last name DeWolf gave as "DuBray," was born in Essex, England, and came to the United States in 1870. Eventually locating to St. Paul, Minnesota, he went into the saloon business with fellow Englishman Thomas Hay. In March 1875, he enlisted as a private in the U.S. Army and served as a general service clerk in the headquarters of the Department of Dakota in St. Paul until July 1875. From July 9, 1875, to December 31, 1878, he was employed by First Lieutenant Charles A. Varnum, the Seventh Cavalry's regimental quartermaster, for $100 per month as a clerk in the quartermaster department at Fort Abraham Lincoln and as an interpreter in the field during several expeditions in the Nez Perce War.

Thereafter, he served as a general service clerk with the rank of sergeant during a second enlistment from 1878 to 1882 in the headquarters of the Department of the South at Newport Barracks, Kentucky, having followed Major Greene to that post.

As DeWolf mentioned in his letter of March 20, during their brief stay together at Fort Seward on the way to Fort Abraham Lincoln in March 1876, duBray wished to obtain a commission as a second lieutenant in the army. Beginning in May 1875, duBray spent seven years pursuing the appointment. He was highly recommended by numerous officers who knew him during his service, but his applications to the Adjutant General's Office and Secretary of War's Office were eventually denied because of the army's G.O. No. 62, limiting second lieutenant applicants to those of "21 minimum years of age, but not over 30 years of age and not married." He left the army in excellent standing in October 1883. In the years after his army career, he became a gun salesman in the Cincinnati, Ohio and Covington, Kentucky areas and later moved his family to California in 1910. He and his wife are buried in Cypress Lawn Memorial Park in Colma, California. Register of Enlistments in the U.S. Army, 1798–1914 (for 1875 and 1878), RG 94, microfilm M233, vol. 73 (1871–1877, D–G), p. 59 and roll 41, vol. 78 (1878–1884), p. 12, respectively, AGO, NARA; ACP, 1882, Box 798, Arthur W. duBray file, AGO, NARA; Office of the Quartermaster General, 1818–1905, Reports of Persons and Articles Hired in 1877, Box 499, entry 0475 and Lt. Charles A. Varnum, RQM and AAQM, 7th Cavalry, "Report of Persons and Articles employed and hired at Fort Abraham Lincoln, D. T. 1877," Box 493, entries 99–153, 136, RG 92, NARA; Arthur W. duBray, application for appointment as 2nd lieutenant, USA, 3544 ACP, June 28, 1880 and 5641 ACP, April 18, 1882, RG 94, AGO, NARA. See New York Passenger Lists, 1820–1957 (Aug. 22, 1870), microfilm M237, roll 333, line 2, list no. 802. See also Minnesota Territorial and State Censuses, 1849–1905 (for 1875); *U.S. City Directories, 1821–1989* for St. Paul, Minn. (for 1873 and 1874), Covington, Ky. (for 1884–98), and Cincinnati, Ohio (for 1899–1910); U.S. Federal Census for Hamilton Co., Ohio, 1910; and California Death Index, 1905–1939, and San Francisco Area Funeral Home Records, 1895–1985 (for 1927 and 1928); and cemetery location, all available at www.findagrave.com (accessed Mar. 25, 2015) and www.ancestry.com (accessed Jan. 9, 2015).

36. First Lieutenant William Reynolds Maize (1841–91?). Originally from Pennsylvania, he enlisted as a private in the Nineteenth Pennsylvania Volunteer Infantry in 1861. He became a second lieutenant in the Seventy-Eighth Pennsylvania Volunteer Infantry and was cited for "gallant and meritorious service" at the Battle of Stone River, Tennessee, where he was wounded. After the war, he was transferred to the Second Infantry, then to the Twentieth Infantry in 1870. At that time, he was assigned to Dakota Territory, first at Fort Pembina and then Fort Seward in 1872. Because of his health, Maize requested leave from the army in 1876; he eventually retired in 1891. Brown, *Fort Seward*, 59. See also Heitman, *Historical Register* (1903), 685.

37. Custer and his wife, Elizabeth, were en route from Chicago to Fort Abraham Lincoln after his five-month leave in the East. The snow was so bad that the train was

stalled on the tracks and unable to proceed for three weeks. Eventually, horse-drawn sleighs were used to transfer the passengers off the train and to their destination. Such storms were the norm for winters on the Dakota plains. Dr. E. W. DuBose, post surgeon, noted in his annual report of 1875 at Fort Seward that "the winters are long and extremely cold and rapid changes in the temperature are common, sometimes as much as 40° in 24 hours" and that "[t]he snowfall is not great, but it is not uncommon to have it in May and October. . . . In winter, severe and blinding storms of wind and snow are . . . frequent occu[r]rences." DuBose listed the temperature range at Fort Seward in March 1874 as having a low of 25°F and a high of 58°F. Recent total snowfall in March at Jamestown, from data collected over the period of 1981–2010, averaged 7.2 inches over 5.2 days, with an average March low temperature of 18°F. Brown, *Fort Seward*, 41 (for DuBose's weather observations); see also "1981–2010 Climate Normals," *Current Results*, weather and science facts, Weather for Eastern North Dakota, National Oceanic and Atmospheric Administration (NOAA), National Centers for Environmental Information (formerly National Climatic Data Center), available at www.currentresults.com (accessed July 17, 2016).

38. She was the wife of Captain William Fletcher of the Twentieth Infantry at Fort Totten (see chap. 2, n. 31).

39. This suggests that DeWolf's foot injury, noted in his diary entry of March 10, was not serious. Most likely, this was a contusion (severe bruise) or sprain and not a fracture. That he would still have some swelling from such an injury is not uncommon.

40. Lieutenant Colonel Lewis Cass Hunt (1824–86), a Michigan native, was the commanding officer of Fort Totten when the DeWolfs lived at that post. Hunt's actual rank at the time was lieutenant colonel in the Fourteenth Infantry (though he was promoted to colonel later in his career). DeWolf refers to him as "General" in his letter, honoring Hunt's highest brevet rank (brigadier general of the U.S. Volunteers in the Civil War), given for "gallant and meritorious service during the war" in the battles of Fair Oaks, Virginia, and Kingston, North Carolina. Referring to brevet rank was an unofficial courtesy among officers during that era. Hunt was a graduate of the U.S. Military Academy in 1843 (thirty-third in his class) and served in several regiments before he joined the Ninety-Second New York Volunteer Infantry in the Civil War. Hunt's wife, Abby Pearce Casey Hunt, became friends with Fannie DeWolf, Edna Ferguson, and many of the other officers' and medical staff's wives at the post. Hunt's later military service took him to the Texas and New Mexico regions. He suffered from chronic dysentery and died at Fort Union in New Mexico, only six months after Abby died at their home in Michigan. Hunt is buried in Fort Leavenworth National Cemetery. Brown, *Fort Seward*, 58–59; Heitman, *Historical Register* (1903), 556; www.findagrave.com (accessed Feb. 24, 2013).

41. Dr. James B. Ferguson (1840–1926). As the post surgeon at Fort Totten, he (and his wife, Edna) had a son born at that post in October 1875. Ferguson's medical log at Fort Totten from 1875 to 1876 reveals much about the daily activities of both medical and social life at the fort. The Fergusons and DeWolfs were good friends

during the DeWolfs' time there. Ferguson appears to have been a well-liked and competent physician, as evidenced by his long-time service as a contract physician. Born in Peterborough, Ontario, Canada, he enlisted in the Civil War as a private and hospital steward in the Sixth New York Cavalry's Company G in 1861. Ferguson was captured in 1862 in Virginia but was released on parole and served as a hospital steward until being mustered out in 1864. He graduated from Jefferson Medical College at Philadelphia in 1866. A career citizen physician/surgeon in the army, Ferguson served as an acting assistant surgeon at numerous posts in Dakota Territory. He finished out his career in private practice and as a first lieutenant in the Medical Reserve Corps. In 1926 Ferguson died at St. Paul, Minnesota, where he and his wife had moved after his retirement from the army in 1911. New York Civil War Muster Roll Abstracts, 1861–1900, 3775–83, Box no. 816, microfilm roll 472, www.ancestry.com (accessed June 6, 2015); Fort Totten, Post Returns, 1867–1877, M617, roll 1282, AGO, NARA; see also *Directory of Deceased American Physicians, 1804–1929* and *Minnesota Death Index, 1908–2002*, both available at www.ancestry.com (accessed June 6, 2016).

42. DeWolf was referring to Captain Thomas Mower McDougall (1845–1909) of Company B of the Seventh Cavalry. The son of (Brevet) Brigadier General Charles McDougall, he served in the Civil War, initially as an aide-de-camp for General J. P. Hawkins and later with the Tenth Louisiana Volunteers (Forty-Eighth U.S. Colored Infantry), and was wounded at Lakeville, Mississippi. He later served with several infantry regiments in the West and the South after the war years, before being assigned to the Seventh Cavalry in 1870. He "commanded Company B of the 7th Cavalry in the [Little Big Horn] expedition and was assigned to protect the pack train on June 25" (Luce, "Diary and Letters," 11). This latter duty was a result of his being late to the morning officers' meeting, which saved him from being with Custer, and he subsequently survived the hilltop fight with Reno and Benteen. After eighteen years of service in the Dakota Territory, McDougall retired from the military in 1890 as a result of chronic liver disease from malaria fever. He died in 1909 and is buried in Arlington National Cemetery in Washington, D.C. See Nichols, *Men with Custer*, 215.

43. Rumors and gossip continually circulated among the enlisted men and officers with regard to the campaign's actual plans and personnel. In this instance, DeWolf refers to the rumored reasons for Custer's summons to Washington in the telegram the officer had received the day prior. Some thought that Custer might be seeking a promotion in rank and a new administrative position away from the Seventh Cavalry, when in reality, his summons was to testify in the Clymer-Belknap Hearings. In penning about this potentially unique situation facing Custer, DeWolf was not making an erroneous interpretation but merely noting the rumors, as evidenced by his declaration that these were "only surmises and not to be trusted explicitly." Utley, *Cavalier in Buckskin*, 163–64; Hutton, *Phil Sheridan*, 309; Koster, "Belknap Scandal," *Wild West*; Smith, *Grant*, 593–95; Brands, *Man Who Saved the Union*, 560–62.

44. First Lieutenant William Thomas Craycroft (1847–1906), Company B, Seventh Cavalry. A native of Kentucky, he graduated from the U.S. Military Academy in

1869 and served his entire military career in the Seventh Cavalry. Fortunately for Craycroft, he missed the Little Big Horn debacle, as he was on detached service purchasing horses in Kentucky for the regiment from April to September of that year. After his retirement from the Seventh Cavalry in 1878 because of "disability in line of duty," he worked in an industrial school and later in the insurance and newspaper businesses. He died in Dallas, Texas, in 1906. Heitman, *Historical Register* (1903), 337; Nichols, *Men with Custer*, 66.

45. Acting Assistant Surgeon Henry H. Rugar. An 1865 graduate of Jefferson Medical College in Philadelphia, Pennsylvania, as a civilian contract physician he was first assigned to Fort Seward in March 1876 as post surgeon, becoming an assistant surgeon under Dr. James Ferguson at Fort Totten later that year. Rugar later became a prominent citizen in the area, where he went into private practice and was also a representative in the state legislature. See Brown, *Fort Seward*, 67–68; and Wertenberger, "Fort Totten," 139, 145.

46. The post hospital at Fort Seward was substantial. Its main building was completed in 1874, although "the ward ha[d] not yet been completed" according to Captain Patterson in his annual report to his superiors. Despite the site of the hospital being well adapted for that purpose, Patterson thought it to be "out of all proportion to the size of the Garrison." Nonetheless, the two-story structure was of good construction and appears to have been in accordance with the official hospital regulations and plans required by the U.S. Army for its military posts by the mid-1870s, with the added luxury of its own stable for the hospital cows. Although the medical staff at Seward had a nice facility in which to treat their patients, no doubt DeWolf would have been shocked to learn (and perhaps he did) that the floors had covered a previous "temporary and unauthorized latrine." Just two years prior, Patterson had learned that the carpenters who worked on the building were defecating among the floorboards, and he had swiftly issued an order banning that practice. Brown, *Fort Seward*, 30–31.

47. Echerson has not been identified.

48. Amanda B. Forbes, stepmother of Patterson's wife, Mary Elizabeth Forbes Patterson. Mary's father, former Minnesota military and civil government official William H. Forbes, was the Indian agent at Fort Totten and had remarried after the death of Mary's mother. After he died at Fort Totten on July 20, 1875, his second wife, Amanda, along with Mary's full sisters, Jennie Forbes and Mrs. Annie Littson, came to live with the Pattersons at Fort Seward. Brown, *Fort Seward*, 36–37; Rokus, "John H. Patterson," 20, 25–26 (available at www.civilwar.org, accessed Dec. 20, 2013).

49. DeWolf's descriptions of his daily routine coincide with the known schedule of everyday activities at Fort Seward, which was typical of the military posts on the western frontier. Brown notes the schedule of roll calls and service in 1876 in his history of the fort. Reveille/first call was at 5:15 A.M. (immediately after daybreak per official army regulations), with breakfast call at 6:30 A.M. and sick call and fatigue call at 7:00 and 7:30 A.M., respectively. As DeWolf notes, this gave him time for a more leisurely breakfast, which he most likely enjoyed with his fellow medical staff

officers while the enlisted men and officers had morning inspection at 9:00 A.M. Dinner call was at 12:30 P.M. Retreat was at 9:00 P.M. (at sunset per official army regulations) and taps at 9:20 P.M. However, for the officers, entertainment continued into the night in various forms, such as music and social visits among the upper social classes. For the Fort Seward 1876 spring schedule, see Brown, *Fort Seward*, 47; for hours of service and roll calls, see War Office, *Revised U.S. Army Regulations*, Art. XXVIII/no. 230–36, pp. 39–40.

50. DeWolf's mention of the lack of these two activities at this point is interesting. Card playing and drinking helped the soldiers and officers pass the long hours at night and were also enjoyed in between official daily garrison duties. While DeWolf did not imbibe alcohol in quantity or often, he did partake of an occasional drink and enjoyed playing cards, as he notes in some of his later letters (see letter of March 25).

51. Brown notes that there were a total of nineteen garrison courts-martial held at Fort Seward during 1876. The charges included "Absent Without Leave, Drunk on Duty, theft of a Springfield Rifle, [and] Conduct to the Prejudice of Good Order and Military Discipline," as well as a court-martial for one man who "did behave himself in a disgusting manner by breaking wind at the table." Brown, *Fort Seward*, 49.

52. First Lieutenant James Calhoun (1845–76), Company C, Seventh Cavalry. Calhoun, "brother-in-law to General Custer" (Luce, "Diary and Letters," 13), was married to George and Tom Custer's sister, Margaret. A native of Cincinnati, Ohio, he had joined the Twenty-Third Infantry at age eighteen, after graduating from an independent New York military academy. Calhoun eventually became an officer and was later assigned to the Seventh Cavalry in early 1871, serving with his brothers-in-law until his death with them at the Little Big Horn. The doctor clearly thought well of the lieutenant. Calhoun is buried at Fort Leavenworth. See Nichols, *Men with Custer*, 47.

53. James Henton (d. 1895) was born in England and served in the U.S. Army Sixth Infantry between 1853 and 1858 as a private and later a sergeant. During the Civil War, he served in the Fourteenth Infantry as a sergeant, participated in the Battle of Gettysburg, and was later promoted to the rank of captain in 1865. He transferred to the Twenty-Third Infantry in 1866, rising to the rank of lieutenant colonel. See Heitman, *Historical Register* (1903), 525.

54. Arthur W. Kelly was a sutler at Jamestown, Dakota Territory, having arrived there in 1872. He had contracted with the military to provide supplies to the garrison at Fort Seward and, later, other posts in the region. Brown, *Fort Seward*, 26.

55. Seidletz Powders are a milder laxative (or purgative) for constipation and "cleansing of the bowels," commonly used in nineteenth-century medicine and well into the twentieth century. This combination of two powders (tartaric acid and a mixture of sodium bicarbonate and Rochelle salt, or sodium potassium tartrate) was named after a village in Bohemia whose mineral springs had similar laxative effects. Such mineral water salts and the other contents of Seidletz Powders were milder than other known purgatives, such as castor oil and rhubarb. Seidletz Powders were also used in

a variety of other conditions in which "purging" was thought to be of benefit, such as indigestion, heartburn, and even headaches. However, as with any medicinal substances, side effects such as headaches could occur, and it appears that DeWolf, while taking the Seidletz for one purpose, ended up with the side effect it was supposed to cure. Chase, *Dr. Chase's Recipes*, 125, 157; Agnew, *Medicine in the Old West*, 98–99.

56. In his limited editing of DeWolf's diary and letters, Edward S. Luce footnoted this March 21 letter as having "some uncertainty regarding the name of Lunis." He noted that it was "his best judgment, although it could have been Lewis or some name similar to it" (Luce, "Diary and Letters," 14) and that DeWolf mentions Lunis numerous times in his letters. Luce surmised that Lunis was probably an enlisted man or a contract carrier of mail. Luce was correct in the latter, as North Dakota historian Dana M. Wright (as well as Bill Brown) avers that Edward H. Lohnes operated an express service between Jamestown/Fort Seward and Fort Totten and later became a prominent citizen in the Devil's Lake area after marrying an Indian woman on the reservation there. As DeWolf indicates, he was awaiting mail when Lunis arrived at Seward, and so it is highly probable that the latter is actually Edward H. Lohnes and that the doctor misspelled the name, as he occasionally did with other persons. Also, although there was a Benjamin Lewis stationed at Fort Seward from August 1875 to November 1876, he was a private in Company A of the Twentieth Infantry, and thus it is most reasonable to assume he is not the "Lunis" referred to by DeWolf.

Lohnes was born in 1844 in New York, his father a Pennsylvanian of German descent, his mother's side of the family being Irish. He served in the First Regiment of the New York Mounted Rifles in the Civil War and beginning in 1867 with the Thirty-First U.S. Infantry and then the Twentieth Infantry at Fort Totten until his discharge there in 1870. Upon leaving the army, Lohnes operated the aforementioned mail express service. He later served as a wood and beef contractor at Fort Totten and as a county commissioner in Ramsey County near Sweetwater Lake from 1883 to 1889, where he farmed until 1904; he also served in the lower house of the North Dakota legislature. Notes of Sep. 13, 1958, Box 5, no. 15, "Trails—Fort Totten to Fort Seward," Wright Papers, SHSND; Libby, "Edward H. Lohnes," *North Dakota History* 3 (1958); Libby, *North Dakota History* (1910), 213–14; Brown, *Fort Seward*, 34, 37.

57. Edward Walker has not been identified. The organization that Walker belonged to and how DeWolf knew him are unknown at this time. No record to date has been found of an Edward Walker who was a resident of Watertown or a member of the Pequossette Masonic Lodge during the time of the DeWolfs' residence there. However, DeWolf's statement suggests that Walker was a fellow Mason.

58. The exact association under discussion is unclear. There was a Masonic lodge in Greenfield, but why he would wish to eventually move there or what other association DeWolf might have that would have caused a potential interest in joining is not known.

59. It is not surprising that duBray became queasy upon hearing DeWolf's stories about the dissecting room. Famed Boston surgeon Dr. John Warren (1753–1815),

who lectured at Harvard Medical School during and after the Revolutionary War, wrote of the importance of dissection to medical curricula, although he also noted the unpleasantness to which DeWolf alluded: "At the first view of dissections, the stomach is apt to turn, but custom wears off such impressions. It is anatomy that directs the knife in the hand of a skillful surgeon, & shews him where he may perform any necessary operation with safety to the patient . . . which enables the physician to form an accurate knowledge of diseases." Quoted in Green, *Broad Foundation*, chap. 1, para. 8, www.countway.harvard.edu/chm/rarebooks/exhibits/broad_foundation/index.html.htm (accessed July 28, 2009).

60. Liquor was readily available to off-duty soldiers at Fort Seward to spend their little pay on. There were numerous saloons in the nearby city of Jamestown, often called "Jimtown," located just across the James River and founded by merchants serving the Northern Pacific Railroad and the military. In 1874, there were only six or eight wooden houses in Jamestown; in 1876, many of the saloons were still tent establishments. The saloons created constant problems in military discipline and health issues at Fort Seward, as DeWolf indicates here and in his March 22 letter about the inebriated officers harassing the telegraph operator in town. For further discussion of Jamestown's saloons and resulting conflicts between soldiers and civilians, see Brown, *Fort Seward*, 11, 20–21, 26–28, 51.

61. The treatment of frostbite in the 1870s is similar to that of today, with some changes in the initial treatment steps. Gradual rewarming of the affected limb remains the central caveat of treatment. In the nineteenth century, the exposed part was to be either "slowly rubbed with snow, or bathed with cold water, either in the open air or in a cold room . . . [and] after half an hour, two or three tea-spoons of weak brandy and cold water [were] to be given." Billroth, *General Surgical Pathology*, 251; Chase, *Dr. Chase's Recipes*, 228–29 (quotation); see Miller, *Domestic Medical Practice*, 831. However, modern-day recommendations involve immersing the injured tissue in a warm water bath at 104–107.6°F (40–42°C), then lightly wrapping or splinting the injured part to prevent further tissue damage from the ice crystals that have formed. Rubbing or massage of the involved part is contraindicated, although debridement of any skin blisters is still recommended. See Golant et al., "Cold Exposure Injuries"; and DeLee et al., *Orthopaedic Sports Medicine*, 1:547–49. Waiting several days (sometimes even up to three months) to ascertain the areas of demarcation of nonviable tissue, i.e., blackening/necrosis, and to determine what level of debridement and/or amputation is necessary remains the standard of care. Despite amputation of toes and foot portions, many soldiers functioned quite well.

62. Elmira has not been identified.

63. This is a reference to the Pequossette Lodge of Free Masons that DeWolf joined while he attended Harvard Medical School (see the introduction to this volume).

64. DeWolf does not mention the exact building in which he stayed at Fort Seward. Although not an officer, as an acting assistant surgeon DeWolf was still considered part of the staff. Because duBray was a general service clerk and Maize and

McDougall were officers, and DeWolf noted he was living with them, most likely they all stayed in the officers' quarters. These quarters consisted of three buildings, each containing two main rooms "15 × 15 feet each, a dining room, a kitchen, a laundry and a hall. Servant rooms were in the attic" (Brown, *Fort Seward*, 9). With two to three officers per room, it was somewhat crowded but cozy, as DeWolf describes. DeWolf's comments indicate that he was not a smoker. The levity in his last sentence exemplifies his good sense of humor and positive attitude, seen throughout his letters.

65. This is probably the *Norwalk Reflector*, one of the newspapers in Fannie's hometown and most likely sent to her by her sister and brother-in-law, Emma and David Hall, before she forwarded it to James. News from the East was a welcome break from the daily monotony at the various posts.

66. Dr. James Peleg Kimball (1840–1902) was one of the most renowned U.S. Army surgeons of the late nineteenth century. Born in Berkshire, New York, he attended Hamilton College, graduated from Albany Medical College in 1864, and then joined the Union Army, serving as an assistant surgeon for two New York volunteer units for the remainder of the Civil War. He practiced as a private physician for about a year, but his calling was for a career in the army as a surgeon, and he was fortunate enough to pass the army medical board's oral examination process in 1867. He was eventually assigned as the post surgeon at Fort Buford, Dakota Territory, later that year and served there until 1870. He married Sarah Eddy of Albany in 1869. After serving three years at Little Rock, Arkansas, Kimball eventually became good friends with Custer and Terry and served at Custer's request as chief medical officer during the 1873 Yellowstone (Stanley) expedition for the Northern Pacific Railroad route. After serving at Fort Abraham Lincoln with Custer, he was transferred in 1876 to Fort Brady, Michigan, thereby saving him from the disastrous fate that befell Custer and his regiment at the Little Big Horn. Thereafter, Kimball served at various army posts in the western frontier, including New Mexico, then in the Spanish-American War. He also became an assistant surgeon general for the army and was appointed the medical director of the army's Department of the Omaha, serving there until 1901. He was promoted to the rank of colonel in January 1902 and died that spring in Onteora-in-the-Catskills, New York. For a full review of his life, see the excellent biography by his wife, Maria Brace Kimball, *Soldier-Doctor of Our Army: James Peleg Kimball*.

67. General Alfred Howe Terry (1827–90) was the "commander of the Department of Dakota, with headquarters in Fort Snelling at St. Paul, Minnesota" (Luce, "Diary and Letters," 5). Terry was a native of Connecticut who graduated from Yale Law School in 1848 and served as the clerk of the superior court of New Haven County. During the Civil War, he commanded a volunteer regiment from his home state and later became a Union brigadier general for his leadership in the capture of Fort Fisher at Wilmington, North Carolina, in January 1865. He remained in the army after the war and became the commander of Dakota Territory from 1866 to 1869 and again from 1872 to 1886, leading the Dakota Column of the 1876 Indian expedition initially

leaving Fort Abraham Lincoln and acting as Custer's direct superior. He is buried in Grove Street Cemetery in New Haven, Connecticut. His original field notes from the 1876 Sioux campaign are located in the archives of the State Historical Society of North Dakota; his letters to his sisters during the campaign are part of the Western Americana Collection, Beinecke Library, Yale University, and have been published as Willert's *Terry Letters*. Additional biographical details can be found in Warner's *Generals in Blue* and Eicher and Eicher, *Civil War Commands*, 524.

68. Orville Babcock, President Ulysses S. Grant's private secretary, was implicated in a national whiskey tax underpayment scandal, one of several scandals that marred President Grant's administration. Brands, *Man Who Saved the Union*, 556–60; Smith, *Grant*, 590–93.

69. General George Crook (1828–90), "commander of the Department of the Platte" (Luce, "Diary and Letters," 17), was a career army officer serving in the Civil War and later in the western Indian wars; he led the southern Wyoming column during the 1876 campaign. He is buried in Arlington National Cemetery in Washington, D.C. See Magid, *George Crook: From the Redwoods to Appomattox* and *The Gray Fox*; Robinson, *Crook on the Western Frontier*; Bourke, *On the Border*; Warner, *Generals in Blue*; and Eicher and Eicher, *Civil War High Commands*. Also, Michno's *Deadliest Indian War . . . The Snake War* and Gray's *Centennial Campaign—The Sioux War* relate Crook's involvement in those conflicts.

70. Despite this letter's sensitive nature, it is surprising that DeWolf would mark it as "private," since all his letters to his wife are private correspondence. Here, DeWolf cautions his wife in regard to gossip among the army wives at the post and asks for her not to discuss what he shared in his letter with anyone, even her friends.

71. This is a reference to a deed that DeWolf mentions in a later letter. He was in the process of purchasing a portion of his family's farm in Pennsylvania from his mother, Achsah, who by this time had remarried after his father's death (see introduction, n. 37). His mother had already sold off the family farm in parcels to some of her other sons, as well as some of the neighbors (see introduction, n. 38). DeWolf's comments here suggest that he was perturbed about the in-progress transaction and agreement for the purchase.

72. This provides additional information about DeWolf's physical stature, supplementing the other personal information and descriptions on his pension army records (see introduction, n. 15).

73. DeWolf's comments suggest that perhaps an incident at Fort Totten gave him cause to caution his wife about locking the front door of her quarters. However, no correlating letter from Fannie to her husband has been found.

74. DeWolf is providing an update on former trooper George Zimmerman. Although Zimmerman was a civilian, he was afforded continuation of treatment until his recovery for his service and because there was no civilian physician available in the area. Because he was discharged from the service while in the hospital, per army regulations, the post surgeon, Henry H. Rugar, would have made out a

discharged soldier's final statements for pay and clothing. War Office, *Revised U.S. Army Regulations*, Art. XLIV/no. 1286, p. 311.

75. Mary Elizabeth Forbes Patterson died in 1883 at Fort Supply in Oklahoma and is buried in the Calvary Cemetery at St. Paul, Minnesota. Brown, *Fort Seward*, 45, 60; Rokus, "John H. Patterson," 23–25 (available at www.civilwar.org).

76. DeWolf notes here that Lieutenant Craycroft intended to retire from the army as a result of health reasons, probably symptoms of cerebral vascular insufficiency, as he eventually died of a stroke. Craycroft was instead assigned to detached service in Kentucky, purchasing horses for the army until September 1876. He appears to have changed his mind about retirement, though his reason is not known, and delayed his retirement from the service, being on sick leave until 1878 because of disability. Nichols, *Men with Custer*, 66.

77. Common among civilians, straw hats were also permitted for use in the field. Although not favored as much by the officers, straw hats were worn on the campaign by some staff members and were very popular among the enlisted men. The hats usually cost between twenty-five and fifty cents. Several well-known photos of Seventh Cavalry officers with Custer, taken at Fort Abraham Lincoln and in the field in 1874 and 1875, provide evidence that some officers wore the hats. Later on in the Little Big Horn campaign, sutlers sold these hats to the soldiers at the Heart and Powder River camps. McChristian, *U.S. Army*, 155; Sarf, *Little Bighorn Campaign*, 146; Chorne, *Following the Custer Trail*, 152, 181; Reedstrom, *Custer's 7th Cavalry*, 114.

78. Second Lieutenant Alfred Reynolds (1849–1925) was from Pennsylvania and graduated twenty-eighth in his class at the U.S. Military Academy in September 1870. He served as post adjutant/treasurer at Fort Totten; Fort Totten Post Returns, Oct. 1875, NARA, 196. He was appointed as a second lieutenant in the Seventeenth Infantry in 1874 and was promoted to first lieutenant in 1889, to captain in 1891, and eventually to major in the Twenty-Second Infantry in 1899, and he served in both the Spanish-American War and the Philippines insurrection. In 1900, he was transferred to the Twentieth Infantry and was appointed as an assistant to the inspector general in 1901. Promoted to the rank of colonel in 1906, he assisted in recovery efforts in the San Francisco earthquake. He retired in 1912. Reynolds is buried in San Francisco National Cemetery. See www.findagrave.com (accessed Aug. 17, 2013); see also Heitman, *Historical Register* (1903), 824.

79. DeWolf is referring to another political situation in the army command structure. General Sherman had moved army headquarters from Washington, D.C., to St. Louis, Missouri, in 1874 as a result of his political and personal feuds with Secretary Belknap. Although they had been colleagues during the Civil War (Belknap had accompanied Sherman during the 1864 March to the Sea campaign in Georgia), their relationship later soured during the 1870s after Belknap was appointed secretary of war. Sherman had disagreements with Belknap concerning army policy and believed that he was interfering in the commander's authority on many army issues. Only after

Belknap resigned his position in President Grant's administration did Sherman move army headquarters back to Washington, D.C. See Hutton, *Phil Sheridan*, 296–99; and Athearn, *William Tecumseh Sherman*, 268–69.

80. William Harmon (1835–1903), a former U.S. Army officer, was the appointed post trader at Fort Abraham Lincoln between 1875 and 1880. Although DeWolf calls Harmon a former captain, he only attained the rank of lieutenant during his military service. A native of Maine, he moved with his family to Minnesota in 1850. During the Civil War, he served in the First Minnesota Volunteer Regiment and eventually was promoted to lieutenant. After the war, Harmon eventually served with the army at the Grand River Agency in Dakota Territory but resigned his commission after he met and married a Sioux woman, Zoe "Lulu" Picotte, the daughter of the respected Sioux Matilda Picotte Galpin (also known as Eagle Woman That All Look At). He became a trading post agent with that agency, although after his tenure at Fort Lincoln he and his family became merchants in nearby Bismarck and later Miles City, Montana. He also eventually became a friend of Theodore Roosevelt. Harmon died in Milwaukee, Wisconsin. For further information, see the First Minnesota Volunteer Infantry Regiment website, www.1stminnesota.net (accessed Feb. 17, 2013); see also Heitman, *Historical Register* (1903), 501.

81. Membership and participation in various societies and clubs was common among the upper social classes at the various army posts. The Pedro Club was a favorite pastime of the officers and medical staff at Fort Totten, including the DeWolfs. Pedro is "one of several card games resembling seven-up in which five points are scored for winning the five trumps in a trick." *World Book Dictionary*, 2:1536.

82. Captain Abram A. Harbach (1841–1933) was the commander of Company K of the Twentieth U.S. Infantry, stationed at Fort Totten. Harbach was a native of Pittsburgh, Pennsylvania, and served in the Eleventh Iowa Infantry during the Civil War, being breveted a captain for "gallant and meritorious service in the Battle of Gettysburg." He transferred to the Twentieth Infantry in 1866 and was appointed regimental adjutant of the regiment in 1867. He served as the post quartermaster/commissary at Fort Totten. He founded Fort Pembina, North Dakota, in 1874, along with Captain Lloyd Wheaton in Company I of the same regiment. He married Lilian Otis in July 1895. Harbach later rose to the rank of lieutenant colonel in the Third U.S. Infantry, served in Minnesota in the late 1890s, was promoted to colonel in the First Infantry in 1899, and was made a brigadier general in 1902, shortly before his retirement. He lived in Rochester, New York, in his later years and died on November 22, 1933, in Santa Barbara, California. He is buried in Arlington National Cemetery, Section 7, Grave 8009. Blegen, "New Historical Marker for Fort Pembina near Pembina Airport," *Minnesota History* (December 1931): 438; Matsen, "The Battle of Sugar Point: A Re-examination," *Minnesota History* 50 (Fall 1987): 274. For more details regarding his service record, see Heitman, *Historical Register* (1903), 499; and Fort Totten Post Returns, Oct. 1875, NARA, 196.

83. Erastus (1851–1917), James's younger brother, was living in Mehoopany/Forkston.

Erastus was buying remaining portions of the family farm from their mother, and after James's death at the Little Big Horn, he eventually purchased James's portion from Fannie. DeWolf was sending money to his brother, as Erastus was acting as overseer/trustee for their mother in the transactions. Sometime before 1880, Erastus moved his family (his wife, Elizabeth, and their sons) to Manistee County, Michigan. They later moved to Washington after 1900. Erastus died in Seattle on December 14, 1917. Author's personal communication with Michael Hogan, DeWolf descendant, Mar. 8, 2015.

84. Colonel Theodore Thaddeus Sobieski Laidley (1822–86), a native of Virginia, was a graduate of the U.S. Military Academy and a veteran of the Mexican War and the Civil War. He was an officer in the Ordnance Department his entire career, serving as the commander of seven different government arsenals. He was the commandant of the Watertown Arsenal during DeWolf's tenure there, having that position from 1871 until his retirement in 1882. James and Fannie had been discussing their future once the 1876 Yellowstone campaign was completed, and DeWolf indicated in one letter that he would like to remain with the army as a contract surgeon if possible. This April 4 letter indicates that he was planning to write his former commander, Laidley, about the possibility of returning to the Watertown Arsenal, despite lacking confidence about his being accepted for the position. See Ordnance Hall of Fame website, Fort Lee, Virginia, www.goordnance.army.mil/hof/2000/2008/laidley.html (accessed Feb. 17, 2013); see also Heitman, *Historical Register* (1903), 611.

85. Ella appears to have been a servant at Fort Totten who accompanied the troops to Fort Seward. She worked for DeWolf and Fannie during their time at Totten, as indicated in a later letter the doctor wrote to his wife relating that Ella had desired to return there to assist her (see DeWolf's May 8, 1876, letter in chapter 2). Unfortunately, DeWolf fails to mention her last name, a common occurrence among the officers of the era; see Adams, *Class and Race*, 54. No other information regarding this Ella has been located.

86. William Hemsley Emory (1811–87), a native of Maryland, was the commander of the Department of the Gulf (Louisiana, Arkansas, and Mississippi) in the post–Civil War Reconstruction era. He was a graduate of the U.S. Military Academy and a topographic engineer, explorer, and surveyor, and he served in the Mexican and Civil Wars. For further information regarding his role in the Indian wars era, see Dawson, *Army Generals and Reconstruction*; see also Heitman, *Historical Register* (1903), 405–6.

87. Ernest W. Brenner was the sutler at Fort Totten. Originally from Wurtemburg, Germany, he was a former soldier at Fort Totten who became a hired sutler at the post. He opened a brewery at the fort; however, he "made beer which was so potent that he became unfit to manage his trading post" at the fort. As a result, he was mandated to operate it at a location several miles away, at the Sheyanne River crossing (the former Davis ranch), although he was allowed to continue as the post sutler. Dana M. Wright Papers, SHSND, Series II, Box 5, no. 15, "Trails—Fort Totten to Fort Seward" (quotation); also Wertenberger, "Fort Totten," 139.

88. This was when Custer "was called to Washington to testify before the Clymer-Belknap hearings" (Luce, "Diary and Letters," 54).

89. First Lieutenant Algernon Emory Smith (1842–76) "commanded Company E, of the Seventh Cavalry," at the Battle of the Little Big Horn and was killed with Custer's battalion (Luce, "Diary and Letters," 4). Smith, a native of New York, fought in the Civil War in the 177th New York Infantry with General Terry, was attached to the Seventh Cavalry after the war in 1867, and fought in Custer's Washita campaign and thereafter. He is buried in Fort Leavenworth National Cemetery; his wife, Nettie, died in 1903. See Nichols, *Men with Custer*, 307–8.

90. Second Lieutenant William Van Wyck Reily (1853–76) was born in Washington, D.C. He originally was in the Tenth Cavalry as of October 1875 but was transferred to the Seventh in January 1876. Second Lieutenant Henry Moore Harrington (1849–76) was a native of New York. After graduating from the U.S. Military Academy, he served in the Seventh Cavalry until his death. While Luce noted that Harrington's body "was never found," recent new advanced technical/digital processes and forensic evidence performed on a skull found on the battlefield have now positively identified his remains (Luce, "Diary and Letters," 55). For biographical information for Van Wyck Reily and Harrington, respectively, see Cross, *Custer's Lost Officer*; and Nichols, *Men with Custer*, 275, 140,

91. This was the Powder River Fight of March 17, the only major engagement of the 1876 Big Horn expedition.

92. Pericarditis is inflammation of the pericardium, the membrane covering the heart. Causes include viral, bacterial, and syphilitic infections, as well as tuberculosis, although noninfectious causes are usually associated with other conditions, such as gout, rheumatoid arthritis, scleroderma, mononucleosis, diseases of the kidney, conditions of the blood, myocardial infarctions (heart attacks), and even direct cardiac trauma. Symptoms include pain over the region of the heart, an increased pulse and sometimes difficulty breathing, and a cough; early descriptions included patients often having to sit up in bed to catch their breath and an inability to lie on the left side. Remedies in the late nineteenth century were aimed at treating the symptoms. Mercury often was used to check the inflammation, with opium and laudanum or morphine used for pain. Also, mustard plasters or warm flaxseed poultices were often kept over the heart, and the patient was kept quiet in bed; see *Domestic Medicine Practice*, 389–91. Today, direct causes are treated with appropriate medications: antitubercular agents, anti-inflammatory medications, and antibiotics for infectious causes. If patients are not monitored carefully, fluid accumulation in the pericardium (pericardial effusion) can occur, which can lead to a cardiac tamponade. This places increased pressure on the heart, making it difficult for the heart to beat. The resulting obstruction of heart function requires periocardiocentesis, the immediate evacuation/draining of the fluid pressure on the heart. *Harrison's Principles of Internal Medicine*, 1149–53.

93. Alexander Turnery Stewart (1803–76) was a department store magnate in New York City. Born in Ireland, he eventually became one of the richest men in America

after coming to the United States and establishing his business. In addition to his successful dry goods department store, his firm ran a large mail-order business and was well-known to frontier army members and those in other isolated locations. He died on April 10, 1876. For a detailed biography, see Elias, *Alexander T. Stewart*.

94. Second Lieutenant Herbert Cushman attended the Cadet Naval Academy from 1862 to 1864. Beginning in 1868, he served in the Twentieth Infantry, eventually being promoted to first lieutenant in October 1876. He retired from the army in 1891. While stationed at Fort Totten, he lived with an Indian woman named Julia Otacinpiwin ("Much Desired Woman") from 1876 to 1878, for which he received a general court-martial. DeWolf's comments suggest that Brenner, the civilian post trader and former soldier, was involved in reporting Cushman to his superiors, along with the Devil's Lake Indian agent Paul Beckwith. A letter was eventually received from Secretary of War Alphonso Taft dated March 18, 1876, ordering Cushman to be court-martialed. Although somewhat of a miscreant himself, apparently Brenner disliked Cushman. Also of note here is DeWolf's advice to Fannie to avoid becoming involved in gossip and disputes among the various garrison social factions, since the DeWolfs were considered a part of upper-tier society at the fort. DeWolf's comments also suggest that Lieutenant Cushman had called upon him and his wife in the past. Regarding Cushman, see Brown, *Fort Seward*, 58–59; Heitman, *Historical Register* (1903), 348; and Twentieth Infantry Returns, Fort Totten, October 1875.

95. Billroth's *General Surgical Pathology* and Huxley's *Lessons in Elementary Physiology* were listed as recommended texts for students at the Harvard Medical School in its 1873–74 catalog. Author's personal communication with Mr. Jack Eckert, public services librarian, Center for History of Medicine, Francis A. Countway Library of Medicine, Harvard Medical School, Oct. 18, 2013.

96. James McLaughlin, appointed Indian agent at Devil's Lake Agency in June 1876.

Chapter 2.
Fort Abraham Lincoln, D.T.

1. Bismarck was founded in 1872 by settlers and Northern Pacific Railroad personnel at what was then called the Missouri Crossing, where the Lewis and Clark expedition had crossed. The Mandan Indians had occupied the area from the late 1500s to the 1780s. Bismarck began to grow when the Northern Pacific Railroad reached there a year later, with the U.S. Army building Camp Hancock and the nearby associated posts of Forts McKeen and Abraham Lincoln (see n. 21, this chapter), all constructed to protect railroad workers and the settlers flooding into the region. The city started out as a ramshackle "village of 150 cottonwood shacks and tents"; it became the capital of North Dakota in 1889. As evidenced by his April 16 letter, DeWolf did not think much of its appearance in 1876 either. For a description of its early history, see Barnard, *I Go with Custer*, 77–82.

2. Captain Henry Smith Howe (1831–1910), Seventeenth Infantry, was the commander of Camp Hancock. Born in Massachusetts, Howe served in the Minnesota

Cavalry during the Civil War, initially as a private, then as a sergeant, before mustering out as a first lieutenant in 1866. Later that year, he was appointed as a second lieutenant in the Seventeenth Infantry, becoming a captain in 1875; he served with that unit until his retirement in 1892. He and his wife, Harriet M. Howe (1836–1910), are buried in Arlington National Cemetery. Camp Hancock Post Returns, Oct. 1875–Apr. 1876, NARA; Heitman, *Historical Register* (1903), 547 (service record); www.findagrave.com (accessed Aug. 17, 2013).

3. Dr. Henry Renaldo Porter (1848–1903), a native of New York, was a contract surgeon for the U.S. Army and the lone doctor out of the three with the Seventh Cavalry to survive the Battle of the Little Big Horn. He initially attended the University of Michigan Medical School but graduated from Georgetown University Medical School in 1872. After completing a three-month internship at the Columbia Hospital for Women and Lying-In Asylum in Washington, D.C., he signed on as a contract surgeon for the U.S. Army and served in the Arizona Territory campaigns, moving on to Camp Hancock in Bismarck in 1873 after signing another contract with the army. He also established a private practice in Bismarck, which he resumed when he left the army after the 1876 Sioux campaign. Assigned with DeWolf to Major Marcus Reno's right wing, he set up the field hospital at the Reno/Benteen defensive hill position, gallantly treating the wounded during the fight at the Little Big Horn. Excellent detailed synopses are found in Walker's *Dr. Henry R. Porter* (pp. 57–59), the first published full-length biography on Porter, and also in Stevenson's *Deliverance from the Little Bighorn* (pp. 57–96), which details his actions and service at the Little Big Horn. DeWolf's letters clearly reveal that Porter and he had become good friends in the short time of their service together with Custer; see chapter 3 for further details.

4. Colonel Clement A. Lounsberry (1843–1926) "was a lieutenant colonel in the Twentieth Michigan Infantry during the Civil War." Originally from Indiana, Lounsberry became a journalist after the war and had headed a newspaper in Minnesota before moving to Bismarck in May 1873 and establishing the *Bismarck Tribune*. As a prominent citizen of the rapidly growing town, he "was postmaster at Bismarck, 1876–1885." First serving as a private in the First Michigan Volunteers (having worked in Michigan as a farm laborer), he was captured and imprisoned by the Confederates. However, after being released, and despite being wounded twice in later campaigns, he was eventually promoted to lieutenant colonel and later colonel before the end of the war. He commanded the famed First Michigan Sharpshooters and the Second Michigan Infantry at the surrender of Petersburg, Virginia, in April 1865. Lounsberry published the first full newspaper account of the Little Big Horn disaster on July 6, 1876, after the news reached Bismarck in the late hours of the evening before. Historian Sandy Barnard has examined the historical record and relates convincing evidence that refutes Lounsberry's long-standing claim to be the intended newspaper correspondent for the Little Big Horn campaign, as well as his alleged excuse of a family illness as the reason for Kellogg's taking his place for that assignment. Luce, "Diary and Letters," 4 (both quotations). For a detailed biographical sketch,

see Hyde, "Clement A. Lounsberry," *History of the Great Northwest*, 372–74. See also Barnard, *I Go with Custer*, 78, 80 (Lounsberry's arrival in Bismarck), 99–106, 151–60 (correspondent controversy and aftermath).

5. George Brown Dandy (1830–1911). As he often did, DeWolf used one of Dandy's brevet ranks from the Civil War. Dandy was also commonly referred to by his middle name. At the time he met DeWolf, Dandy was actually a major in the army and served as the quartermaster at Fort Abraham Lincoln. At the outbreak of the Civil War, he was a captain and served as an assistant quartermaster general, then became colonel of the 100th New York Volunteer Infantry in August 1862. Throughout the Civil War, he was cited for "distinguished and gallant conduct" in several engagements. Dandy later served in the Quartermaster Department of the U.S. Army, at Fort Phil Kearney at the Big Horn Mountains from 1866 to 1868, Fort Abercrombie from 1871 to 1873, and Fort Abraham Lincoln from 1873 to 1875. In 1873, he married Anne Eliza Slaughter of East Grand Forks, Minnesota. Dandy was a cousin to J. W. Raymond, the business partner of George Fairchild in Bismarck, and Fairchild's sister-in-law, Charlotte Viets, was married to Dr. Henry Porter. Later in his career, Dandy oversaw the Quartermaster's Subsistence Department at Yuma, Arizona, before retiring from the U.S. Army in 1894. Dandy lived his last years in Omaha, Nebraska, before moving to New York City, where he died on January 15, 1911. He is buried in Arlington National Cemetery. Heitman, *Historical Register* (1903), 352; "George Brown Dandy: Brigadier General, United States Army," Arlington National Cemetery website, www.arlingtoncemetery.net/gbdandy.htm (accessed Feb. 23, 2013, and July 25, 2016); Fort Abercrombie, Post Returns, 1871–1873, and Fort Abraham Lincoln, Post Returns, 1873–1875, microfilm M617, AGO, NARA. For information about the Raymond and Fairchild connections, see Walker, *Dr. Henry R. Porter*, 36.

6. The individual to whom DeWolf is referring has not been ascertained. One possibility is Richard Edward Thompson, a second lieutenant in the Sixth Infantry (d. 1933, buried in the San Francisco National Cemetery), since he was to serve on General Terry's staff in the Dakota Column as the acting commissary of subsistence (ACS) for the expedition. However, neither Terry nor he had arrived at Fort Lincoln by this time, and the Dakota Column staff was not yet assembled for the expedition; 6th Infantry, Regimental Returns, 1875–1876, microfilm M665, NARA. The more likely candidates with these last names would have been George A. Wilson of Company K, Morris G. Thompson of Company C, or Peter Thompson of Company E, who were all privates in the Seventh Cavalry. This seems likely since DeWolf specifically indicated in his diary entry that "the latter returned from the 7th" in reference to the last two men. In addition, as DeWolf did not identify these last two names as officers by listing their rank, as he did with the immediately preceding three named men, this further suggests that Wilson and Thompson were privates. For brief biographical sketches of Wilson and the two Thompsons, see Nichols, *Men with Custer*, 361 and 329, respectively. While there are privates with these last names

from the companies of the Seventh Infantry for the 1876 expedition (A, B, E, H, I, and K), those companies were under Colonel Gibbon in the Montana Column and not at Fort Lincoln at this time. The other officers named Wilson, such as Second Lieutenant James L. Wilson of the Fourth Artillery and Captain Robert P. Wilson of the Fifth Cavalry, to which DeWolf might have been referring were not at Fort Abraham Lincoln or Camp Hancock at this time; see Hedren, *Great Sioux War*, 88, 106. The other less likely candidate is Captain Lewis Thompson of Company L of the Second Cavalry (d. July 19, 1876, buried at New Hope, Pennsylvania), who was with Colonel John Gibbon's Montana Column for the expedition and committed suicide a few days after assisting in the burial of the Seventh Cavalry dead on the Little Big Horn battlefield. See Overfield, *Little Big Horn*, 100–189.

7. Camp Hancock (1872–94) was established at Bismarck in 1872 by the U.S. Army to protect the "supplies, equipment and engineering crews of the Northern Pacific Railroad." Renamed a year later for George Winfield Hancock, who was the commander of the Department of Dakota at the time, it originally consisted of several log and wooden buildings, including barracks, officers' quarters, a storehouse, a tented hospital, surgeon's quarters, and a guardhouse. The Seventeenth Infantry garrisoned the post until 1877, when it became a quartermaster's depot and signal office (continuing to serve those functions until 1894). As he indicates here, DeWolf stayed only for a day at Camp Hancock before transferring across the river to Fort Abraham Lincoln. The post surgeon's quarters is the only remaining building today, and it serves as a museum for the Camp Hancock State Historic Site. See Barnes, *Forts of the Northern Plains*, 109; see also State Historical Society of North Dakota, "Camp Hancock State Historic Site," http://history.nd.gov/historicsites/hancock/ (quotation) and Bismarck Historical Society, "Camp Hancock," http://www.bismarckhistory.org/?id=33 (both accessed Feb. 22, 2013).

8. Second Lieutenant Charles S. J. Chubb of Company D of the Seventeenth Infantry was second in command to Captain Henry S. Stowe at Camp Hancock. Chubb served as the post adjutant and post treasurer of the Quartermaster Department; he was on recruiting service in September 1875 at Fort Rice, as well as the Standing Rock and Cheyenne Agencies. Camp Hancock Post Returns, Feb. 1876, and Seventeenth Infantry Regimental Returns, Oct. 7, 1875, NARA. For Chubb's commission record, see Heitman, *Historical Register* (1903), 301.

9. Corporal William Finnegan of Company B of the Sixth Infantry was stationed with the Sixth Infantry detachments at Fort Abraham Lincoln in November 1875; he was appointed acting hospital steward at Camp Hancock, serving in that capacity from January to April 1876 before being ordered to return across the river to rejoin his company. Camp Hancock Post Returns, Jan.–Apr. 1876, NARA.

10. Major William Smith was the paymaster on duty in the Department of Dakota. He was assigned to pay troops on the Missouri River posts from his base at Sioux City, Iowa, which included Forts Rice and Abraham Lincoln, Camp Hancock, and Forts Stevenson and Buford. Originally from Vermont, he served in the volunteer

forces from Minnesota during the Civil War. He was appointed assistant paymaster of the volunteers in May 1861, breveted a lieutenant colonel in March 1865 for "faithful and meritorious" service during the war, and honorably mustered out of the service in 1866. The following year, Smith joined the regular army and was promoted to the permanent rank of major and appointed as paymaster. Promoted to brigadier general on March 10, 1890, he became the paymaster general and served in that position until his retirement from the army on March 26, 1895. Heitman, *Historical Register* (1903), 904; *Army and Navy Journal*, July 12, 1873, 760.

11. First Lieutenant James M. Burns, Company A, Seventeenth Infantry, Fort Abercrombie, 1875. Burns was later appointed post commissary at Fort Abraham Lincoln in April 1876. A native of Ohio, he served as a private and sergeant in the First West Virginia Volunteers. At the Battle of Newmarket, "under a heavy fire of musketry from the enemy, he voluntarily assisted a wounded comrade . . . thereby saving him from capture," a feat for which he was later awarded the Medal of Honor. In 1867, he began his service in the Seventeenth Infantry during the Indian wars as a second lieutenant, was promoted to first lieutenant in 1874, rose to the rank of captain in 1889, and transferred to the Seventh Infantry in 1899. For Burns's service record, see Heitman, *Historical Register* (1903), 265 (quotation); see also Fort Abercrombie Post Returns, June 1875, and Fort Abraham Lincoln Post Returns, Apr. 1876, NARA.

12. Fort Abercrombie (1858–77) was constructed on the Red River in northeastern North Dakota to protect the "Gateway to the Dakotas" for settlers and merchants proceeding west and also north into Fort Garry at present-day Winnipeg, Manitoba. It was attacked during the Minnesota Sioux uprising of 1862 and later played an important part in the protection of railroad laborers and sending troops for service during the 1870s Indian wars campaigns. Two reconstructed blockhouses, a partial reconstructed stockade, the restored original guardhouse, several "ghost framed" buildings, and a museum/visitor's center constitute the present Fort Abercrombie State Historic Site. For a detailed synopsis of its history, see Barnes, *Forts of the Northern Plains*, 101–4. Frazier, *Forts of the West*, 109.

13. Dr. Elbert Judson Clark (1847–1921), acting assistant surgeon. As a contract surgeon in the army, he was at the Cheyenne River Indian Agency prior to being sent to Fort Abraham Lincoln for the 1876 campaign. He was assigned to the supply depot, which spared him from the Little Big Horn disaster. He eventually returned to private practice in Winnebago, Illinois, from the 1880s through 1900. He and his wife later moved to Cleveland, Ohio, where he died in 1921. See U.S. School Catalogs, 1765–1935 (Northwestern University, 1871); U.S. Federal Census 1860, 1880, 1890, 1900, and 1910 for Rockford/Winnebago, Illinois; *Directory of Deceased American Physicians, 1804–1929*; and *Ohio Deaths, 1908–1932, 1930–2007*, all from www.ancestry.com. See also S.F.O. No. 5, Brig. Gen. Terry, May 14, 1876, AGO, DeWolf Collection, WSL/LIBI; and Gray, *Centennial Campaign*, 271.

14. Kimball was Custer's first choice to head the Medical Department for the Dakota Column for the 1876 campaign, as Custer knew the surgeon from his service

on the 1873 Yellowstone expedition and they subsequently became friends. However, in March 1876 Dr. Kimball was designated by Army Headquarters of the Dakota Department for assignment as the medical director at Fort Brady, in Sault Ste. Marie, Michigan. Kimball, *Soldier-Doctor of Our Army*, 65–66, 82–84.

15. The "boat" that DeWolf mentions here was either the *Denver* or the *Union*, which were the two steamboats that ferried people and supplies across the Missouri River between Bismarck, the railroad warehouse, and the area's two military posts (Camp Hancock and Fort Abraham Lincoln). The *Far West* was a third steamboat, used only for long-distance trips because of its larger size and better condition. The two smaller boats were constantly in need of repair, as DeWolf mentions in his letter. The ferry landing at Fort Abraham Lincoln was not extensive either. Chorne, *Following the Custer Trail*, 5; Chambers, *Fort Abraham Lincoln*, 59.

16. Captain Edward Worthington Smith (1832–83) of the Eighteenth Infantry was a native of Vermont and a Civil War veteran twice decorated for "gallant and meritorious service in the assault on Fort Wagner, South Carolina and . . . at Petersburg, Virginia," rising to the ranks of brevet lieutenant colonel and then brevet brigadier general of the Illinois Volunteers in 1865. Smith remained in the regular army after the war and was assigned to the Eighteenth Infantry in 1870. He served as an acting assistant adjutant general on General Terry's staff of the Dakota Column for the Little Big Horn campaign, was breveted a lieutenant colonel in the Fifteenth Infantry during the war, and continued to serve on the western frontier until his death at Fort Lewis on May 21, 1883. He is buried at Greenwood Cemetery in his hometown of St. Albans, Vermont. For Smith's service record, see Heitman, *Historical Register* (1903), 896 (including quotation); see also www.findagrave.com (accessed Feb. 23, 2013); and Hedren, *Great Sioux War*, 98.

17. First Lieutenant James Ezekiel Porter (1847–76) was a native of Maine and graduated from the U.S. Military Academy in 1869. He served with the Seventh Cavalry until his death at the Little Big Horn with Company I, presumed killed with Custer but with "his remains never positively identified," leaving behind his wife and two young sons. Luce, "Diary and Letters," 4 (quotation). For a more detailed biographical sketch, see Nichols, *Men with Custer*, 264–65.

18. Dr. Robert George Redd (1842–1908) was born in Knox County, Kentucky, and was a graduate of both the Ohio College of Medicine in Cincinnati in 1869 and Bellevue Medical College in New York in 1871. After being in private practice for two years, he joined the U.S. Army as a contract physician, serving as an acting assistant surgeon in Kentucky and the Carolinas, at Fort Lincoln, and eventually at Fort Keogh, Miles City, Montana, in 1877 with the Fifth Infantry. He resigned from the army in 1881, became the mayor of Miles City in 1889, and then served as a Montana state senator from 1889 to 1892, all while maintaining a private medical practice. He was also a member of the Freemasons. Because of poor health, Redd returned to his native Kentucky for the last twelve years of his life and resided with his brother in the town of Crab Orchard. He died there in 1908 and is buried in the

Crab Orchard Cemetery. Fort Abraham Lincoln Post Returns, Dec. 1875–May 1876, NARA; biographical information from obituary notice, *Mt. Vernon* (Ky.) *Signal*, Feb. 26, 1909, historic newspaper archives, Kentucky Virtual (Digital) Library, University of Kentucky, http://kdl.kyvl.org (accessed Feb. 28, 2013, and July 26, 2016).

19. Dr. Johnson Van Dyke Middleton (1834–1907) was born in Washington, D.C. He was an army surgeon, serving as an assistant surgeon during the Civil War, and was breveted a major in 1865 for "faithful and meritorious service." He served as the post surgeon at Fort Abraham Lincoln during 1876, being promoted to major in June that year. Later in his military career, he was promoted to colonel and served as the chief surgeon of the Department of California after his service in the Philippines campaign in 1898, retiring from the army that year. He died in 1907 and is buried in Oak Hill Cemetery, Washington, D.C. Fort Abraham Lincoln Post Returns, Jan.–May 1876, NARA. See www.findagrave.com; see also Heitman, *Historical Register* (1903), 708 (quotation and service record).

20. The dispensary was the building used for the medical clinic at Fort Abraham Lincoln, as there was no hospital in the cavalry post, the actual hospital being in the infantry post section up on the hill. The building, a small structure measuring 17 feet by 40 feet, has not been reconstructed at Fort Abraham Lincoln to date. U.S. Army blueprint drawings of it are shown in Chambers, *Fort Abraham Lincoln*, 96–98. The hospital was much larger than the dispensary, its two stories measuring 44 feet by 152 feet with a rear wing of 16 feet by 40 feet. Similar to other military post hospital buildings of the period, it followed a standard design for the main portion. Like the dispensary, this building has not been reconstructed; however, a photograph and blueprints of the large structure are shown in Chambers, *Fort Abraham Lincoln*, 61–62.

21. Established on the hill above the Missouri River in 1872, Fort McKeen was originally named for Colonel Henry B. McKeen, a Civil War officer killed in the Battle of Cold Harbor; it was established to protect the laborers constructing the Northern Pacific Railroad. "When the cavalry quarters were built between the hill and the river, the name of the post was officially changed to Fort Abraham Lincoln. However, many continued to refer to the infantry quarters at Fort McKeen" (Luce, "Diary and Letters," 4). The infantry post portion consisted of twenty-five structures, including three blockhouses and two long palisades. Companies of the Sixth and Seventeenth Infantry Regiments were stationed there during the 1870s. One of the blockhouses has been reconstructed, and archaeological investigations have been done in past years as well. It is part of the current Fort Abraham Lincoln State Historic Site. See Chambers, *Fort Abraham Lincoln*, 61–62; and Barnes, *Forts of the Northern Plains*, 105–9.

22. In late April 1876, the medical staff at Fort Abraham Lincoln consisted of the post surgeon, Dr. Middleton of the regular U.S. Army, and four civilian contract surgeons: the acting assistant surgeons Elbert J. Clark, James Madison DeWolf, Isaiah H. Ashton, and Robert G. Redd. The latter group increased to five with the addition of Henry R. Porter in early May. Fort Abraham Lincoln Post Returns, Apr. 1875, NARA.

23. Second Lieutenant William H. Low Jr. (1848–86) of Company C of the Twentieth Infantry commanded the Gatling gun battery. Originally from Whitehall, New York, he graduated from the U.S. Military Academy in July 1868. He served his career in the Twentieth Infantry, rising to the rank of first lieutenant in 1877; he died on July 24, 1886, and is buried in Custer National Cemetery, Section C, Big Horn County, Montana. Heitman, *Historical Register* (1903), 644.

24. Second Lieutenant Frank Xavier Kinzie (1852–1909) of Company F of the Twentieth Infantry was second in command of the Gatling gun battery with Lieutenant Low. A native of Illinois, he was appointed a second lieutenant in the Twentieth Infantry on October 1874; he was at Fort Pembina, Dakota Territory, in 1876 before going to Fort Abraham Lincoln and the eventual 1876 campaign. He married Julia F. Mallory on October 1876 in Cook County, Illinois, and later served at Fort Clark in Texas. Kinzie resigned from the army on January 1, 1879, and worked for the firm of Mallory and Brother. He is buried in Graceland Cemetery, Chicago. Heitman, *Historical Register* (1903), 602; *Album of Genealogy*, 355–58; Fort Pembina, Post Returns, 1876, and Fort Clark, Post Returns, 1878, NARA; www.findagrave.com listing for Graceland Cemetery, Cook Co., Ill. (accessed Nov. 14, 2013).

25. DeWolf misidentifies the individual here; he was actually referring to Captain Louis A. Sanger of the Seventeenth Infantry, who commanded Company G at Fort Abraham Lincoln at the infantry post up on the hill (i.e., the former Fort McKeen). He was stationed there along with his fellow officer of the same company, First Lieutenant Josiah Chance, who had also served on Custer's 1874 Black Hills expedition; see Fort Abraham Lincoln Post Returns, Feb. 1876, NARA; see also Seventeenth Infantry Regimental Returns, Apr. 1876, NARA. Sanger was born in Maine and served in the Seventeenth Infantry's Company C, First Battalion during the Civil War, initially enlisting as a private in 1861 and rising to the rank of captain by July 1865. He was breveted a major that year "for gallantry and meritorious service in the Battle of Gettysburg." He died on December 23, 1884. Heitman, *Historical Register* (1903), 859 (quotation and service record).

26. First Lieutenant Josiah Chance (1839–85), Company G, Seventeenth Infantry. Chance was born in Ohio and served in the Thirteenth Ohio Infantry's Company H as a private and in the band during the Civil War from 1861 to 1862, then as a bugler in the First Ohio Cavalry the following two years, before becoming a captain in Company C of the 127th U.S. Infantry in 1864. He was mustered out the following year after the end of the war. In 1867, he was appointed a second lieutenant in the Seventeenth Infantry, being promoted to first lieutenant in 1873. He was serving at Fort Abraham Lincoln during the 1876 campaign. He died on December 12, 1885, and is buried in Oakwood Cemetery, Fremont, Ohio. Fort Abraham Lincoln Post Returns, Feb. 1876, NARA; Heitman, *Historical Register* (1903), 294; see also www.findagrave.com (accessed Nov. 14, 2013).

27. Noted as "Custer's favorite and most trusted scout" by Edward Luce ("Diary and Letters," 60), Bloody Knife initially worked for the American Fur Company.

After enlisting as a scout in the U.S. Army in 1868, he later met Custer, and they developed a close friendship during the first Yellowstone expedition, in 1873. Numerous sources contain detailed information regarding his life and involvement in the Little Big Horn, including Gray, "Arikara Scouts with Custer," 443–78; Innis, *Bloody Knife*; and Libby, *Arikara Narrative*. For accounts of Bloody Knife made after his death, see Larson, *Gall*, 257n21.

28. DeWolf is referring to Captain Thomas Weir, who was in command of Company D of the Seventh Cavalry, using Weir's brevet rank of lieutenant colonel; see Heitman, *Historical Register* (1903), 1015. Weir was originally from Ohio but grew up in Albion, Michigan, and graduated from the University of Michigan in 1861. He became a career army officer and was a decorated Civil War veteran, serving with the Third Michigan Cavalry. "Weir came up to the Little Big Horn with Benteen the afternoon of June 25 and, being annoyed with the inactivity of Reno and Benteen, was the first to start with his Company D in the direction of the Custer engagement" (Luce, "Diary and Letters," 60). For years, historians have extensively debated and reexamined the controversy over his dispute with Benteen and Reno and his attempt to go to Custer's aid near the end of the battle. Some claim that he had planned to eventually tell Mrs. Custer the details of this episode, but he died later that year, allegedly because of either "alcohol" or "fatigue and exposure" brought on by the Sioux campaign. For a brief synopsis of this controversy, see Sarf, *Little Bighorn Campaign*, 222–24. See also Hammer, "Interview with Winfield S. Edgerly," in *Custer in '76*, 55–57; and Graham, *Custer Myth*, 215–17 (1995 reprint), which contains a letter written by Edgerly. For a more detailed biographical sketch of Weir, see Nichols, *Men with Custer*, 350–51.

29. Pleurisy is an inflammation of the pleura membrane, which covers the lungs and lines the internal surface of the chest. Symptoms include fever, chills, chest pain, and difficulty breathing, although vomiting and headache also can occur. In the 1870s, causes were attributed to "obstructed perspiration, through exposure to cold, . . . sleeping out doors, or on the damp ground; wet clothes, exposure to the cold air when in a state of perspiration . . . and even by drinking strong liquors, by the stopping of the usual evacuations, etc., etc." Treatments included the application of heat, vapor baths, bathing the feet in warm water, emetics "given immediately, two table-spoons of the sudorific tincture, or half a tea-spoon of the sudorific powder," warm herb tea, and even "salt, cayenne, and brandy, well simmered, and made strong, [which were said to] form an excellent application for pleuritic pains." Today, pleurisy is known to usually occur as a complication of pneumonia, tuberculosis, some arthritic conditions, and other infectious diseases, and it is treated according to the specific cause, including the use of antibiotics and analgesics. Chase, *Dr. Chase's Recipes*, 248–49 (both quotations); *Harrison's Principles of Internal Medicine*, 1265.

30. Private David O'Keefe, Company E, Seventh Cavalry. O'Keefe was listed as sick in the hospital at Fort Totten in the April 1876 returns of that post; he had been sentenced there to two years of confinement with forfeiture of pay for desertion, by

order from Headquarters of the Department of Dakota at St. Paul, Minnesota, as of January 12, 1876. DeWolf had obviously attended him in the hospital with Dr. Ferguson earlier in the year, before DeWolf's departure with the Seventh Cavalry to Fort Seward and eventually Fort Abraham Lincoln. However, there is no other mention of O'Keefe in DeWolf's notebook or the Fort Totten returns during the early spring months. Fort Totten Post Returns, Apr. 1875, NARA. Metzdorf is unidentified at this time, with no listing in the post returns at Totten or for the Seventeenth Infantry and Seventh Cavalry Companies E and L stationed there.

31. Captain William Fletcher (born in New York) served in two Ohio infantry companies from June 1846 to July 1848, then in the First Artillery from 1848 to 1858. From 1859 to 1861, he served in the Eighth Infantry and rose to the rank of sergeant; during the Civil War he served in the Eleventh Infantry, and he was appointed a first lieutenant in 1862 and was breveted a captain for "gallantry and meritorious service in the 2nd Battle of Bull Run, Virginia." He transferred to the Twentieth Infantry in 1866, was promoted to captain later that year, and retired from the army in 1887. Heitman, *Historical Register* (1903), 425 (quotation and service record). See also Fort Totten Post Returns, Oct. 1875, NARA, 196.

32. Captain Myles Moylan (1838–1909) was from Massachusetts, though his birthplace is listed as Galway, Ireland. Captain of Company A of the Seventh Cavalry, he was involved in the Reno valley and hilltop fights at the Little Big Horn. Luce was slightly mistaken regarding the date of Moylan's Medal of Honor, which he listed as awarded in 1877 (Luce, "Diary and Letters," 61); Moylan actually was awarded the Medal of Honor in 1894 for the September 30, 1877, action at the Battle of Bear Paw Mountain against the Nez Perce Indians in Montana. He died in San Diego, California, and is buried in Greenwood Memorial Park Cemetery. For a more extensive biographical sketch, see Nichols, *Men with Custer*, 236–37.

33. This reference and another in his letter of May 8 (in addition to Porter's July 28, 1876, letter to Fannie DeWolf) confirm that DeWolf had a revolver during the campaign as well as during the Little Big Horn battle. Although Porter had firearms during the expedition, had been in the Arizona campaign with Crook in 1872–73, and was an experienced hunter and marksman, for unknown reasons, he chose not to arm himself for the battle. Nichols, *Reno Court of Inquiry*, 189 (Porter's testimony).

34. The post office building at Fort Abraham Lincoln, which DeWolf seemed to have visited on a daily basis, also contained the telegraph office and served as a stage stop. It was actually located at the infantry post portion of the fort. Chambers, *Fort Abraham Lincoln*, 68.

35. Isaiah Heylin Ashton (1849–89), acting assistant surgeon. Ashton was born in Philadelphia, Pennsylvania, to John and Mary Heylin Ashton. Ashton served as a contract physician for the U.S. Army in 1875–76. Although he was with the Dakota Column on the expedition to the Little Big Horn, he was not involved in the battle, having been assigned to the supply depot several days earlier. He married Kate Thompson of St. Paul in 1877. After traveling the country and going abroad, in 1882 he and

his wife moved to Irvington in Westchester County, New York, where he established a private practice. Ashton suffered from ill health for much of his life, which required wintering in the South (no specific diagnosis is mentioned, although it may have been rheumatoid arthritis). He was described as an "ambitious and enthusiastic physician" who cared deeply about his patients. Ashton died on February 18, 1889, from peritonitis, which had developed from internal injuries he sustained after being thrown from his horse wagon eight days earlier. He is buried in Sleepy Hollow Cemetery, Sleepy Hollow, New York. New York State Medical Association, *Transactions*, 895–96; www.findagrave.com (accessed Dec. 11, 2014).

36. This was the famed Seventh Cavalry band, which Custer loved to have accompany him in the field when possible. The band had its own quarters at Fort Abraham Lincoln, a barracks building measuring 23 feet by 50 feet. Headed by Chief Musician Felix V. Vinatieri, the band consisted of sixteen members, which was in accordance with the army regulations for regimental bands. In addition to its official post duties of playing at military inspections and drills, the band also played for the enjoyment of the officers and their wives in the evenings and even took part in some of Bismarck's public social and theatrical events. As Luce ("Diary and Letters," 5) noted, "The 7th Cavalry Band accompanied the march (i.e., the Terry/Custer Dakota column) as far as the base of supply established near the mouth of the Powder River on the Yellowstone River. All wagons were also left at the base and only pack transportation taken beyond that point." See Reedstrom, *Custer's 7th Cavalry*, 84; Fougera, *With Custer's Cavalry*, 81–82; and Gleason, "Mounted Band." For a roster of the band, see Overfield, *Little Big Horn*, 153; see Nichols, *Men with Custer*, 374, for biographical sketches of the respective band members. For a blueprint of the band quarters, see Chambers, *Fort Abraham Lincoln*, 82–83. See also War Office, *Revised U.S. Army Regulations*, Art. XII/no. 81–83, p. 19, regarding band stipulations.

37. Major Marcus A. Reno (1834–89) was a native of Illinois who commanded the Seventh in Custer's absence. During the Civil War, "he served as a colonel and was breveted a brigadier general" (Luce, "Diary and Letters," 62). His controversial actions in the Little Big Horn have been debated for years, although no charges were brought by the court of inquiry in 1879. His dismissal from the army in 1880 involved an alleged "peeping Tom" incident concerning the daughter of the Seventh Cavalry's commander, Colonel Samuel D. Sturgis, at Fort Meade, South Dakota. For an excellent full-length biography, see Nichols, *In Custer's Shadow*.

38. Although DeWolf does not indicate the nature of the letter or fully identify this person, it is likely to be Dr. William E. Bryant, who served as an acting assistant surgeon at Camp Lyon in Idaho Territory from December 1866 to August 1867. DeWolf served as the hospital steward at Camp Lyon during that time and so would have known Bryant; see Camp Lyon Post Returns, Dec. 1866–Aug. 1867, NARA (see introduction, n. 50). The other possible, although less likely, candidate could be Dr. Charles Borromer Byrne, as DeWolf was not always accurate in his memory of spelling names. Byrne would have known DeWolf from both Camp Lyon and

Camp Warner, where they served during the same time periods: Byrne served as an assistant surgeon at Camp Lyon from October 1868 to at least March 1869, while DeWolf was at that post, and later served as acting surgeon at Camp Warner from April 1871 to June 1873, when Hospital Steward DeWolf and his wife were married there. Byrne's letter of February 22, 1872, attested to DeWolf's "thorough efficiency and capacity as a hospital steward" (Byrne to Surgeon General, Washington, D.C., Feb. 22, 1872, SGO, DeWolf Collection, WSL/LIBI; also quoted in Noyes, "Frontier Army Doctor," 21). As a first lieutenant in the army, Byrne initially was appointed in charge of the hospital at Warner per S.O. No. 98 and also served as post treasurer per Post Order No. 41 in April 1871; he was promoted to captain by November 1871 and served until being "relieved of duty" July 1873 by S.O. No. 113, being transferred from "Regular duty to casualty Duty." Camp Warner Post Returns, Apr. 1871–July 1873, NARA. Despite these ties to Byrne, the spelling that DeWolf uses in his letter suggests that this was most likely a reference to Bryant.

39. Though not allowed to wear a uniform, contract surgeons were permitted to purchase items from the military stores, as evidenced by DeWolf buying blue material from the Fort Lincoln Quartermaster Department.

40. Dr. William J. Sloan, medical director of the Department of Dakota, was stationed at St. Paul, Minnesota. Born in Pennsylvania, Sloan served as an assistant surgeon in 1837; he was promoted to major in 1855 and served in the Department of New Mexico, including at Fort Union, from 1856 to 1860. As the medical director, he assigned surgeons, assistant surgeons, and contract surgeons to their various army posts during the Indian wars period. He rose to the regular rank of colonel as a surgeon by 1877 and was breveted a brigadier general in 1866 "for meritorious and distinguished service at several posts in New York harbor where cholera prevailed during the war." He died on March 17, 1880. For his commission record, see Heitman, *Historical Register* (1903), 891 (quotation and service record); for a brief comment on his role in the 1876 campaigns, see Gillett, *Army Medical Department*, 69–70.

41. This was forty-eight men of the Seventeenth Infantry's Company C, under the command of Captain Malcolm McArthur from Fort Wadsworth, according to my personal communication on March 6, 2013, with historian/researcher Bill Hoskins, director of the Siouxland Heritage Museums in Sioux Falls, South Dakota, who did extensive research on Fort Wadsworth/Sisseton for the State of South Dakota Game, Fish and Parks Department. See also Seventeenth Infantry Returns, Apr. 1876, NARA; and Schuler, *Fort Sisseton*, 50. Fort Wadsworth, renamed Fort Sisseton (1864–89), is located near present-day Lake City, South Dakota, in the northeastern section of the state. Built after the 1862 Minnesota Sioux uprising to protect settlers in the region, the fort was originally named in honor of General James S. Wadsworth, who was killed in the Battle of the Wilderness that same year. The fort was renamed in late 1876, in honor of the local friendly Sisseton Sioux tribe. Fourteen of the original fort's stone buildings remain, forming the core of Fort Sisseton State Park. Barnes, *Forts of the Northern Plains*, 159–61. For a more in-depth history of the fort,

see Johnson, *Chilson's History of Fort Sisseton*; see also Schuler, *Fort Sisseton*. Grice's *History of Weather Observations, Fort Sisseton* provides a detailed history of the fort and the method of weather observations recorded there by U.S. Army surgeons at the hospital.

42. In "going to the [medical] dictionary," as DeWolf suggested his wife do, she would have learned that this unfortunate unnamed trooper was accidentally shot in the nates, which is the correct term for the buttocks (gluteal muscles). The ball passed on to the tailbone (coccyx). See *Stedman's Medical Dictionary*, 923.

43. Throughout his letters, DeWolf describes the extreme changes in weather conditions he encountered in his travels. The heavy rainstorm he comments about here, which lasted until April 25, was somewhat heavier than the average for April during the mid-1870s in the Dakota Territory. Dr. DuBose's report at Fort Seward for 1875 noted that for the previous two years, the average accumulation of rainfall in April was 0.22 inches. In comparison, according to data compiled from 1981 to 2010 by the National Oceanic and Atmospheric Administration (NOAA) National Climatic Data Center, the average monthly precipitation for North Dakota in April was 1.2 inches at Jamestown (the Fort Seward area) and 1.3 inches at Bismarck (Fort Abraham Lincoln area). Additionally, an extensive 2000 study by Cary Mock, examining precipitation climatology from the 1870s to the late 1880s in the Great Plains states, with a primary focus on the Dakota Territory, documented much drier springs and summers in the early to mid-1870s, particularly 1873–75. The chief surgeon at the various posts of that era was required to meticulously record meteorological data of these conditions and temperatures, although those activities began to be taken over (per an act of Congress) by the U.S. Signal Corps in the 1870s, and the Smithsonian Institution was also involved in compiling information in years prior. The methodology and location of weather instrumentation for recording rainfall and average temperatures for the Dakotas at several of the historic army posts during the Indian wars era have been extensively examined and published in recent years by Gary K. Grice for the National Climatic Data Center. See Brown, *Fort Seward*, 41–42 (DuBose's report); Average United States Weather (annual and monthly totals for states and cities), North and South Dakota, available at *Current Results: Weather and Science Facts, NOAA*, www.currentresults.com/Weather/North-Dakota/precipitation-april.php (accessed Aug. 29, 2012, Mar. 2, 2013, and July 17, 2016); Mock, "Rainfall"; Grice, *History of Weather Observations, Fort Randall*; Grice, *History of Weather Observations, Fort Sisseton*; and Grice, *History of Weather Observations, Fort Sully*. For a history of the U.S. Signal Corps and the Smithsonian Institution's involvement in meteorology data collection, see Raines, *Getting the Message Through*, 46–73.

44. This refers to only one company that arrived, Company G of the Twentieth Infantry, from Fort Ripley, Minnesota, directed to be on detached service by S.O. No. 28 from the Department of Dakota. The contingent consisted of three commissioned officers (Captain William S. McCaskey, First Lieutenant John A. Hanley, and First Lieutenant John J. Crittenden) and twenty-two enlisted men, along with

one enlisted man and one musician of the Twentieth Infantry, both of the Omaha Department. This detachment left Fort Ripley on April 20; see Fort Ripley Post Returns, including Commissioned Officers Present and Absent, Apr. 1876, nos. 33 and 43, NARA. Fort Ripley (1849–77) was originally built by the U.S. Army to keep the peace between the Winnebagos (now known as the Ho-Chunks) and the Dakota and Chippewa (Ojibwe) tribes. Today, nothing remains of the fort except ruins of the powder magazine, located on the active training grounds of the Minnesota National Guard at Camp Ripley along with the Minnesota Military Museum. Barnes, *Forts of the Northern Plains*, 23–27. For a more detailed history, see Baker, *Muster Roll*. Boulay's *History of Weather Observations, Fort Ripley* relates the history of the fort and the medical staff's U.S. Army weather observations.

45. Fort Buford (1866–95) in northwestern North Dakota was built to protect travelers to Montana and the West and, later, laborers building the Northern Pacific Railroad. It served as a supply base for the Indian wars campaigns during the 1870s. Today, at Fort Buford State Historic Site, the restored commanding officer's quarters, enlisted men's barracks, powder magazine, and "ghost frame" of the guardhouse can be seen. Barnes, *Forts of the Northern Plains*, 109–13; Frazer, *Forts of the West*, 110. For an extensive history, see Remele, *Fort Buford*.

46. While DeWolf obviously enjoyed playing cards, the doctor indicates several times in his letters that he did not approve of the gambling often involved. Apparently, those couples in the social circles that Fannie and he enjoyed and were part of at Fort Totten were of the same opinion. Although gambling routinely took place at the frontier posts, army regulations at the time did not contain any reference to it in the Articles of War. Not until the 1880s would gambling be explicitly prohibited at the posts. Regarding drunkenness, regulations stipulated that "any commissioned officer found drunk while on his guard, party, or other duty, shall be cashiered," while soldiers "so offending shall suffer such corporeal [*sic*] punishment as shall be inflicted by the sentence of a court-martial." War Office, *Revised U.S. Army Regulations*, Articles of War, Sec. 1, no. 45, p. 492.

47. Suitable public lands at or near each post were set aside for post gardens to grow vegetables for the garrison troops. Although "desiccated compressed mixed vegetables or potatoes" (referring to cakes of crushed beets, onions, and other vegetables) could be substituted for the beans, peas, rice, or fresh potatoes that were included in each soldier's daily personal food ration allowance, fresh vegetables could be purchased by each soldier out of the company fund. The fund consisted of money that was credited to each company in an amount equivalent to the value of provisions each company chose not to withdraw out of its total allotment of monthly rations, such as sugar, bacon, and pork. The funds actually came from the post fund, which was an assessment (tax) imposed on each post sutler "not to exceed 10 cents per month for each officer and soldier in the company" and overseen by the Commissary Department. However, individual soldiers also often contributed to it out of their own pay. Despite post gardens and other initiatives aimed at improved nutrition for the troops,

there were "632 cases of scurvy reported at the various U.S. military posts" between 1868 and 1874. The post gardens at Fort Abraham Lincoln were located behind the granary at the north end of the compound and have not been excavated to date. Ibid., Art. XXIII/no. 198, p. 35 (first quotation) and Art. XLIII/no. 1188, no. 1190, no. 1191, pp. 243–44 (post fund and rations substitutions, respectively); Ashburn, *History*, 130 (second quotation); author's personal communication with Dan Schelske, park manager, Fort Abraham Lincoln Park, May 15, 2013 (regarding post gardens at Fort Abraham Lincoln). See also Barnard, *Ten Years with Custer*, 219.

48. DeWolf shared his personal opinions on various officers and some of the behind-the-scenes relationships and aspects of the army. However, this was the only time he commented about the politics of the expedition. Whether he knew the actual cost to the government regarding its Indian policy in all facets is unknown; most likely, he did not. DeWolf also never indicated his personal thoughts on the moral issues of the government's Indian policy (or lack thereof).

49. A surgeon's field kit included amputating knives and saws, various forceps, lancets, probes, needles and thread, a stethoscope, syringes, tourniquets, and various other instruments, such as trepanning drills (for skull fractures). Examples of these can be seen in Dr. Henry Porter's extensive medical kits, including those issued by the U.S. Army, in the collections of the State Historical Society of North Dakota. Army surgeons and contract surgeons were issued their own set of instruments, although they were forbidden to transfer these for personal use per order of the army's Office of the Surgeon General. Strict inventory records were also kept by medical personnel. War Office, *Regulations for the Medical Department of the Army, 1863*, 30, 31; Agnew, *Medicine in the Old West*, 22, 138, 234–35; Walker, *Dr. Henry R. Porter*, 52–53, 185–88, 196.

50. This was the 1872 folding campaign hat, which was made of blended fur felt and could be folded up on the sides and fastened by hooks in less inclement weather. The latter gave the headgear an unusual yet characteristic bicorn look, as can be seen in period photos. The enlisted men's hats were nearly identical to those of the officers, though they lacked the black silk lining on the edges. Although issued and widely used up through the 1876 campaigns, these hats were despised by the troopers because of the lack of ventilation and the black color. In 1876, a ventilated, smaller-brimmed hat was issued. McChristian, *U.S. Army*, 45–46, 55, 165–66.

51. Second Lieutenant Winfield Scott Edgerly (1846–1927) was a native of New Hampshire. After graduating from the U.S. Military Academy in 1870, he joined the Seventh Cavalry that year. He married Grace Cory Blum of New York in St. Paul, Minnesota, in October 1875. Edgerly was on scouting duty and survived the Reno hilltop fight. He went on to a distinguished military career, becoming a brigadier general. He died in his hometown of Farmington and is buried in Arlington National Cemetery. For a detailed biographical sketch, see Nichols, *Men with Custer*, 95. For his later comments regarding the battle, see Hammer, *Custer in '76*, 53–55; and Graham, *Custer Myth*, 219–21.

52. Per official U.S. Army regulations, ambulances were to be used only for the sick and wounded and not for other transportation purposes. However, this restriction was often ignored on the frontier. See War Office, *Revised U.S. Army Regulations*, Art. XLIV/no. 1331, p. 317; Fougera, *With Custer's Cavalry*, 169; and Koster, "Belknap Scandal," 64. For DeWolf's opinion of Custer's dogs being transported in the ambulance during the 1874 Black Hills expedition, see his letter of May 23, 1876. For a useful history of the transport of wounded soldiers and the development of the ambulance, see Stewart, *Moving the Wounded*.

53. This is a surprising outburst from the mild-mannered, calm, and usually diplomatic DeWolf, who rarely used profanity (only two times in his letters). Perhaps the monotony of the daily post routine was getting to him.

54. Probably the *St. Louis Republican*; see chap. 3, n. 13.

55. DeWolf's reference is unclear. His description suggests a recreational area, possibly Sully's Hill at Devil's Lake by Fort Totten. The huge hill was named for Alfred Sully, a brevet brigadier general of volunteers during the Civil War, whose troops camped there during an 1865 expedition. Two years later, the fort was built with timber cut from the hill. Today, Sully's Hill is a national game preserve for bison, elk, deer, and birds, with a visitor's center and hiking trails through woods and prairies. In the Victorian era of the fort, this and the area around Fort Totten provided places for officers, their wives, and others to enjoy picnics and leisurely walks. Perhaps Glencroft's slide was an area where people slid down the hill during the winter. Unfortunately, despite a meticulous search, no information has yet been located to identify the nature and location of Abbis, Glen Alin, and Glencroft's slide.

56. Ella was a servant who apparently was at Fort Totten and then Fort Seward (see chap. 1, n. 85).

57. Fort Fetterman (1867–82), a sprawling post in mid-eastern Wyoming consisting of log structures, was built to protect travelers on the Bozeman Trail. It was named for Captain William J. Fetterman, who was killed in the infamous 1866 battle with Indians near Fort Phil Kearny. General Crook used the fort as the base for his expeditions to the Powder River during the 1876 Sioux campaign. Fort Fetterman State Historic Site preserves the only two remaining original buildings. Barnes, *Forts of the Northern Plains*, 180–84; Frazer, *Forts of the West*, 181. For a more thorough history, see Lindmier, *Drygone*.

58. Colonel John Gibbon (1827–96) of the Seventh Infantry was assigned to lead the expedition's Montana Column. Born in Philadelphia, Gibbon later moved to North Carolina with his family and graduated from the U.S. Military Academy in 1847. He served in the Florida Seminole Indian wars and the Mexican War and was a captain of the Fourth Artillery in Kansas at the start of the Civil War. He remained loyal to the Union despite his brothers' fighting for the Confederacy, and was wounded at Fredericksburg and again at Gettysburg during Pickett's Charge. He received several brevet appointments throughout the war, attaining the rank of brevet major general in March 1865 for gallant service in the capture of Petersburg, Virginia. After the

war, he reverted to the regular army rank of colonel, eventually being assigned to the Seventh Infantry in 1869. His Indian wars service included not only the Little Big Horn campaign but also the Nez Perce War of 1877. He retired from the army in 1891 and lived in Baltimore until his death in 1896 of pneumonia. He is buried in Arlington National Cemetery. "John Oliver Gibbon," Arlington National Cemetery website, www.arlingtoncemetery.net/jgibbon.htm (accessed Aug. 9, 2013, and July 26, 2016); U.S. Department of Agriculture, Forestry Service, Nez Perce National Historic Trail website, www.fs.usda.gov/npnht/ (accessed Aug. 9, 2013); Heitman, *Historical Register* (1903), 452.

59. This term refers to the horde of prospectors, miscreants, and land seekers who flooded into the Black Hills seeking gold, land, and fortune after the Black Hills expedition of 1874.

60. Dr. Charles Andrew Stein (1848–1920) was the senior staff veterinary surgeon for the Seventh Cavalry at the Powder River Camp; see Overfield, *Little Big Horn*, 152. A native of New Orleans, Louisiana, with German ancestry, Stein and his wife, Mary (whom he married in 1871), resided in the city with their family. In 1875, he was appointed junior veterinarian to the Seventh Cavalry's Company B at Shreveport, but he was soon promoted to senior veterinarian and joined Terry, Custer, and the regiment at Fort Lincoln in the spring of 1876 for the Sioux expedition. After that campaign, he resigned his commission and moved his family to St. Paul, Minnesota, where he continued a private veterinary practice at least until 1891; see *U.S. City Directories, 1821–1989* (for St. Paul, Minnesota, 1881–91), www.ancestry.com (accessed May 5, 2015). Nothing is known about his remaining years, other than that he died on June 21, 1920, in New Orleans. For a detailed review of his duties and involvement in the Little Big Horn campaign, see Gray, "Veterinary Service." DeWolf apparently did not think much of Stein.

61. Charley Reynolds was born in Kentucky, although he grew up in Illinois, where his father practiced medicine. He served in the Civil War in the Tenth Kansas Infantry. After the war he became a scout and hunter in the upper Missouri regions. He signed on for the Yellowstone expeditions of 1873 and 1875 and the Black Hills expedition of 1874, and he was employed by the Seventh Cavalry as a civilian guide in April 1876. He was referred to as "Lonesome Charley," as he often kept to himself, but he was genial and well liked by almost everyone who met him and "had the reputation of being a silent man, of great bravery, unusual sense and unimpeachable character." His services as a scout and guide were sought after because of the "fauna and flora and geological formations [that] were familiar to him" and his excellent hunting skills. He was at the Crow's Nest with Custer and Varnum on the early morning of the battle and "was killed with Major Reno's battalion during the retreat on the afternoon of June 25" (Luce, "Diary and Letters," 5). See Brininstool, "Charley Reynolds," in *Troopers with Custer*, 306 (first quotation), 316 (second quotation); see also Nichols, *Men with Custer*, 277, which includes an extensive list of published sources on Reynolds.

62. Captain John Francis Weston (1845–1917) of the Seventh Cavalry was stationed at Fort Totten and in command of Company L from October 1875 until December 10, 1875, just after he was promoted from lieutenant to captain and appointed as the commissary of subsistence on November 29, per orders from Headquarters of the Department of Dakota. Weston was originally from Kentucky and served in the Fourth Kentucky Volunteer Cavalry during the Civil War, reaching the rank of major by 1864. He later was awarded the Medal of Honor for gallantry at Wetumka, Alabama, for leading a detachment that defeated an enemy force and captured their steamboats loaded with supplies. After the war, he served in the Seventh Cavalry until becoming a staff officer with the Commissary Department. He continued in the commissary, being promoted to major in 1892, colonel (and serving as the assistant commissary general of subsistence) in 1898, and then brigadier general of volunteers, serving in Cuba during the Spanish-American War. In 1900 he returned to the regular army and was appointed brigadier general and commissary general, then major general in 1905, serving in the Philippines until 1909, when he retired as commander of the Department of California. He is buried at Arlington National Cemetery. Fort Totten Post Returns, Oct.–Dec. 1875, NARA; Heitman, *Historical Register* (1903), 1021; Official Army Register for 1914, War Department Records, AGO, NARA, 498.

63. The horses at Fort Abraham Lincoln were kept at the stables and granary area and were not allowed to graze, because of their great number and the impracticality of gathering them quickly when needed. Chambers, *Fort Abraham Lincoln*, 99, 116.

64. Captain Frederick W. Benteen (1834–98) had attained the rank of colonel of volunteers during the Civil War but, as Luce noted, "like many others was required to accept a reduced rank in the regular army after the war" (Luce, "Diary and Letters," 41). Part of the Seventh since its 1866 organization, Benteen commanded a battalion of three companies (D, H, and K) at the Little Big Horn. Benteen's personality conflict with Custer was well-known and, along with his alleged actions at the Little Big Horn and testimony at the Reno court of inquiry, has been the subject of continuous debate and numerous publications. Benteen retired from the army in 1888 because of poor health and was breveted a brigadier general in 1890. He died in Atlanta, Georgia, though he is now buried in Arlington National Cemetery. For a more detailed biographical sketch, see Nichols, *Men with Custer*, 20–21, which also includes references to Benteen's personal papers and several published works regarding the Benteen-Custer feud. For a full-length biography, see Donovan, *Brazen Trumpet*. For additional essays regarding the controversy over his actions at the Little Big Horn, see Graham, *Custer Myth*, chap. 4; Unger, *ABCs of Custer's Last Stand*, chap. 20; and Smith, "Benteen."

65. Fort Rice (1864–78), in mid-southern Dakota Territory, was initially built on the Missouri River for the expedition against the Sioux in 1864. It served as the command base for the three Yellowstone expeditions of the 1870s and was also home to four companies of the Seventh Cavalry. Nothing remains of the fort today other than markings of building foundations, although there are interpretive signs and

Notes to Pages 89–90

markers for a walking tour at the Fort Rice State Historic Site in North Dakota. Barnes, *Forts of the Northern Plains*, 116–18; Frazer, *Forts of the West*, 113.

66. First Lieutenant William Winer Cooke (1846–76). Easily recognized by his distinctive long double-side whiskers, Cooke served as the Seventh Cavalry's regimental adjutant from 1872 to his death at the Little Big Horn, and he was among Custer's most loyal officers. Born in Mt. Pleasant (near Hamilton), Ontario, he served in the New York Volunteer Cavalry during the American Civil War. He was breveted a lieutenant colonel in 1867, which accounts for the title by which DeWolf refers to him in this letter. Cooke joined the Seventh Cavalry in 1866 and served with Custer in the 1868 Washita, 1873 Yellowstone, and 1874 Black Hills campaigns. At the Little Big Horn, he penned the famous "Come quick, Bring Packs" message from Custer to Benteen. He is buried in Hamilton. For a more detailed biography, see Nichols, *Men with Custer*, 62. Regarding reinterment arrangements for his remains, see M. V. Sheridan to Lt. Cooke's father, July 16, 1877, AGO, Consolidated File no. 4163, WSL/LIBI.

67. First Lieutenant Henry James Nowlan (1837–98), the son of a British officer, was born in Corfu in the Ionian Islands. He graduated from the Royal Military Academy at Sandhurst and initially served in the British army. He eventually came to America and enlisted in the New York Cavalry in 1863, serving in the Civil War. In 1866 he was appointed as a second lieutenant in the Seventh Cavalry. He served as the quartermaster for the Yellowstone Depot during the entire 1876 campaign and was on detached service there at the time of the Little Big Horn fight. He is buried in Little Rock National Cemetery in Arkansas. Fort Abraham Lincoln Post Returns, Jan.–May 1876, NARA; G.O. No. 1, Brig. Gen. Alfred H. Terry, HQ, Dept. of Dakota, May 14, 1876, WSL/LIBI. For a more detailed biography, see Nichols, *Men with Custer*, 248.

68. Grace Cory Blum Edgerly was the wife of Second Lieutenant Winfield S. Edgerly.

69. DeWolf is referring to the Stanley Stockade, built for the Yellowstone expedition of 1873, which was led out of Fort Rice by Colonel David Sloan Stanley (1829–1902), commander of the Twenty-Second Infantry regiment. This expedition "was designed for the protection of engineering surveyors of the Northern Pacific Railroad." Expedition troops included companies from the Eighth, Ninth, Seventeenth, and Twenty-Second Infantries, with artillery squads from the latter regiment, and ten companies of the Seventh Cavalry, commanded by Custer. The stockade for the transfer of supplies was constructed as "a strong bastioned stockade upon the south bank of the Yellowstone, eight miles by land above Glendive's Creek," easily accessed by the steamboats *Far West* and *Josephine*. The Dakota Column camped at the stockade for five days, from June 11 to June 15, 1876. Nothing remains of the stockade today, although the site is marked with signs leading to the original location; see Chorne, *Following the Custer Trail*, 158. For the official army account of the expedition, see Stanley, *Report on the Yellowstone Expedition*, 3 (first quotation), 5 (second quotation).

70. Captain Otho Ernest Michaelis, ordnance officer, Department of Dakota, Dakota Column. A native of Germany and later a resident of New York, Michaelis served in the Signal Corps as a second lieutenant in 1863, then as a first lieutenant in 1864, and was breveted a captain for "faithful and meritorious service" in 1865. After the war, he became a captain in the Ordnance Department, serving out west; he was eventually promoted in the Ordnance Department to major in 1889. He died on May 1, 1890. For his commission record, see Heitman, *Historical Register* (1903), 707. For his 1876 campaign staff position, see Overfield, *Little Big Horn*, 109; and Hedren, *Great Sioux War*, 98, 120.

71. Robert Cloud Seip (1840–78) was the post trader at Fort Abraham Lincoln from 1874 to 1875. He served at Fort Snelling in 1867 and also served for several years as the chief clerk to (Brevet) Colonel Asa Peabody Blunt, quartermaster for the department in the Washington, D.C., area, where he was a member of the Dawson Masonic Lodge No. 16. Shortly after Seip and his wife arrived at Fort Abraham Lincoln, their daughter Ella died of diphtheria (on August 27, 1874); she was buried in the post cemetery at Fort Abraham Lincoln. See *Bismarck Tribune*, Sep. 2, 1874, p. 8; see also Chambers, *Fort Abraham Lincoln*, 55. Seip died in Bismarck on January 8, 1878. His remains were brought back to D.C., where he was buried after a funeral at the Masonic temple; see Seip obituary, *Washington (D.C.) Post*, Jan. 26, 1878, and *Evening Star*, Jan. 15, 1878.

72. DeWolf apparently drew an extra month's pay in advance. Troops were to be paid in a time frame not to exceed two months. War Office, *Revised U.S. Army Regulations*, Art. XLV/no. 1338, p. 351; Barnard, *Ten Years with Custer*, 219.

73. DeWolf was obviously envious of this development, as he had already expressed to Fannie his own desire to return to Fort Totten on assignment and undoubtedly believed he should have been selected instead of Redd.

74. This is not at all surprising, as Middleton was a regular army medical officer while Redd was a contract surgeon and had never served in the regular army. Petty jealousies among staff personnel (regardless of department) were common, certainly not a new occurrence in the history of the military.

75. DeWolf's assignment order is found in S.F.O. No. 5, Headquarters, Department of Dakota, camp near Fort Abraham Lincoln, May 14, 1876, vol. 191, AGO, photocopy in WSL/LIBI.

76. Dr. John Winfield Williams (c. 1839–89) was the chief medical officer for the expedition; he was also appointed to oversee the battery and Captain Baker's company, Sixth Infantry (S.F.O. No. 5, ibid.). Born in Washington, D.C., he was commissioned as a second lieutenant in the Medical Corps in 1862 and served as an assistant surgeon in the Fourteenth U.S. Infantry during the Civil War in the Army of the Potomac. He was breveted a major in 1865. After the war, he served with the army in Arizona Territory. He became the chief medical officer of the Seventh Cavalry for Custer's Black Hills expedition in 1874 and then served in the same capacity for General Terry (Luce, "Diary and Letters," 5), organizing the triage and evacuation of casualties from the Battle of the Little Big Horn. He died in 1889 while still on

active duty in Chalmette, St. Bernard Parish, Louisiana, and is buried in Chalmette National Cemetery, Sec. 23, Site 12195. Heitman, *Historical Register* (1903), 1041; also findagrave.com, Memorial Record no. 64592431 (accessed Nov. 14, 2013).

77. Chief Medical Officer Williams offered Porter a contract as an acting assistant surgeon for the upcoming Yellowstone expedition, which Porter accepted; see S.F.O. No. 5 (see n. 75, this chapter). Porter had attended the troops at Camp Hancock under a civilian contract with the army, offered in late September 1875 per the Dakota Department's medical director, Dr. Sloan. Stevenson, *Deliverance*, 148, 188n3; letters between William J. Sloan and Henry R. Porter, Porter Papers, NARA, Sep. 28, 1875 and Oct. 1, 1875 respectively; see also Camp Hancock Post Returns, Oct. 1875–Apr. 1876, NARA.

78. DeWolf notes here that Custer did not want Ashton assigned to the cavalry, since he had less military experience than the other physicians and contract surgeons. Williams eventually assigned Clark and Ashton to the supply depot, where they attended several sick soldiers, per DeWolf's June 8 letter. Gray, *Centennial Campaign*, 274.

CHAPTER 3.
MISJUDGMENT AND THE TRAIL TO DISASTER

1. This is actually Camp No. 1 (in contradistinction to previous Custer Trail studies). DeWolf's numbers identifying the camps along the expedition trail are one number higher than those given in previous studies on the Custer Trail, including Carroll, *Frank Anders* and Chorne, *Following the Custer Trail*. This is a result of the doctor having considered and labeled Camp No. 1 as the camp at Fort Abraham Lincoln.

2. Captain George W. Yates (1843–76), commander of Company F and a native of New York, served in the Civil War in the Fourth Michigan Infantry and saw action at Antietam, Fredericksburg, and Gettysburg; he also served with the Forty-Fifth Missouri Infantry and Thirteenth Missouri Cavalry. After the war, he joined the Second Cavalry and eventually was assigned to the Seventh, serving in the Black Hills expedition of 1874 before being killed at the Little Big Horn. He is buried in Fort Leavenworth National Cemetery. See Nichols, *Men with Custer*, 365.

3. As DeWolf noted, the first camp after leaving Fort Abraham Lincoln was on the Heart River, some 12 miles west of the fort. This was a "delightful spot for a camp," according to *Bismarck Tribune* correspondent Mark Kellogg, who accompanied the expedition. It encompassed approximately 1,000 acres of level ground, surrounded by cottonwood trees, plenty of firewood, and good drinking water. Perhaps the only drawback was the infestation of rattlesnakes, of which the troops routinely disposed in a systematic "skirmish line" manner before setting up camp. For further details, see Barnard, *I Go with Custer*, 170; and Chorne, *Following the Custer Trail*, 18–23.

4. As the chief engineer, Lieutenant Maguire, related, odometers were attached to the four-mule ambulance that carried his instruments and men. Historians have noted that this means of measurement recorded how far the wagons had traveled

each day but was not entirely accurate as to the exact "straight line" distance between two locations, since the terrain was extremely difficult to navigate. Varied elevations, deep ravines, and dangerous river crossings often caused unplanned detours, all of which added to the measurements. Nonetheless, such measurement means provided a rough indication of the distances traveled. Studies have shown that surviving written records by various individuals on the expedition all essentially corroborate each other, minor discrepancies and variations notwithstanding. Carroll, *Frank Anders*, 130; Gray, *Custer's Last Campaign*, 184–88; Stewart and Luce, "Reno Scout," 21–22.

5. Myles Keogh (1840–76), the commander of Company I, was a native of Ireland. He served in over thirty engagements in the Civil War, during which he attained the rank of major and was breveted a lieutenant colonel. After the war, he joined the Seventh Cavalry and was eventually promoted to captain, serving until his death at the Little Big Horn. Luce noted that Keogh's horse Comanche "was the only living part of the regiment found on the Custer Battlefield after the battle"; this is not entirely accurate, as there were other wounded horses found on the battlefield, which were then shot to end their suffering. Keogh is buried in Fort Hill Cemetery in Auburn, New York. Luce, "Diary and Letters," 42 (quotation). See also Nichols, *Men with Custer*, 177–78; and the expansive biography by Langellier et al., *Myles Keogh*.

6. Captain Thomas Henry French (1843–82) was a native of Maryland who served in the Tenth Infantry during and after the Civil War and was assigned to the Seventh Cavalry in 1871. He participated in the Yellowstone expedition of 1873 and survived the Little Big Horn, commanding Company M on the Reno-Benteen hilltop. The following year he served in the Nez Perce campaign. He died at Fort Leavenworth and is buried in the National Cemetery there. See Nichols, *Men with Custer*, 109–10. For the definitive study on the men of Company M, see MacLean, *Custer's Best*.

7. DeWolf's initial impression of Reno's unfriendly demeanor confirms what others at the time mentioned and wrote about the major. DeWolf likely perceived him as such because of Reno's aforementioned inquiries and suspicions regarding the medical staff keeping soldiers off duty on the sick list. For further commentary on Reno's personality, see Nichols, *In Custer's Shadow*, vii–x.

8. Second Lieutenant Benjamin Hubert Hodgson (1848–76) was born in Philadelphia and graduated from the U.S. Military Academy in 1870. He joined the Seventh Cavalry shortly thereafter and served until his death at the Little Big Horn. Hodgson and Reno were friends, the latter becoming distraught when Hodgson "was killed on June 25 in his attempt to cross the Little Bighorn River" to get to the high ground of the defense hill. Reno went to great lengths to retrieve his friend's body despite the raging battle. Hodgson also became good friends with DeWolf in the short time they knew each other. Luce, "Diary and Letters," 42 (quotation). For a more detailed biographical sketch, see Nichols, *Men with Custer*, 149–50; for accounts of his death, see Hardorff, *Custer Battle Casualties II*, 93–98.

9. Now known as Camp No. 2 (though DeWolf numbers it as their third camp). This camp was located about 3 miles south of present-day I-94, just south of the railroad

track (2 miles west of the Sweet Briar Station of the original Northern Pacific Railroad) and 10 miles east of the present-day town of New Salem. There Custer sent his wife, Elizabeth, back to Fort Lincoln with an escort of the scouts and the paymaster, as she had been allowed to accompany him that far on the expedition. See Chorne, *Following the Custer Trail*, 24; see also Carroll, *Frank Anders*, 130.

10. Camp No. 4. This camp was located about a mile south of the southwest corner of New Salem.

11. Reynolds was nicknamed "Lucky Man" by the Indians as a result of his hunting prowess. The large amount of game killed by the "solitary rifle of this extraordinary hunter became a subject of much discussion among the neighboring Indian tribes" as well as "widespread familiarity among envious hunters." He supplied meat for the officers in addition to his role as a guide on the Little Big Horn expedition. Brininstool, "Charley Reynolds," in *Troopers with Custer*, 312–13 (both quotations); see also Sarf, *Little Bighorn Campaign*, 134.

12. This hailstorm was actually much more violent than DeWolf notes here—which is surprising, given his usual attention to detail. General Terry noted that "it terrified the drenched and bawling herd of beef cattle into a wild stampede! Man and beast alike sustained bruises from this untoward assault from the skies. . . . The Cavalry mounts, struck repeatedly, whinnied and snorted in wild-eyed fright and uncertainty," causing the infantrymen to take cover under the wagons and the cavalrymen to bring their horses close to the latter for protection. Chorne, *Following the Custer Trail*, 33 (quotation).

13. While DeWolf again does not divulge the full name of the periodical, the newspaper he mentions is very likely either the *St. Louis Republican* or the *Omaha Republican*, both major newspapers in the western regions and Chicago at the time. The *St. Louis Republican* was in publication from 1873 to 1876, originating from Missouri's first newspaper in 1808. The *Omaha Republican* was in operation from 1858 to 1883. A review of the State Historical Society of North Dakota's guide to historical newspapers and Hugh J. Reilly's *Bound to Have Blood* suggest that no other newspapers in the region had any form of the name "Republic" or "Republican" at the time. If DeWolf received the *Republican*, he would have read either the April 2 or the May 1 monthly issue, which contained the articles "Judiciary Committee Not Ready with the Belknap Impeachment Articles" and "Emigrants Killed by Indians [in the Black Hills]." Conversely, if his issue was the April 29 edition of the *Omaha Republican*, DeWolf would have read editorials of that paper's criticism of the U.S. Army and the government's treatment of the Indians. Whatever the case, as DeWolf's gratitude to his wife suggests, the newspaper must have provided a welcome opportunity to read and relax at night after the monotonous long days of riding on the campaign. Digital images of the *St. Louis Republican*, Apr. 2 and May 1, 1876, Collections of the State Historical Society of Missouri, http://statehistoricalsocietyofmissouri.org/cdm/compoundobject/collection/dmr4/id/8337 (accessed June 28, 2013); Reilly, *Bound to Have Blood*, chaps. 3 and 4.

14. DeWolf is suggesting that his wife make legal arrangements. For what reason and why at this particular time are not known, although it would be reasonable to speculate that he might have been considering the worst-case scenario, should he be killed on the campaign. Lovni might have been an attorney, either in Fannie's hometown of Norwalk or perhaps in Watertown. However, the Watertown and Norwalk city directories during the time DeWolf and his wife lived in the latter town do not include anyone by that name.

15. Captain Stephen Baker (d. 1904), Company B, Sixth Infantry. Baker served in the Sixth Michigan Infantry during the Civil War, rising through the ranks to become quartermaster sergeant. After the war, he served in the regular army Sixth Infantry as a lieutenant, then as the regimental quartermaster in 1867–68. He was promoted to captain in June 1874, became a major in the Fourth Infantry in 1897, and retired from the army in 1899. See Heitman, *Historical Register* (1903), 185; Overfield, *Little Big Horn*, 110; and "Stephen Baker," Arlington National Cemetery website, www.arlingtoncemetery.net/stephen-baker.htm (accessed June 28, 2015).

16. Second Lieutenant John Jordan Crittenden (1854–76), Twentieth Infantry. Born in Frankfort, Kentucky, he was dismissed from the U.S. Military Academy in 1874 because of academic insufficiency. In October 1875 he was assigned to the Twentieth Infantry at Fort Abercrombie, in present-day North Dakota, where his father, Lieutenant Colonel Thomas L. Crittenden, was commandant. While there, he lost an eye in a hunting accident. He was killed with Custer's detachment at the Little Big Horn and is buried there in Custer National Cemetery. Biographical information from Nichols, *Men with Custer*, 69.

17. Captain Robert Patterson Hughes (d. 1909), Company E, Third Infantry, aide-de-camp to Terry. Hughes served in several Pennsylvania Infantry units during the Civil War and was breveted a colonel "for gallantry and meritorious service in the assault on Fort Gregg, Virginia." He was assigned to the Third Infantry in 1875. Hughes rose to the rank of major general in 1902, retiring from the army the following year. Brother-in-law to General Terry, he is buried in the Terry family plot in Grove Street Cemetery, New Haven, Connecticut. Heitman, *Historical Register* (1903), 552–53 (quotation and service record); Hedren, *Great Sioux War*, 120; Overfield, *Little Big Horn*, 109; www.findagrave.com (accessed Aug. 17, 2013).

18. Captain Edward Worthington Smith of Company G of the Eighteenth Infantry (brevet lieutenant colonel) served as an acting assistant adjutant general under Terry; see chap. 2, n. 16.

19. First Lieutenant Eugene Beauharnais Gibbs (1833–82) of Company C of the Sixth Infantry was aide-de-camp to Terry. Originally from Rhode Island, he served as a captain in the Second California Infantry during the Civil War. After the war, he was a second lieutenant in the Eighth Infantry in 1867 and then first lieutenant two years later, eventually being assigned to the Sixth Infantry in 1871 and promoted to captain in 1880. He died on April 25, 1882, and is buried in Island Cemetery, Newport,

Rhode Island. See Hedren, *Great Sioux War*, 120; Overfield, *Little Big Horn*, 109; and www.findagrave.com (accessed July 27, 2016). For Gibbs's service record, see Heitman, *Historical Register* (1903), 453.

20. First Lieutenant Edward Maguire (1847–92) was an ordinance officer. Originally from Nashville, Tennessee, Maguire graduated ninth in his class from the U.S. Military Academy in September 1863. He was assigned as a second lieutenant to the engineers in 1867 and was promoted to first lieutenant in 1869 and to captain in 1881. He died on October 11, 1892, in Philadelphia. Maguire's map, drawn the day after the battle, is the first known map of the battlefield. Donahue, *Drawing Battle Lines*; Hedren, *Great Sioux War*, 120; Overfield, *Little Big Horn*, 109; Heitman, *Historical Register* (1903), 684. For a discussion on the several variations of the Maguire map, see Unger, *ABCs of Custer's Last Stand*, 67–77, 119–20, 258–59; and King, *Massacre*. Maguire's field diary notes are in Carroll, *Frank Anders*. For Maguire's testimony in the 1879 Reno court of inquiry, see Nichols, *Reno Court of Inquiry*, 7–18; see Donovan, *Terrible Glory*, 361, for comments regarding the testimony.

21. DeWolf was referring to Private Henry A. Abbotts (b. 1853), Company E, Seventh Cavalry. Abbotts was assigned as a temporary hospital steward (attendant) to DeWolf on May 6, according to S.O. 34, HQ, 7th Cav., May 6, 1876, NARA. For a biographical sketch, see Nichols, *Men with Custer*, 1.

22. In the first of his four *Tribune* columns, published May 17, 1876, Kellogg listed DeWolf's name as "Woolsey" among the acting assistant surgeons on the staff roster. DeWolf is obviously miffed by what he perceived as a sarcastic nickname. The reason for the apparent petty quarrel between the doctor and the reporter is not known, although DeWolf provides a possible hint. Kellogg displayed privilege among the officer staff, and rightly so, as he was the only correspondent on the expedition. Perhaps during the course of conversation in the officer's mess, DeWolf was not amused by a joke or possibly Kellogg's opinion of the campaign and/or perception of the various staff members. All of this is speculation, of course. The exact reason may never be known, since nothing further is mentioned or alluded to by either DeWolf or Kellogg in their written correspondence for the remainder of the campaign. For commentary on Kellogg's status and also a full description of the first column and the "Woolsey" listing, see Barnard, *I Go with Custer*, 109–10, 165–69.

23. Kellogg penned opinions and observations about many of the officers and men in his columns during the expedition. Both his and DeWolf's comments corroborate the general perceptions about Custer and Terry by others (the known extreme dislike and jealousies between Custer, Benteen, and Reno notwithstanding). Also, as DeWolf notes and photos of this and the earlier Custer expedition of 1874 show, buckskin clothing, particularly coats, was popular among the officers and other staff during the campaign. For Kellogg's description of Terry and Custer, see Barnard, *I Go with Custer*, 168.

24. Sutures and needles were a part of the surgeon's kit in the nineteenth century.

Absorbable catgut was preferred, although sutures of silk, linen, and even iron, lead, or silver wire were used. Wilbur, *Civil War Medicine*, 14, 43; for linen sutures, see Agnew, *Medicine in the Old West*, 135.

25. For the roster of the fifty-one Indian scouts, see Nichols, *Men with Custer*, 387–88.

26. Camp No. 5 can be seen from above on the decks overlooking the site at the current rest stop on I-94, in Morton County, North Dakota. Chorne, *Following the Custer Trail*, 41.

27. A coulee, as it is commonly known in the western United States and Canada, is "a deep ravine or gulch that is usually dry in summer." *World Book Dictionary*, 1:473.

28. Camp No. 6, known as Head Hay Creek, is 4 miles northwest of I-94, also in Morton County, near Haymarch Town. Just to the southeast are the Twin Buttes called "Maiden's Breasts," which can be seen from the highway as well, of which various hilarious remarks were made by the passing soldiers in the expedition. Chorne, *Following the Custer Trail*, 44–49.

29. Camp No. 7 in Stark County is west of Hebron, North Dakota, about 13 miles north of I-94. Chorne, *Following the Custer Trail*, 50.

30. DeWolf does not name this soldier. However, Gray has identified him as the trumpeter John Connell, Company B, Seventh Cavalry. He was subsequently on detached service at the Yellowstone Depot to recover from his wound and missed the battle at the Little Big Horn. Gray, *Centennial Campaign*, 272; for a biographical sketch, see Nichols, *Men with Custer*, 60.

31. DeWolf does not specify the exact nature of the medication he consumed here; most likely he is referring to an aperient pill, i.e., a laxative. Aperient pills were a mild purgative taken in pill form because in "some adults, liquid medicines produce nausea and pills are the only form in which aperients can be exhibited" (Chase, *Dr. Chase's Recipes*, 371). See *World Book Dictionary*, 1:95. The less likely candidates would be some type of cathartic powder, such as charcoal or Culver's root; these are valuable but powerful aperients used for quicker results, as the former "immediately removes offensive exhalations from the intestines and renal discharges and purifies the breath," while Culver's root "is effective in fevers and removing black and morbid matter from the bowels" (Chase, *Dr. Chase's Recipes*, 338). Neither would be the medication that DeWolf used, though, as he clearly indicates taking a pill.

32. This is the grave of Sergeant Henry C. Stempker of Troop L of the Seventh Cavalry, who died of "chronic diarrhea" and was buried at this site on August 25, 1874, during the 1874 Black Hills expedition. The grave remains near the location of Camp No. 7 today, although it is on private property. Chorne, *Following the Custer Trail*, 56–58. Reporter Mark Kellogg also noted Stempker's grave in his Big Horn diary; see Barnard, *I Go with Custer*, 114, 201.

33. The Camp No. 8 site, in Stark County, North Dakota, is a mile west of Young Man's Butte and overlooks the scenic Knife River. Chorne, *Following the Custer Trail*, 56–58.

34. Glycerin, or glycerol, is "a colorless, sweet, syrupy liquid obtained from animal and vegetable oils," used for making gargles for sore mouths and throats or applied to the skin for a soothing effect. *World Book Dictionary*, 1:909 (quotation); Miller, *Domestic Medical Practice*, 1073; *Stedman's Medical Dictionary*, 592. Alum is "a whitish mineral salt used in medicine and in dy[e]ing, sometimes used to stop bleeding," although more formally defined as "any one of the double salts formed by a combination of a sulfate of aluminum, iron, manganese, chromium, or gallium with a sulfate of lithium, sodium, potassium, ammonium, cesium or rubidium and . . . used locally as [a] styptic" (i.e., to stop bleeding). *World Book Dictionary*, 1:62 (first quotation); *Stedman's Medical Dictionary*, 48 (second quotation).

35. Here DeWolf hints at the lack of compassion from some officers and the accepted distinguishing of social status between them and the enlisted men, as well as the blatant misuse of government ambulances (see DeWolf's letter of May 23, 1876). Custer's use of ambulances for dogs and animals instead of soldiers shows his arrogance, which he had displayed through similar behavior during the 1874 Black Hills expedition. Grafe and Horsted, *Exploring with Custer*, 21.

36. Camp No. 9 was on the Green River in present-day Stark County, adjacent to the I-94 rest stop at this locale. It was among the nicest areas of all the camps on the expedition, as it had an excellent supply of wood, sufficient water for bathing and fishing, and extensive pasturage for grazing of the horses. See Kellogg diary entry of May 23 in Barnard, *I Go with Custer*, 200–201; see also Chorne, *Following the Custer Trail*, 62.

37. Camp No. 10 was near Crow Ridge, a high butte with a sandstone cropping on the top, overlooking the Heart River valley and 2 miles north of present-day South Heart, North Dakota. DeWolf's opinion of the actual site of the camp differs from that of the earlier Anders/Carroll account provided in Chorne's *Following the Custer Trail*, because the portion of the Heart River here is described as much "wider and deeper" and the site is larger to accommodate the large size of the expedition's men, wagons, and horses. DeWolf's mention of a horse that almost drowned seems to support the latter contention. Chorne, *Following the Custer Trail*, 68–70.

38. Porter was an experienced hunter and enjoyed it; see Walker, *Dr. Henry R. Porter*, 93–94.

39. DeWolf relates the danger of hunting parties that had to go out for the command, a risky endeavor for all the columns on the campaign. For example, three privates out hunting at Gibbon's Rosebud camp were killed by a party of Sioux on May 23, as DeWolf mentioned in his June 8 letter. Gray, *Custer's Last Campaign*, 156.

40. Here DeWolf references Custer's penchant for flair. The troops' enjoyment of it can be derived from DeWolf's various references to the band in his almost-daily letters, as well as from others who kept journals, such as Mark Kellogg. See Kellogg diary entry of May 27, in Barnard, *I Go with Custer*, 202; and Gleason, "Mounted Band," 82–84.

41. This would be Devil's Lake, which Fort Totten overlooked.

42. Camp No. 11 was located on a branch of the Heart River about 3 miles south of present-day Belfield, in Stark County. Descriptions of this area from Lieutenant Maguire, Mark Kellogg, and others relate that it had nice grass and a good stream but no wood. Troops had to rely on the supply of timbers that the engineers brought along, both for firewood and for multiple bridge crossings. For Kellogg's description, see Barnard, *I Go with Custer*, 178 (and diary entry of May 25, 1876, pp. 202–3); see also Maguire's diary entry, quoted in Chorne, *Following the Custer Trail*, 78.

43. The site of Camp No. 12 is in Billings County, North Dakota, at the entrance to the Davis Creek valley. It is part of the Little Missouri National Grassland Wildlife and Scenic Tour. Chorne, *Following the Custer Trail*, 82.

44. Private John R. Colwell. There is no John Caldwell listed for either Company L or Company E of the Seventh Cavalry at this time.

45. There is no William A. Lomy listed in Company E rosters at this time. However, there was a William J. Logue (1841–1919) in Company L; see Nichols, *Men with Custer*, 196, for further biographical information. Most likely DeWolf misspelled the name here and inadvertently placed him in the wrong company list.

46. There are two Hendersons listed in the Company E roster: John and Sykes. The latter name is the more likely candidate, given its similarity with the listed name of Zach.

47. There is no John S. Henley listed on the Company E roster or for any of the Seventh Cavalry rosters at this time. This trooper is probably the other Henderson in Company E (see previous note), since the first name is John and the last name begins with the same letter.

48. There is no William B. Jones listed in Company E at this time. There were two privates listed with the last name Jones: Henry of Company I and Julien of Company H. Nichols, *Men with Custer*, 168. William B. Jones is listed by DeWolf as a sergeant in Company E; possibly he had been discharged, like George Zimmerman, and was being treated as a civilian until he recovered.

49. The soldier bitten on his finger by the rattlesnake was Private Francis Johnson Kennedy (1854–1924) of Keogh's Company I. He was born in Ireland, enlisted as Francis Johnson in the Seventh Cavalry in 1875, was with the pack train escort, and survived the Reno hilltop fight. He later served in the Seventh Infantry. He married in 1882 after leaving the army, had several children, and resided in St. Paul, Minnesota, until his death. For more biographical details, see Nichols, *Men with Custer*, 176, 395.

The onlooking soldiers' "amusing remarks . . . [and] admiration for the curative powers of whiskey straight" after the administration of 26 ounces of whiskey by Williams and Porter is mentioned by Mark Kellogg, who witnessed this event along with DeWolf. The use of whiskey in the treatment of snakebites was "tried in a number of cases, and always with success . . . [the persons] cured by drinking whisky until drunkenness and stupor were produced." The hypothesis was that whiskey would kill the poison and/or assist in draining it from the body via dehydration and vomiting. We now know that alcohol dilates blood vessels, which results in further absorption of the venom. The decades-old regimen of sucking out the poison and "scarify[ing] the wound with a penknife, razor or lancet . . . and cauterizing the bite freely . . . after it has been well sucked with the mouth or frequently washed or cupped" has also fallen out of favor in recent years. Present-day snakebite treatment guidelines recommend cleansing the wound; using a light nontight elastic wrap just above and below the bite, rather than a tourniquet; keeping the relevant extremity positioned below heart level; transporting the bite victim to the nearest medical facility as soon as possible; and eventual appropriate antivenom therapy. Ice should never be applied and the use of oral suction is no longer advised. Modern suction/cupping devices remain available in commercial snakebite kits, but their use is controversial. For Kellogg's description of Johnson's treatment, see Barnard, *I Go With Custer*, 173–74 (first quotation); Chase, *Dr. Chase's Recipes*, 133–34 (second quotation), 390, 400 (third quotation). See Billroth, *General Surgical Pathology*, 359; see also Agnew, *Medicine in the Old West*, 169; McDougal, "Snakebitten," 125–27; and the following websites (all accessed May 31 or June 2, 2013): www.medicinenet.com/snake_bites/article.htm; http://ememedicine.medscape.com/article/168828treatment; www.wildlife.ca.gov/News/snake (California Department of Fish and Wildlife); www.calpoison.com/public/snakebite.html (California Poison Control); http://phoenix.about.cs/desert/ht/snakebite.htm; www.hitthetrail.com; www.outdoored.com/community/risk_managrment/b/wildmed/archive/2012/07/04/treating-rattlesnake-bites-in-the-field.aspx.

50. Camp No. 13, at Davis Creek, is also on the Little Missouri National Grassland's Wildlife and Scenic Tour. Chorne, *Following the Custer Trail*, 88.

51. The site of Camp No. 14, known as the Camp on the Little Missouri, is in Billings County, south of present-day Medora, across from the current Lutheran Bible Camp. See Chorne, *Following the Custer Trail*, 91. As DeWolf mentioned, this region's terrain was extremely difficult to cross and would become even worse as the expedition reached the Dakota Badlands.

52. Aside from the supposed assistance of the whiskey remedy, Kennedy's quick recovery without apparent disability was most likely because either his bite was from a small rattlesnake or he received no venom from it. Current statistics show that 25 percent of all rattlesnake bites are "dry," i.e., with no venom injected on the first bite. See California Department of Fish and Wildlife website, https://www.wildlife.ca.gov/News/snake (accessed July 27, 2016); see also McDougal, "Snakebitten," 126.

53. Harry Armstrong Reed (1858–76) was a nephew of the Custers. He signed on as a cattle herder for the expedition and was killed with his uncles on Last Stand Hill at the Little Big Horn. Boston Custer and he are both buried in Woodlawn Cemetery in Monroe, Michigan. Utley, *Cavalier in Buckskin*, 171, 191; Merington, *Custer Story*, 306–7; Nichols, *Men with Custer*, 272.

54. These were pockets of burning coal, emitting the characteristic "rotten egg" smell of sulfur. They remain abundant in western Dakota and eastern Montana and

were also noted beyond Camp No. 18 at O'Fallon Creek, as mentioned in Chorne, *Following the Custer Trail*, 124.

55. Camp No. 15 became known as the "Snow Camp" when a gloomy dismal rain turned into snow squalls that pelted and blanketed the ground for two days. The blizzard conditions made it miserable for the troops, horses, and mules. For a synopsis of these two days, see Chorne, *Following the Custer Trail*, 103–33; see also Kellogg's description in Barnard, *I Go with Custer*, diary entry of June 1, p. 204.

56. The army's civilian surgeons were allowed "a public horse, a tent, the necessary servants, and the privilege of purchasing stores from the Subsistence Department" while in the field. War Office, *Revised U.S. Army Regulations*, appx. B, no. 69, p. 518.

57. Private Fredrick Leeper was actually of Company L. He was from Hamilton County, Ohio, and had been in the Seventh Cavalry for four years. As a result of his hand infection, he was spared from the Little Big Horn, convalescing at the Yellowstone Depot. DeWolf also records that he had treated Leeper for constipation on March 15, correctly noting there that Leeper was in Company L; see DeWolf diary/notebook entry, Sick Report, Mar. 1876. See also Nichols, *Men with Custer*, 192; and Chorne, *Following the Custer Trail*, 109. The trooper with the "solidified lung" was Private William Kane of Company C; his condition was most likely pulmonary edema, as he was later diagnosed with valvular heart disease. He, too, was sent to the Yellowstone Depot and missed the Little Big Horn, eventually transferring to Fort Abraham Lincoln on July 19. He probably suffered from mitral valve stenosis, a fibrous or calcific thickening of the valve that funnels oxygenated blood from the left atrium to the left ventricle. It is rarely congenital and usually develops following rheumatic fever. Although two-thirds of mitral valve stenosis patients are female, most are younger and often suffer from symptoms by their fourth decade. Pulmonary edema (swelling and congestion) develops with the sudden increase in flow rate of blood across the narrowed valve opening. This leads to shortness of breath, congestion in the lungs, atrial arrhythmias, and fatigue with activities. Death usually occurs in two to five years unless surgery is performed. Of course, valvular replacement surgery was not available in the 1870s. Kane died at age forty-four in 1879. *Harrison's Principles of Internal Medicine*, 1096–2000; Gray, *Centennial Campaign*, 273. For a biographical sketch, see Nichols, *Men with Custer*, 170.

58. DeWolf hints at his faith and philosophy here. There is no recorded information to date that indicates James and Fannie's adherence to any religious denomination or church. However, his comments here, his overall demeanor, and the fact that he gave Fannie an engraved cross, as seen in her photo, suggests that they held to some religious faith.

59. Luce notes that John Gibbon, serving under Terry's command, had left Fort Ellis around April 1 with ten companies and that they were "marking time along the Yellowstone awaiting the arrival of the troops from Fort A. Lincoln." Luce, "Diary and Letters," 7. Gibbon was actually a colonel of the Seventh Infantry during the 1876 Sioux War and was not made a brigadier general until 1885, but Luce's note uses his later brevet rank. For an account of Gibbon's trek to the Yellowstone Depot, see

Hedren, *Great Sioux War*, 47–48; Hutton, *Phil Sheridan*, 302–4; and Gray, *Custer's Last Campaign*, 131–78.

60. This portion of the trail turns south at the North Dakota–Montana border and continues on to the Powder River. The site of the camp is 1.5 miles east of Montana Highway 7 and 8 miles south of Wibaux, Montana. Chorne, *Following the Custer Trail*, 114.

61. The Stanley Stockade (see chap. 2, n. 69).

62. Gray, *Custer's Last Campaign*, 158. DeWolf was correct in his prediction, as Gibbon only reported seeing several war parties. As occurred during the Powder River Fight in March, Crook's first deployment, it was Crook who would see initial action at Rosebud Creek on June 17.

63. The expedition was heading in a southern direction, and so this camp was located on the Wibaux-Fallon County line, about 1.5 miles east of Montana Highway 7; Chorne, *Following the Custer Trail*, 118. This region held some of the worst and most difficult terrain, hence the name "Badlands." In his more descriptive assessment for one of his columns, Kellogg related, "The scenery in the Bad Lands, that possesses the most picturesque and the most attractive, is that portion lying near the Powder River. The formations are more grotesque, more forcible, grander, and a considerable growth of spruce and cedar trees exist on the ranges, but the marching is more tedious, because of the rough formation; grasses are hardly seen, naught but sage brush, cactus, prairie dog villages and rattlesnakes are produced as one reached the head of this region that HIS SATANIC MAJESTY must have had supervision of during its creation." He summarized this declaration in his diary entry for June 5: "Worse road have had & worst country. Chief products sagebrush, cactus & rattlesnakes." Barnard, *I Go with Custer*, Kellogg Column no. 4, pp. 185–87 (first quotation), and diary entry for June 5, p. 205 (second quotation).

64. Camp No. 18 at Cabin/Pennel Creek, is northwest of Baker, Montana, on Montana Highway 7, in a location that was difficult to reach but not completely inaccessible. Chorne, *Following the Custer Trail*, 122.

65. First Sergeant James Hill (1826–1906) of Captain Thomas McDougall's Company B, Seventh Cavalry. Born in Scotland, he initially served in the Seventy-First Highland Light Infantry and later served in the U.S. Civil War. He fought gallantly in the Reno hilltop fight, according to McDougall. Hill died in Ohio of liver disease at the age of seventy-four. Overfield, *Little Big Horn*, 157 (troop roster listing). For a biographical sketch, see Nichols, *Men with Custer*, 149.

66. Camp No. 19, the O'Fallon Creek camp site, is a quarter mile west of Ismay, Montana, north of U.S. Highway 12. Chorne, *Following the Custer Trail*, 125.

67. Private David McWilliams (b. 1849) of Benteen's Company H, Seventh Cavalry. McWilliams's injury placed him in the Powder River Camp hospital and thereby saved him from possible injury or death at the Little Big Horn. Born in Scotland but married to a woman from Kentucky, he enlisted in the Seventh Cavalry in 1866, serving until his discharge in 1880. McWilliams's wound missed vital neurovascular structures; even with penetration through the soft tissues of the gastrocnemius

(calf) muscle or Achilles tendon, such partial tears and single-track gunshot wounds often heal well. However, he was extremely lucky in avoiding infection. His ability to resume a full career in the cavalry for another twelve years suggests that the wound was not extensive. For biographical details, see Barnard, *I Go with Custer*, 205; Overfield, *Little Big Horn*, 176; and Nichols, *Men with Custer*, 224.

68. The Powder River Camp, Camp No. 20, is near Locate, Montana, 3 miles north of old U.S. Highway 12 and south of I-94; Chorne, *Following the Custer Trail*, 131. At this point, DeWolf's diary contains no record of camps 20 through 24, because he was not with Custer and the main column, being assigned to go on the special Tongue River scout with Reno's wing (see n. 70). While the doctor's diary entries provide information about the various struggles and camp sites on the Tongue River scout expedition, he apparently had no time to write to his wife during those days, as there are no extant letters between June 8 and June 21.

69. Heliotrope is a perennial flowering plant that produces clusters of vivid rich cherry/pink or lavender flowers. The sweet-smelling fragrance has given the heliotrope its nickname "cherry pie plant." They are still abundant in the northern plains states today and are popularly used in gardens. *Perennials*, 46, 78–79.

70. This was the controversial Reno Scout. See Hardorff, "Reno Scout"; Hedren, *Great Sioux War*, 104–5; Nichols, *In Custer's Shadow*, 151–60; Stewart and Luce, "Reno Scout"; Willert, "Another Look"; and Moore, *Where the Custer Fight Began*, 28–29. DeWolf's diary only provides the daily movements and some brief details of this miniexpedition. However, John S. Gray has compiled an excellent table and discussion summarizing DeWolf's recording of mileage during the Reno reconnaissance scout, which Gray personally traced and measured; see Gray, *Custer's Last Campaign*, 184–87.

71. Hardtack was among the standard rations issued to the soldiers by the U.S. Army during the Civil War and subsequent Indian wars. It was a plain flour-and-water biscuit, similar to but harder than the present-day soda cracker. Soldiers often crumbled it in their coffee to soften it and make it more palatable. John Billings, a veteran of the Civil War, noted that two hardtack biscuits "in [his] possession measure[d] 3 1/8 inches × 2 and 7/8 inches, and nearly half an inch thick." Shipped and distributed to the regimental commissaries, hardtack often became infested with maggots and weevils during storage. Once again, DeWolf hints at the difference in social status between the commissioned officers and staff and the enlisted men, as the former dined better in camp. Billings, *Hardtack and Coffee*, 113–18.

72. The Dakota Column's Gatling guns have always been an intriguing and controversial topic of discussion among those who study Custer and the Little Big Horn. The three-gun battery was manned by a provisional company of two officers and twenty-four enlisted men of the Twentieth Infantry, commanded by Second Lieutenant William H. Low of Company C and his second-in-command, Second Lieutenant Frank X. Kinzie of Company F. The controversy arose from the premise that Custer might have avoided full disaster had he not declined Terry's offer to take the guns with him, believing that they would slow him down, especially since he lacked a healthy, serviceable horse to haul them. Although this is vigorously debated

by many, there is unquestionable merit to the encumbrance premise, as evidenced by DeWolf's relation of the difficulties in hauling the Gatling gun on the Reno Scout. For the definitive history of the Gatling Gun battery, see Noyes, "Guns 'Long Hair' Left Behind"; and Noyes, "Guns Custer Left Behind." For the return of the Twentieth Infantry Gatling gun detachment, see Overfield, *Little Big Horn*, 144–45.

73. Luce writes, "It is not clear whether this word was intended to be 'grass' or 'game.' The presence of large bodies of Indians with their pony herds could create a scarcity of either." Luce, "Diary and Letters," 9.

74. Gibbon's command was camped "on the north bank of the Yellowstone River opposite the mouth of the Rosebud Creek" between June 14 and 21. Ibid.

75. The "old trading fort" was, as Luce notes, most likely Fort Van Buren. "Built about 1835 for the American Fur Company by Samuel Tullock" on the Yellowstone River near the mouth of Rosebud Creek. The fort was named for the eighth U.S. president. Its operator, Charles Larpenteur, burned the fort in 1842 and built nearby Fort Alexander to take its place. In his 1876 journal, Lieutenant James H. Bradley described the evidence of the fire, as well as the remaining portions of seven stone chimneys and a ridge where the palisade stood. Luce, "Diary and Letters," 9 (quotation); Stewart, *March of the Montana Column*, 80, 113–14; for both forts, see also http://files.usgwarchives.net/mt/statewide/military/forts.txt (accessed Aug. 11, 2013 and July 27, 2016).

76. The officers and staff received abundant whiskey supplies on the expedition, including DeWolf, although he was not a huge consumer of alcohol. However, the enlisted men received whiskey only when the sutlers were permitted to dispense liquor at the accessible camp sites, such as the Rosebud and previously at the Heart and Powder Rivers. Sutler John Smith and his employee, John Coleman, sold whiskey and other goods to the soldiers, who often squandered their hard-earned pay and imbibed as much drink as they could. Kellogg noted that the "Paymaster is paying off the troops, this p.m., and the 'boys' will have a 'stake' in their pockets for a much longer period than they usually keep one there." Kellogg diary entry of May 17, in Bernard, *I Go with Custer*, 171. See Chorne, *Following the Custer Trail*, 152, 182; and DeWolf, letter to Fannie, June 17.

77. First Lieutenant George Edwin Lord (1846–76) of the Sixth Infantry was born in Boston and adopted at an early age by Reverend Thomas Lord of Maine. He graduated from Bowdoin College in that state in 1866 and from Chicago Medical School (now Northwestern University) in 1871. Lord served as an acting assistant surgeon (contract surgeon) in the Department of Dakota at various posts, including Fort Abraham Lincoln in 1875. That year, he passed the army medical board examinations and was appointed as an assistant surgeon. Assigned to the Sixth Infantry, he served at Fort Buford in Dakota before returning to Fort Abraham Lincoln in early 1876. He was eventually assigned to take Williams's place as the chief medical officer on Custer's Seventh Cavalry staff and the Yellowstone/Little Big Horn expedition in June that year. See Nichols, *Men with Custer*, 197–98; and Noyes, "Custer's Surgeon."

78. Sunstroke (heatstroke or hyperpyrexia) involves the shutdown of the body's

heat-controlling or cooling mechanisms because of a combination of overheating and dehydration. Direct exposure to the sun is not an absolute requirement. Sunstroke occurs in temperatures of 90°F or higher, with humidity in the minimum range of 60–75 percent. Initial symptoms include disorientation, confusion, incoherent speech, cessation of sweating, flushed skin, cardiac arrhythmia (rapid heartbeat), and low blood pressure. A patient's temperature is usually at or above 105°F (as measured today). Unconsciousness and death will occur rapidly if emergency treatment is not rendered. Sunstroke is treated essentially the same way today as it was in the late nineteenth century, with some minor exceptions. The afflicted person should be taken out of the sun, his clothes removed, and the mechanism reversed by cooling and rehydration, placing wet cold towels on the body, and fanning. In modern medicine, full-body ice immersion and intravenous fluids are administered in an attempt to reduce the person's core body temperature to around 100°F as quickly as possible. Sunstroke was common among soldiers and men who worked in the heavy heat of the West. In addition to the aforementioned measures, some nineteenth-century sources also note the use of leeches to bleed and then recommend to "send for a surgeon"—analogous to transporting the patient to a hospital as soon as possible. Also, DeWolf is referring here to the fact that "whiskey," i.e., consumption of alcohol, contributes to dehydration, though he indicates that the two soldiers mentioned were dehydrated only by their sunstroke, as neither had partaken of any whiskey. Moreover, their sunstroke was caught in the early stages, as DeWolf describes their conditions as mild. Agnew, *Medicine in the Old West*, 170; Chase, *Dr. Chase's Recipes*, 387; Billroth, *General Surgical Pathology*, 249; *Harrison's Principles of Internal Medicine*, 56–57; Roy and Irvin, *Sports Medicine*, 481–82.

79. Although pronghorn antelope and bighorn sheep are still abundant in the northern plains states, the American buffalo population has not fared as well. Buffalo herds in North America were estimated as high as 60 million in the early 1800s and the northern herd about 2 million at the time of the Great Sioux War. The latter had been reduced to an estimated 250,000 by 1882. By 1890, the population was decimated to an estimated 1,000 or fewer animals, having been killed off for food, sport, and the highly desired hides for eastern business markets during the expansion of the railroads and eventual introduction of the cattle industry. Through preservation efforts that began in the twentieth century, an estimated 500,000 buffalo remain in North America today in private and public herds. The former are raised for food, while public herds are preserved at various national and state parks such as Custer State Park, Badlands National Park in South Dakota, and Theodore Roosevelt National Park in North Dakota, as well as an estimated 19,000 free-roaming buffalo in Yellowstone National Park. On the plight of the American buffalo, see Hedren, *After Custer*, 92–110; and Lott, *American Bison*, 167–85.

80. This was DeWolf's last letter to his wife. He and many of his colleagues clearly believed there would be no contact with the Indians and predicted that the campaign would end soon.

CHAPTER 4.
"IF HE HAD GOTTEN A FEW FEET FURTHER..."

1. The accounts of these early morning reconnoiters at the Crow's Nest on June 25, as described by those who were there, are contained in multiple sources. See Graham, *Custer Myth*, 20–23, 31–33, 342 (for narratives of the Crow scout White Man Runs Him, the Arikara scout Red Star, and Varnum's letter of July 4, 1876, to his parents, respectively); Hammer, *Custer in '76*, 59–60 (for Varnum's 1909 interview with Walter Camp); and Gray, *Custer's Last Campaign*, 220–41 (for a meticulous review of accounts and an itinerary-chronology of the Crow's Nest activities). See also Donovan, *Terrible Glory*, 200–209; Philbrick, *Last Stand*, 139–41; and Sarf, *Little Bighorn Campaign*, 180–85.

2. Nichols, *In Custer's Shadow*, 171; Gray, *Custer's Last Campaign*, 245.

3. Walker, *Dr. Henry R. Porter*, 55–56; Noyes, "Custer's Surgeon," 18.

4. For discussion/speculation of some theories, see Unger, *ABCs of Custer's Last Stand*, 54–55. Currently, despite a meticulous search of primary documents, no author has discovered any comment on Custer's medical personnel assignments by any of the officers who survived the Little Big Horn battle.

5. For Benteen's testimony, see Nichols, *Reno Court of Inquiry*, 403; for his statement to the *New York Herald*, Aug. 8, 1876, see Graham, *Custer Myth*, 227.

6. Gray, *Custer's Last Campaign*, 253–55 (Varnum's sighting), 257, 273–75 (Gerard's sighting). Some historians believed that Frank Gerard saw the fleeing Sioux Indians at the lone tepee, but Gray established that Gerard's sighting was a second one occurring not at the lone tepee but beyond that location at a ridge overlooking the Little Big Horn valley.

7. Ibid., 275.

8. Reno to E. W. Smith, July 5, 1876, in Overfield, *Little Big Horn*, 44 (quotations); for Reno's testimony, see Nichols, *Reno Court of Inquiry*, 44.

9. Nichols, *Reno Court of Inquiry*, 516.

10. Gray, *Custer's Last Campaign*, 272.

11. Quoted in Overfield, *Little Bighorn*, 44.

12. The location of the skirmish line is discussed in Moore, *Where the Custer Fight Began*, 121–32.

13. Nichols, *Reno Court of Inquiry*, 284, 564.

14. For Porter's testimony, see ibid., 190, 196. See also Walker, *Dr. Henry R. Porter*, 56; and Stevenson, *Deliverance*, 45–46, 180. This was most likely Private Henry Klotzbucher. See also Nichols, *Men with Custer*, 182; and Brininstool, *Troopers with Custer*, 51.

15. For Porter's testimony, see Nichols, *Reno Court of Inquiry*, 196, 205, 212.

16. Ibid., 562.

17. For accounts of their deaths, see Nichols, *Reno Court of Inquiry*, 88–89 (Reynolds); Brininstool, *Troopers with Custer*, 318–20 (Reynolds); Graham, *Custer Myth*, 140 (Hodgson); Barnard, *Ten Years with Custer*, 296 (Hodgson); and Hardorff, *Custer*

Battle Casualties II, 93–98, 124–25, 125–26 (Hodgson, Dorman, and Reynolds, respectively). Distraught over the death of his close friend Hodgson, Reno later ordered a small contingent of soldiers to retrieve the officer's body during a lull in the fighting.

18. Nichols, *Reno Court of Inquiry*, 197.

19. Brininstool, *Troopers with Custer*, 53. Slaper (1854–1931), a private in Troop M, was under the command of Captain Thomas H. French in Reno's battalion. Originally from Cincinnati, he was a safe maker before enlisting in the cavalry in 1875. Despite his part in obtaining water for the wounded during the Reno hilltop defense, he was not one of the Little Big Horn battle recipients of the Medal of Honor. Slaper provided an extensive account of his experience of the battle for Brininstool in 1920. He died in Sawtelle, California, and is buried in Los Angeles National Cemetery. See Nichols, *Men with Custer*, 109, 306.

20. Barnard, *Ten Years with Custer*, 296.

21. Nichols, *Reno Court of Inquiry*, 151. The official government transcript of the Reno court of inquiry of 1879 has several published versions, which are essentially the same. Some offer minor variations because several reporters from different newspapers contributed to it, but they are essentially the same in relating the lieutenant's testimony. The transcript is also contained in Unger, *Reno Court of Inquiry*.

22. Utley, *Reno Court of Inquiry* (first paragraph) and Carrol, *Custer's Chief of Scouts* (second paragraph), both quoted in Hardorff, *Custer Battle Casualties II*, p. 121, no. 377, no. 379.

23. Hardorff, *Custer Battle Casualties II*, p. 121, no. 378.

24. Nichols, *Reno Court of Inquiry*, 350. Sergeant Edward Davern (1844–96), a private in Company F at the time of the Little Big Horn battle, was from Ireland and went on to serve in the Seventh Cavalry. After his army career, Davern died in Washington, D.C., and is buried in Arlington National Cemetery. See Nichols, *Men with Custer*, 79.

25. Nichols, *Reno Court of Inquiry*, 54, 56.

26. "The Story of Sergeant Kanipe, One of Custer's Messengers," (from *Daily Record* [Greensboro, N.C.], Apr. 27, 1924), in Graham, *Custer Myth*, 249. Sergeant Daniel A. Kanipe (1834–79) of Company C of the Seventh Cavalry was originally from North Carolina and had been a farmer before enlisting in the cavalry in 1872; he had not served in the Civil War. After the Little Big Horn, he served with the Seventh Cavalry until 1882 and then was employed by the U.S. Revenue Service for twenty years. Kanipe died in 1926 in his hometown of Marion, North Carolina. For a more detailed biographical sketch, see Nichols, *Men with Custer*, 170. For Kanipe's Little Big Horn accounts, see Hammer, *Custer in '76*, 91–98; Graham, *Custer Myth*, 140, 247–50; and Unger, *Custer's First Messenger?*

27. Brust et al., *Where Custer Fell*, 55–59; Nichols, *Reno Court of Inquiry*, 278–79, 335; Nichols, *Men with Custer*, 1, 57 (Abbott and Clear, respectively).

28. Hardorff, *Custer Battle Casualties II*, p. 122, no. 383.

29. Stevenson, *Deliverance*, 53–71, 80–83; Walker, *Dr. Henry R. Porter*, 57–59, 61–63; Nichols, *Reno Court of Inquiry*, 189–90, 207 (Porter's testimony).

30. Graham, "General Godfrey's Narrative," in *Custer Myth*, 143. In later years, Porter thought this the most accurate account of the action at the Little Big Horn, although not without some personal bias on the part of Godfrey toward Reno; see Walker, *Dr. Henry R. Porter*, 60.

31. Graham, "General Godfrey's Narrative," in *Custer Myth*, 146.

32. Graham, *Custer Myth*, 376 ("General Godfrey Describes the Burials," from *The Century*, 1892).

33. The published literature concerning the burials and care for the wounded is vast. A less-known description is the original letter of the chief medical officer, Dr. J. W. Williams, concerning the "ambulance" beds used after the battle. In this three-page letter, Williams describes the mule "litter ambulances" or travois devised to transport the wounded to the junction of the Little Big Horn and Big Horn Rivers and eventually to the steamboat *Far West*. The description also contains Williams's hand-drawn sketch of a mule and the litter. Statement of J. W. Williams, June 25, 1876, W.O. 94, Medical File B177, AGO, photocopy in WSL/LIBI.

34. Hardorff, *Custer Battle Casualties*, p. 147, no. 249.

35. H. R. Porter to Mrs. Fanny DeWolf, July 28, 1876, DeWolf Collection, WSL/LIBI.

36. For Porter's testimony, see Nichols, *Reno Court of Inquiry*, 188–89. While going down into the bottom, Porter said, "[Major Reno] asked me if I didn't want his gun. He had a gun on the pommel of his saddle, or over his shoulder. I don't remember which. He asked me if I didn't want it, and I told him 'no.'"

37. H. R. Porter to Mrs. Fanny DeWolf, Sep. 14, 1876, DeWolf Collection, WSL/LIBI.

38. Nichols, *Reno Court of Inquiry*, 207.

39. Porter's biographer cites the scout Charley Reynolds's last words of warning to Porter during the fight in the timber in the moments before Reynolds was killed, in which Reynolds purportedly shouted, "Look out Doctor, the Indian's are shooting at you!" in reference to Porter being an easy target because of the "white" linen duster he was wearing (Walker, *Dr. Henry R. Porter*, 56). This would actually have been a cream color, as such linen dusters appeared almost white in the hot sun. Porter confirms that DeWolf was wearing this same attire and therefore made a similar target.

40. Extract of Monthly Report of Sick and Wounded, Station in the Field, on Little Big Horn River, M.T., June 1876 (concerning Acting Assistant Surgeon James DeWolf), Dec. 8, 1876, SGO, no. 149 (A–B), DeWolf Collection, WSL/LIBI.

41. P. H. Sheridan to Alfred H. Terry, Mar. 26, 1877, AGO, WSL/LIBI.

42. P. H. Sheridan to secretary of War, May 7, 1877, AGO, WSL/LIBI (emphasis in the original).

43. P. H. Sheridan to M. V. Sheridan, May 16, 1877, AGO, WSL/LIBI.

44. P. H. Sheridan to Alfred H. Terry, Apr. 18, 1877, AGO, WSL/LIBI.

45. M. V. Sheridan to Lt. Cooke's father, July 16, 1877, and M. V. Sheridan to Mrs. L. M. Johnson, May 14, 1877, NARA, Consolidated File 4163, AGO, 1876, photocopy in WSL/LIBI. Transportation of the bodies to Fort Leavenworth was to be at the

families' and/or their friends' expense. The Fort Leavenworth designation was later discontinued and the bodies of the officers allowed to be buried where their families desired, again at their own expense.

46. Graham, *Custer Myth*, 377; Nichols, *Men with Custer*, 177.

47. G.O. 101, Nov. 8, 1877, E. D. Townsend, adj. gen., per W. T. Sherman, AGO, WSL/LIBI. For an extensive history of Fort Custer, see Upton, *Fort Custer*. See also Barnes, *Forts of the Northern Plains*, 38–40; Polka, *Fort Custer*; Frazer, *Forts of the West*, 79–80; and Upton, *Indian as a Soldier*.

48. Michael V. Sheridan to editor, *Chicago* Tribune, July 30, 1877 (as quoted in Hardorff, *Custer Battle Casualties II*, p. 29, no. 37 (both quotations). For Sheridan's report, see Graham, *Custer Myth*, 373, 375.

49. For Sheridan's report, see Graham, *Custer Myth*, 375. At the initial internments, Porter said he "cut a lock of hair from the head of each officer and gave it to their families on [his] return home." Hardorff, *Custer Battle Casualties II*, p. 27, no. 27 (Porter, *St. Louis Globe Democrat* undated clipping), p. 23, no. 386 (Reno's supposition).

50. List of Officers Remains Taken to Fort Lincoln, July 12, 1877, AGO, WSL/LIBI.

51. Michael V. Sheridan to Mrs. Fanny DeWolf, July 16, 1877, DeWolf Collection, WSL/LIBI.

52. *Norwalk Reflector*, Aug. 16, 1876; also noted in *Huron County Chronicle* (Norwalk, Ohio), Aug. 18, 1876.

53. The letter was signed by Albert F. Heaynes [Haynes], secretary of the Pequossette Lodge, and lodge committee members Charles H. Bradlee, Charles T. Perkins, and Samuel F. Steams. Pequossette Lodge of Free Masons to Mrs. Fannie DeWolf, Sep. 27, 1876 (resolutions and tribute), Sep. 30, 1876 (letter), Microfilm Whole No. 2144, NPL.

54. David T. Hall (b. 1832–d. 1906) was born in New York and eventually moved to the Norwalk area. He was married to Emma Downing (1840–1914), who was born in Norwalk. He served in the 123rd Ohio Volunteer Infantry during the Civil War, becoming an insurance agent in Norwalk afterward. He and Emma had five children; Minnie Hall (1856–1947), who married William B. Darling; Frank Hall (1858–75); Charles Henry (1860–62); Harry T. Hall (1862–after 1930); and George Oliver Hall (1880–1930). David, Emma, and their children are buried with James and Fannie in the Hall-DeWolf family plot in Greenlawn Cemetery at Norwalk. Personal correspondence with Henry Timman, Huron Co. historian, Norwalk, Ohio, Apr. 23, 2009, and Oct. 4, 2013.

55. *Norwalk Experiment*, Aug. 6, 1877; *Norwalk Reflector*, Aug. 8, 1877 (the quotation is from both newspapers).

Epilogue

1. Erb and Erb, *Voices in Our Souls*, 184–85. See also Siebert, *History of Ohio State University*, 5:14, 258, 262–64; and http://archive.org/stream/historyofohiosta41ohio

/historyofohiosta41ohio_djvu.txt (accessed Oct. 7, 2013). Verne Dodd died in 1957, and Dodd Hall at Ohio State University is named for him; see http://library.osu.edu/blogs/mhcb/2012/06/18/dodd-hall/ (accessed Oct. 7, 2013).

2. Department of the Interior, Bureau of Pensions, Washington, D.C., July 16, 1912, and May 19, 1918, War Department Records, AGO, DeWolf Collection, WSL/LIBI.

3. Erb and Erb, *Voices in Our Souls*, 167, 170, 176, 194. Information also from author's personal visit and interview with Gene and Ann DeWolf Erb, June 25, 2013.

4. DeWolf's grave in the Woodlawn Cemetery Directory is Sec. 20, Lot 155, Grave 1.

Appendix A

1. Jedediah Hyde Baxter (d. 1890) was a Vermont native and a Civil War veteran surgeon in the Twelfth Massachusetts Volunteers. Baxter was a colonel and served as chief medical purchaser at this time, appointed to that position in 1872. Heitman, *Historical Register* (1903), 200.

2. Major Rodney Smith was the paymaster on duty in the Department of Dakota. Originally from Vermont, Smith was promoted to major and appointed as paymaster during the Civil War in 1864 in Kentucky. While his counterpart, Major William Smith, served the posts farther west in Dakota Territory (see chap. 2, n. 10), Rodney Smith's region for troop payments included Forts Snelling and Ripley in Minnesota and Forts Abercrombie, Wadsworth, Seward, Totten, and Pembina in Dakota Territory. He was later promoted to colonel in the Paymaster Department in 1886 and retired from the army in June 1893. Heitman, *Historical Register* (1903), 903; see also *Army and Navy Journal*, July 12, 1873, 760.

Bibliography

ARCHIVAL MATERIALS
Firelands Historical Society Museum, Norwalk, Ohio
James M. DeWolf, *Synopsis of Services Performed, Volunteer Service* (photocopy)
James M. DeWolf Papers

National Archives and Records Administration, Washington, D.C.
Available online at www.ancestry.com
Adjutant General's Office Records (RG 94)
Camp Hancock Post Returns, 1872–1877, Microfilm Publication M617, roll 451
Camp Lyon Post Returns, 1865–1869, Microfilm Publication M617, roll 662
Camp Warner Post Returns, 1865–1874, Microfilm Publication M617, roll 1349
Fort Abercrombie Post Returns, 1858–1877, Microfilm Publication M617, roll 1
Fort Abraham Lincoln Post Returns, 1872–1880, Microfilm Publication M617, roll 628
Fort Clark Post Returns, 1866–1881, Microfilm Publication M617, roll 214
Fort Pembina Post Returns, 1870–1881, Microfilm Publication M617, roll 899
Fort Ripley Post Returns, 1866–1877, Microfilm Publication M617, roll 1027
Fort Seward Post Returns, 1872–1877, Microfilm Publication M617, roll 1153
Fort Sisseton Post Returns, 1873–1880, Microfilm Publication M617, roll 1180
Fort Snelling Post Returns, 1874–1884, Microfilm Publication M617, roll 1197
Fourth Infantry Regimental Returns, 1876–1885, Microfilm Publication M665, roll 47
General Index to Pension Files, 1861–1934, Microfilm Publication T-288
Ninth Infantry Regimental Returns, 1870–1879, Microfilm Publication M665, roll 104
Office of the Quartermaster General, 1818–1905 (RG 92)
Registry of Enlistments in the U.S. Army, 1798–1914, Microfilm Publication M233 (available at www.familysearch.org)

Seventeenth Infantry Regimental Returns, 1872–1880, Microfilm Publication M665, roll 184
Seventh Cavalry Regimental Returns, 1874–1881, Microfilm Publication M665, roll 72
Seventh Infantry Regimental Returns, 1874–1884, Microfilm Publication M665, roll 83
Sixth Infantry Regimental Returns, 1869–1878, Microfilm Publication M665, roll 70
Twentieth Infantry Regimental Returns, 1874–1881, Microfilm Publication M665, roll 212
Watertown Arsenal Post Returns, 1874–1883, Microfilm Publication M617, roll 1389

Norwalk Public Library, Norwalk, Ohio
Huron County Chronicles
Norwalk City Directories
Norwalk Experiment
Norwalk Reflector
Notary Public Records, Norwalk Village, Ohio, Huron County
U.S. Census Records, Norwalk Village, Ohio, Huron County

Pennsylvania Historic and Museum Commission State Archives
Available via PHMC Internet access
Land Records–Survey Group and Warrant Reports
Pennsylvania (State) Death Certificates, 1906–1963, Series 11.90, Records of the Pennsylvania Department of Health, Record Group 11

State Historical Society of North Dakota
Dana M. Wright Papers
Fort Totten Medical History Log
North Dakota Newspapers Index (available online)

Watertown Free Public Library, Watertown, Mass.
Watertown City Directories (available online)

White Swan Library, Little Bighorn Battlefield National Monument
DeWolf Collection (including his original diary and a microfilm copy of the diary and letters, as well as photocopies of the DeWolf Papers from the National Archives and Records Administration, Surgeon General of the Army and Adjutant General's Office)
Philip H. Sheridan and Michael V. Sheridan Letters (photocopies of letters from the National Archives and Records Administration, Records of the War Department, Adjutant General's Office)

Wyoming County Historical Society and Genealogical Museum, Tunkhannock, Pa.
Index of Deeds, Wyoming County, Pennsylvania
Tunkhannock Republican
U.S. Census Records for Luzerne County, Pennsylvania
U.S. Census Records for Wyoming County, Pennsylvania
Wyoming Republican

PUBLISHED MATERIALS

Adams, George Worthington. *Doctors in Blue: The Medical History of the Union Army in the Civil War.* Dayton, Ohio: Press of Morningside, 1985.
Adams, Kevin. *Class and Race in the Frontier Army: Military Life in the West, 1870–1890.* Norman: University of Oklahoma Press, 2009.
Agnew, Jeremy. *Medicine in the Old West: A History, 1850–1900.* Jefferson, N.C.: McFarland, 2001.
Album of Genealogy and Biography, Cook County, Illinois. Chicago: Calumet Press, 1909.
Army and Navy Journal. New York: Publication Office, Vols. X, XI, 1873.
Ashburn, Percy M. *A History of the Medical Department of the United States Army.* Boston: Houghton Mifflin, 1992.
Athearn, Robert G. *William Tecumseh Sherman and the Settlement of the West.* Norman: University of Oklahoma Press, 1956.
Bach, Melva M. "Camp Warner Moved to Hone Creek [in] 1867." In *History of the Fremont National Forest*, 14–16. Lakeview, Ore.: Fremont National Forest, U.S. Forest Service, U.S. Department of Agriculture, 1981.
Baker, Robert Orr. *The Muster Roll: A Biography of Fort Ripley, Minnesota.* St. Paul, Minn.: H. M. Smyth, 1970.
Barnard, Sandy. *I Go with Custer: The Life and Death of Reporter Mark Kellogg.* Bismarck, N.Dak.: Bismarck Tribune, 1996.
―――, ed. *Ten Years with Custer: A 7th Cavalryman's Memoirs.* Terre Haute, Ind.: AST Press, 2001.

Barnes, Jeff. *Forts of the Northern Plains*. Mechanicsburg, Pa.: Stackpole Books, 2008.

Barnes, Joseph K. *The Medical and Surgical History of the War of the Rebellion (1861–65), Prepared, in Accordance with Acts of Congress, under the Direction of Surgeon General Joseph K. Barnes, United States Army*. 5 vols. Washington, D.C.: U.S. Government Printing Office, 1870–83.

Bates, Samuel P. *History of the Pennsylvania Volunteers, 1861–1865*. Harrisburg: Pennsylvania State Printer, 1869. Reprint, Wilmington, N.C.: Broadfoot Publishing, 1993.

Bergen, Theodore C. "New Historical Marker Dedicated Fort Pembina Site near Pembina Airport." *Minnesota History* 12, no. 4 (1931).

Billings, John D. *Hardtack and Coffee: Soldier's Life in the Civil War*. 1888. Reprint, East Bridgewater, Mass.: World Publications Group with Konecky and Konecky and JG Press, 1996.

Billroth, Theodore. *General Surgical Pathology and Therapeutics, in Fifty Lectures: A Text-Book for Students and Physicians*. New York: D. Appleton, 1871.

Bode, E. A. *A Dose of Frontier Soldiering: The Memoirs of Corporal E. A. Bode, Frontier Regular Infantry, 1877–1882*. Edited by Thomas T. Smith. Lincoln: University of Nebraska Press, 1994. Reprint, Lincoln: Bison Books, 1999.

Boulay, Peter. *The History of Weather Observations, Fort Ripley, Minnesota, 1849–1990*. St. Paul: Minnesota State Climatology Office, DNR Division of Waters, 2006.

Bourke, John Gregory. *On the Border with Crook*. New York: Charles Scribner and Sons, 2007.

Brands, H. W. *The Man Who Saved the Union: Ulysses Grant in War and Peace*. New York: Doubleday, 2012.

Brininstool, E. A. *Troopers with Custer: Historic Incidents of the Battle of the Little Big Horn*. New York: Bonanza Books, 1952. Reprint, Lincoln: University of Nebraska Press, 1988.

Brown, Bill A. *Fort Seward, Territory of Dakota, Jamestown*. Jamestown, N.Dak.: Two Rivers Printing, 1987.

Brust, James S., Brian C. Pohanka, and Sandy Barnard. *Where Custer Fell: Photographs of the Little Bighorn Battlefield Then and Now*. Norman: University of Oklahoma Press, 2005.

Buckley, John Wells. "The War Hospitals." In *Washington during War Time: A Series of Papers Showing the Military, Political, and Social Phases during 1861 to 1865*, edited by Marcus Benjamin, 138–53. Washington, D.C.: National Tribune Press, 1902.

Carroll, John M. *Custer's Chief of Scouts: Varnum*. Lincoln: University of Nebraska Press, 1987.

———. *Frank Anders: The Custer Trail of 1876.* Glendale, Calif.: Arthur H. Clark, 1983.
Chambers, Lee. *Fort Abraham Lincoln, Dakota Territory.* Atglen, Pa.: Schiffer Publishing, 2008.
Chappell, Gordon. *Brass Spikes and Horsetail Plumes: A History of U.S. Army Dress Helmets, 1872–1904.* 3rd ed. Gettysburg, Pa.: Thomas Publications, 1997.
Chase, A. W. *Dr. Chase's Recipes or Information for Everybody—An Invaluable Collection of Over One Thousand Practical Recipes.* Chicago: Thompson and Thomas, 1867. Revised ed., 1900.
Chorne, Laudie J. *Following the Custer Trail.* Bismarck, N.Dak.: Trails West, 2001.
Connell, Evan S. *Son of the Morning Star: Custer and the Little Bighorn.* New York: History Book Club, 1984. Reprinted 2001.
Cross, Walt. *Custer's Lost Officer: The Search for Lieutenant Henry Moore Harrington, 7th U.S. Cavalry.* Stillwater, Okla.: Cross Publications, 2006.
Cunningham, H. H. *Doctors in Gray: The Confederate Medical Service.* 2nd ed. Baton Rouge: Louisiana State University Press, 1960.
Custer, Elizabeth B. *Boots and Saddles; or, Life in Dakota with General Custer.* Norman: University of Oklahoma Press, 1968.
Custer, George Armstrong. *My Life on the Plains; or, Personal Experiences with Indians.* Norman: University of Oklahoma Press, 1962.
Darling, Roger. *Benteen's Scout to the Left: The Route from the Divide to the Morass, June 25, 1876.* El Segundo, Calif.: Upton and Sons, 2000.
Davison, Kathleen, ed. *Fort Totten Military Post and Indian School, 1867–1959.* Bismarck, N.Dak.: State Historical Society of North Dakota, 1986. 2nd ed., 2010.
Dawson, Joseph G., III. *Army Generals and Reconstruction: Louisiana, 1862–1877.* Baton Rouge: Louisiana State University Press, 1994.
DeLee, Jesse C., David Drez Jr., and Mark D. Miller. *Orthopaedic Sports Medicine: Principles and Practice.* 2 vols. Philadelphia: Saunders, 2003.
DeWolf, Thomas Norman. *Inheriting the Trade: A Northern Family Confronts Its Legacy as the Largest Slave-Trading Dynasty in U.S. History.* Boston: Beacon Press, 2006.
Dobbs, Judy D. *A History of the Watertown Arsenal, 1816–1967.* Watertown, Mass.: U.S. Army Materials and Mechanics Research Center and Via Appia Press, 1977.
Donahue, Michael. *Drawing Battle Lines: The Map Testimony of Custer's Last Fight.* El Segundo, Calif.: Upton and Sons, 2008.
Donovan, James. *A Terrible Glory: Custer and the Little Bighorn, the Last Great Battle of the American West.* New York: Little, Brown, 2008.
Donovan, Terrence J. *Brazen Trumpet: Frederick W. Benteen at the Battle of the Little Big Horn.* Lancaster, Calif.: Mojavewest, 2007.

Dryer, Frederick. *A Compendium of the War of the Rebellion: Compiled and Arranged from Official Records of the Federal and Confederate Armies*. Des Moines, Iowa: Dryer Publishing, 1908.

Dunlop, Richard. "Fighting Doctors of the Frontier." *Westerners' Brand Book* 20 (January 1964): 81–88.

Earls, Alan R. *Watertown Arsenal (Images of America)*. Charlestown, S.C.: Arcadia Publishing, 2007.

Eicher, John H., and David J. Eicher. *Civil War High Commands*. Stanford: Stanford University Press, 2001.

Elias, Stephen N. *Alexander T. Stewart: The Forgotten Merchant Prince*. Westport, Conn.: Praeger, 1992.

Erb, Gene, and Ann DeWolf Erb. *Voices in Our Souls: The DeWolfs, Dakota Sioux and the Little Bighorn*. Santa Fe, N.Mex.: Sunstone Press, 2010.

Ferris, Robert G., ed. "Camp Lyon." In *Soldier and Brave: Historic Places Associated with Indian Affairs and the Indian Wars in the Trans-Mississippi West*, edited by Robert G. Ferris, 100. National Survey of Historic Sites and Buildings 11. Washington, D.C.: U.S. Department of Interior, National Park Service, 1971.

———. "Fort Vancouver National Historic Site." In *Prospector, Cowhand and Sodbuster: Historic Places Associated with the Mining, Ranching, and Farming Frontier in the Trans-Mississippi West*, edited by Robert G. Ferris, 101–3. National Survey of Historic Sites and Buildings 11. Washington, D.C.: U.S. Department of Interior, National Park Service, 1967.

Fougera, Katherine Gibson. *With Custer's Cavalry*. Caldwell, Idaho: Caxton Printers, 1940. Reprint, Bison Books, 1986.

Fox, Richard A., Jr., Melissa A. Connor, and Dick Harmon. *Archaeological Perspectives on the Battle of the Little Bighorn*. Norman: University of Oklahoma Press, 1989.

———. *Archaeology, History, and Custer's Last Stand*. Norman: University of Oklahoma Press, 1993.

Frazer, Robert W. *Forts of the West*. Norman: University of Oklahoma Press, 1965.

Gallagher, Gary W., ed. *The Richmond Campaign of 1862: The Peninsula and the Seven Days*. Military Campaigns of the Civil War. Chapel Hill: University of North Carolina Press, 2000.

Gillett, Mary C. *The Army Medical Department, 1865–1917*. Washington, D.C.: Center of Military History, U.S. Army, 1995.

Gleason, Bruce. "The Mounted Band and Field Musicians of the U.S. 7th Cavalry during the Time of the Plains Indian Wars." *Historic Brass Society Journal* 21 (2009): 69–91.

Golant, A., R. M. Nord, N. Paksima, and M. A. Posner. "Cold Exposure Injuries to the Extremities." *Journal of the American Academy of Orthopedic Surgery* 16 (December 2008): 704–15.

Grafe, Ernest, and Paul Horsted. *Exploring with Custer: The 1874 Black Hills Expedition.* 3rd ed. Custer, S.Dak.: Golden Valley Press, Dakota Photographic, 2005.
Graham, W. A. *The Custer Myth: A Source Book of Custeriana.* New York: Bonanza, 1953. Reprint, Mechanicsburg, Pa.: Stackpole, 1995.
———. *The Reno Court of Inquiry: Abstract.* Harrisburg, Pa.: Stackpole, 1954.
Gray, John S. "Arikara Scouts with Custer." *North Dakota History* 35 (December 1968): 443–78.
———. *Centennial Campaign—The Sioux War of 1876.* Fort Collins, Colo.: Old Army Press. Reprint, Norman: University of Oklahoma Press, 1988.
———. *Custer's Last Campaign: Mitch Boyer and the Little Bighorn Reconstructed.* Lincoln: University of Nebraska Press, 1991.
———. "Medical Service on the Little Big Horn Campaign." *Westerners Brand Book* 24 (January 1968): 81–88.
———. "Veterinary Service on Custer's Last Campaign." *Kansas Historical Quarterly* 43, no. 3 (Autumn 1977): 249–63.
Green, Judy, comp. *A Broad Foundation: Milestones of Medical Education at Harvard.* Part 1, *1783–1900.* Cambridge, Mass.: Francis A. Countway Library of Medicine, Center for the History of Medicine, Harvard Medical Library, Harvard University, 2004.
Greene, Jerome A. *Fort Randall on the Missouri, 1856–1892.* Pierre: South Dakota State Historical Society Press, 2005.
———, ed. *Lakota and Cheyenne: Indian Views of the Great Sioux War, 1876–1877.* Norman: University of Oklahoma Press, 1994.
———. *Washita: The Southern Cheyenne and the U.S. Army.* Norman: University of Oklahoma Press, 2004.
———. *Yellowstone Command: Colonel Nelson A. Miles and the Great Sioux War, 1876–1877.* Norman: University of Oklahoma Press, 2006.
Grice, Gary K. *History of Weather Observations for Fort Randall, South Dakota, 1856–1892.* Report for the Midwestern Regional Climate Center. Asheville, N.C.: Climate Database Modernization Program / NOAA National Climatic Data Center, 2006.
———. *History of Weather Observations for Fort Sisseton, South Dakota, 1866–1889.* Report for the Midwestern Regional Climate Center. Asheville, N.C.: Climate Database Modernization Program / NOAA National Climatic Data Center, 2006.
———. *History of Weather Observations for Fort Sully, South Dakota, 1866–1893.* Report for the Midwestern Regional Climate Center. Asheville, N.C.: Climate Database Modernization Program / NOAA National Climatic Data Center, 2006.

Hammer, Kenneth, ed. *Custer in '76: Walter Camp's Notes on the Custer Fight*. Provo, Utah: Brigham Young University Press, 1976. Reprint, Norman: University of Oklahoma Press, 1990.

Hanley, Mike, with Ellis Lucia. *Owyhee Trails: The West's Forgotten Corner*. Caldwell, Idaho: Caxton Press, 1973.

Hardorff, Richard. *The Custer Battle Casualties: Burials, Exhumations and Reinternments*. El Segundo, Calif.: Upton and Sons, 1989.

———. *The Custer Battle Casualties II: The Dead, the Missing and a Few Survivors*. El Segundo, Calif.: Upton and Sons, 1999.

———. *Indian Views of the Custer Fight: A Source Book*. Norman: University of Oklahoma Press, 2005.

———. "The Reno Scout." *Little Big Horn Associates Research Review* 2 (December 1977): 3–12.

Harrison's Principles of Internal Medicine. New York: McGraw-Hill, 1980.

Hatch, Thom. *Glorious War: The Civil War Adventures of George Armstrong Custer*. New York: St. Martin's Press, 2013.

———. *The Last Days of George Armstrong Custer*. New York: St. Martin's Press, 2015.

Hedren, Paul L. *After Custer: Loss and Transformation in Sioux Country*. Norman: University of Oklahoma Press, 2011.

———. *Fort Laramie in 1876: Chronicle of a Frontier Post at War*. Lincoln: University of Oklahoma Press, 1988.

———. *Great Sioux War, Orders of Battle: How the United States Army Waged War on the Northern Plains, 1876–1877*. Norman: Arthur H. Clark, 2011.

———. *Powder River: Disastrous Opening of the Great Sioux War*. Norman: University of Oklahoma Press, 2016.

———. "The Sioux War Adventures of Dr. Charles V. Petteys, Acting Assistant Surgeon." *Journal of the West* 32 (April 1993): 29–37.

Heitman, Francis B. *Historical Register and Dictionary of the United States Army*. Vol. 1, *From Its Organization September 29, 1789 to September 29, 1889*. Washington, D.C.: U.S. Government Printing Office, 1890.

———. *Historical Register and Dictionary of the United States Army, From Its Organization September 29, 1789 to March 2, 1903*. Washington, D.C.: U.S. Government Printing Office, 1903.

Hennessy, John J. *Return to Bull Run: The Campaign and Battle of Second Manassas*. Norman: University of Oklahoma Press, 1993.

Hoig, Stan. *The Battle of the Washita*. Garden City, N.Y.: Doubleday, 1976.

Howard, Osmond Rhodes, and William H. Rauch. *History of the "Bucktails," Kane Rifle Regiment of the Pennsylvania Reserve Corp (13th Pennsylvania Reserves, 42nd Regiment of the line)*. Philadelphia: Electric Printing, 1906.

Howard-Smith, Logan, and John Fulton Reynolds Scott, eds. *The History of Battery A (Formerly Known as the Keystone Battery) and Troop A*. Philadelphia: J. C. Winston, 1912.

Hutton, Paul Andrew. *The Custer Reader*. Lincoln: University of Nebraska Press, 1992. Reprint, Norman: University of Oklahoma Press, 2004.

———. *Phil Sheridan and His Army*. Norman: University of Oklahoma Press, 1985.

Huxley, Thomas Henry. *Lessons in Elementary Physiology*. 3rd ed. London: Macmillan, 1869.

Hyde, Cornelius W. G., Hugh J. McGrath, and William Stoddard. *History of the Great Northwest and Men of Progress: A Select List of Biographical Sketches and Portraits of the Leaders in Business, Professional, and Official Life*. Minneapolis: Minneapolis Journal, 1901.

Innis, Ben. *Bloody Knife: Custer's Favorite Scout*. Fort Collins, Colo.: Old Army Press, 1973. Reprint edited by Richard E. Collin, Bismarck, N.Dak.: Smokey Water, 1994.

Johnson, Norma. *Chilson's History of Fort Sisseton*. Pierre, S.Dak.: Esco Publishing, 1996.

Kappler, Charles J. *Indian Affairs: Laws and Treaties*. Washington, D.C.: Government Printing Office, 1904.

Kasal, Mark, and Don Moore. *A Guide Book to U.S. Army Dress Helmets, 1872–1874*. Tustin, Calif.: North Cape Publications, 2000.

Kazanjian, Howard, and Chris Enss. *None Wounded, None Missing, All Dead: The Story of Elizabeth Bacon Custer*. Guilford, Conn.: TwoDot, 2011.

Kimball, Maria Brace. *Soldier-Doctor of Our Army: James Peleg Kimball, Late Colonel and Assistant Surgeon-General, U.S. Army*. Boston: Houghton Mifflin, 1917. Reprint, Cambridge, Mass.: Riverside Press, 1971.

King, W. Kent. *Massacre: The Custer Cover Up; The Original Maps of Custer's Battlefield*. Custer Trails no. 3. El Segundo, Calif.: Upton and Sons, 1989.

Koster, John. "The Belknap Scandal: Fulcrum to Disaster." *Wild West: The American Frontier* (June 2010): 58–64.

———. *Custer Survivor: The End of a Myth, the Beginning of a Legend; The Frank Finkel Story*. Palisades, N.Y.: Chronology Books, 2010.

Langellier, John P., Kurt Hamilton Cox, and Brian C. Pohanka, eds. *Myles Keogh: The Life and Legend of an "Irish Dragoon" in the Seventh Cavalry*. Montana and the West Series, no. 9. El Segundo, Calif.: Upton and Sons, 1991.

Larson, Robert W. *Gall, Lakota War Chief*. Norman: University of Oklahoma Press, 2007.

Lawrence, Susan C., Elizabeth Lorang, Kenneth M. Price, and Kenneth J. Winkle, eds. *Civil War Washington*. Lincoln: University of Nebraska–Lincoln, Center for Digital Research in the Humanities. http://civilwardc.org.

Lazarus, Edward. *Black Hills/White Justice: The Sioux Nation versus the United States, 1775 to the Present.* New York: HarperCollins, 1991.
Lee, Robert. *Fort Meade and the Black Hills.* Lincoln: University of Nebraska Press, 1991.
Leech, Margaret. *Reveille in Washington, 1860–1865.* New York: Harper Brothers, 1941.
Libby, Orin G., ed. *The Arikara Narrative of Custer's Campaign and the Battle of the Little Bighorn.* Norman: University of Oklahoma Press, 1998.
———. "Edward H. Lohnes." In *North Dakota History.* Vol. 3, 213–14. Bismarck, N.Dak.: State Historical Society of North Dakota, 1910.
Lindmier, Tom. *Drybone: A History of Fort Fetterman, Wyoming.* Glendo, Wyo.: High Plains Press, 2002.
Lott, Dale F. *American Bison: A Natural History.* Berkeley: University of California Press, 2002.
Lowry, Thomas Power, and Jack D. Welsh. *Tarnished Scalpels: The Court-Martials of Fifty Union Surgeons.* Mechanicsburg, Pa.: Stackpole Books, 2000.
Lubetkin, M. John. *Jay Cooke's Gamble: The Northern Pacific Railroad, the Sioux, and the Panic of 1873.* Norman: University of Oklahoma Press, 2006.
Luce, Edward S., ed. "The Diary and Letters of Dr. James M. DeWolf, Acting Assistant Surgeon, U.S. Army, His Record of the Sioux Expedition of 1876 as Kept Until His Death." *North Dakota History* 25, nos. 1–2 (April–July 1958): 33–82.
MacLean, French L. *Custer's Best: The Story of Company M, 7th Cavalry at the Little Bighorn.* Atglen, Pa.: Schiffer Publishing, 2011.
Magid, Paul. *The Gray Fox: George Crook and the Indian Wars.* Norman: University of Oklahoma Press, 2015.
Matloff, Maurice, ed. *Army Historical Series: American Military History.* Washington, D.C.: Office of the Chief of Military History, U.S. Army, 1973.
Matson, William E. "The Battle of Sugar Point: A Re-examination." *Minnesota History* 50, no. 7 (Fall 1987): 269–75.
McChristian, Douglas C. *Fort Laramie: Military Bastion of the High Plains.* Norman, Okla.: Arthur H. Clark, 2008.
———. *The U.S. Army in the West, 1870–1880: Uniforms, Weapons and Equipment.* Norman: University of Oklahoma Press, 1995.
McDermott, John D. *Red Cloud's War: The Bozeman Trail, 1866–1868.* 2 vols. Norman: Arthur H. Clark, 2010.
McDougal, Len. "Snakebitten." *American Frontiersman* (March 2013): 125–27.
McFeely, William S. *Grant: A Biography.* New York: W. W. Norton, 1981.
Merington, Marguerite, ed. *The Custer Story: The Life and Letters of General George A. Custer and His Wife Elizabeth.* New York: Devin-Adair, 1950. Reprint, New York: Barnes and Noble Books, 1994.

Michno, Gregory. *Deadliest Indian War in the West: The Snake Conflict, 1864–1868*. Caldwell, Idaho: Caxton Press, 2007.
———. *Lakota Noon: The Indian Narratives of Custer's Defeat*. Missoula, Mont.: Mountain Press, 1997.
———. *The Mystery of E Troop: Custer's Gray Horse Company at the Little Bighorn*. Missoula, Mont.: Mountain Press, 1994.
Miller, Frank E., ed. *Domestic Medical Practice: A Household Adviser in the Treatment of Diseases, Arranged for Family Use*. Chicago: Domestic Medical Society, 1912.
Miller, William J., ed. *The Peninsula Campaign of 1862*. 3 vols. Campbell, Calif.: Savis Publishing, 1995–97.
Mills, Charles K. *Harvest of Barren Regrets: The Army Career of Frederick William Benteen, 1834–1898*. Lincoln: University of Nebraska Press, 1985.
Mock, Cary J. "Rainfall in the Garden of the United States Great Plains, 1870–1889." *Climatic Change* 44 (2000): 173–95.
Moore, Donald W. *Where the Custer Fight Began: Undermanned and Overwhelmed; The Reno Valley Fight*. Battle of the Little Big Horn Series, no. 10. El Segundo, Calif.: Upton and Sons, 2011.
Moulton, Candy. *Valentine T. McGillycuddy: Army Surgeon, Agent to the Sioux*. Norman: Arthur H. Clark, 2011.
Nash, Gary B., and Jean R. Soderlund. *Freedom by Degrees: Emancipation in Pennsylvania and Its Aftermath*. New York: Oxford University Press, 1991.
Nevin, David. *The Old West: The Soldiers*. New York: Time-Life Books, 1973.
New York State Medical Association. *Transactions of the New York State Medical Association for the Year 1884–1899*. Vol. 16. New York City, 1890.
Nichols, Ronald H. *In Custer's Shadow: Major Marcus Reno*. Fort Collins, Colo.: Old Army Press, 1999.
———, ed. *Men with Custer: Biographies of the 7th Cavalry*. Hardin, Mont.: Custer Battlefield Historical and Museum Association, 2000.
———. *Reno Court of Inquiry: Proceedings of a Court of Inquiry in the Case of Major Marcus A. Reno at the Battle of the Little Big Horn River on June 25–26, 1876*. Hardin, Mont.: Custer Battlefield Historical and Museum Association, 2007.
Noyes, C. Lee. "Custer's Surgeon, George Lord, among the Missing at Little Bighorn Battle." *Greasy Grass* 16 (May 2000): 13–20.
———. "The Guns Custer Left Behind Would Have Been a Burden." *Wild West, The American Frontier* 27 (June 2014): 70–71.
———. "The Guns 'Long Hair' Left Behind: The Gatling Gun Detachment at the Little Big Horn." *English Westerners' Brand Book* 33, no. 2 (Summer 1999): 1–24.
———. "James M. DeWolf, Frontier Army Doctor." *Frontier Army of Dakota* 26 (October 2012): 20–22.

O'Neil, Thomas E., comp. and ed. *Critical Notes on Line of March: Troops Serving in the Department of Dakota in the Campaign against the Hostile Sioux, 1876, by Frank Lafayette Anders, 1939.* Brooklyn, N.Y.: Arrow and Trooper Publishing, 2009.

Ostler, Jeffrey. *The Lakotas and the Black Hills: The Struggles for Sacred Ground.* New York: Penguin, 2010.

Overfield, Loyd J., II, ed. *The Little Big Horn, 1876: The Official Communications, Documents and Reports with Rosters of the Officers and Troops of the Campaign.* Lincoln: Arthur H. Clark, 1971.

Parker, W. Thornton, ed. *Records of the Association of Acting Assistant Surgeons of the United States Army.* Salem, Mass.: privately printed, 1891.

Pennington, Jack. *The Battle of Little Big Horn: A Comprehensive Study.* El Segundo, Calif.: Upton and Sons, 1999.

Perennials. The Time Life Gardener's Guide. Alexandria, Va.: Time-Life Books, 1988.

Perry, Calbraith B. *Charles D'Wolf of Guadaloupe.* New York: Press of T. A. Wright, 1902.

Petersen, Edward S. "Surgeons of the Little Big Horn." *Westerners' Brand Book* 31 (August 1974): 41–43.

Philbrick, Nathaniel. *The Last Stand: Custer, Sitting Bull, and the Battle of the Little Bighorn.* New York: Penguin, 2010.

Pleasant, Barbara. *Gardening Essentials.* Minnetonka, Minn.: National Gardening Association, 1999.

Polka, George E. *Fort Custer, 1877–1898: Then and Now.* N.p.: privately published, 1994. Reprinted 2008.

Prickett, Robert C. "The Malfeasance of William Worth Belknap, Secretary of War." *North Dakota History* 17, no. 1 (January 1950): 5–51, 97–100.

Radwanski, Paula. *The Civil War: Articles Published in "The Wyoming Republican," 1861–1862.* Tunkhannock, Pa.: Wyoming County Historical Society, 2006.

Raines, Rebecca Robbins. *Getting the Message Through: A Branch History of the U.S. Army Signal Corps.* Washington, D.C.: Center of Military History of the U.S. Army, 1996.

Reedstrom, E. Lisle. *Custer's 7th Cavalry: From Fort Riley to the Little Big Horn.* New York: Sterling Publishing, 1992.

Reilly, Hugh J. *Bound to Have Blood: Frontier Newspapers and the Plains Indian Wars.* Lincoln: University of Nebraska Press, 2011.

Remele, Larry. *Fort Buford and the Military Frontier on the Northern Plains, 1850–1900.* Bismarck: State Historical Society of North Dakota, 1987.

Robinson, Charles M. *Crook on the Western Frontier.* Norman: University of Oklahoma Press, 2001.

Ross, Allen C. (Ehanamani). *Crazy Horse and the Real Reason for the Battle of the Little Big Horn.* Denver, Colo.: Denver WiconiWaste Publishing, 2000.

Roy, Steve, and Richard Irvin. *Sports Medicine: Prevention, Evaluation, Management, and Rehabilitation*. Englewood Cliffs, N.J.: Prentice-Hall, 1983.
Rutledge, Lee A. *Collector's Guide to Military Uniforms, Campaign Clothing: Field Uniforms of the Indian War Army, 1872–1886*. Tustin, Calif.: North Cape Publications, 1997.
———. *Collector's Guide to Military Uniforms, Campaign Clothing: Field Uniforms of the Indian War Army, 1866–1871*. Tustin, Calif.: North Cape Publications, 1998.
Salisbury, E. G. *History of the DeWolf Family*. Halifax, N.S.: privately printed, 1893.
Salisbury, Edward Elbridge, and Evelyn McCurdy Salisbury. "Notes on the Family DeWolf." In *Family Histories and Genealogy*, vol. 2, 123–65. New Haven, Conn.: privately printed, 1892.
Sarf, Wayne Michael. *The Little Bighorn Campaign: March–September 1876*. Great Campaign Series. Conshohocken, Pa.: Combined Publishing, 1993.
Schuler, Harold H. *Fort Sisseton*. Sioux Falls, S.Dak.: Center for Western Studies, Augustana College, 2012.
Scott, Douglas D., Richard A. Fox Jr., and Dick Harmon. *Archaeological Insights into the Custer Battle: An Assessment of the 1984 Field Season*. Norman: University of Oklahoma Press, 1987.
Scott, Douglas D., P. Willey, and Melissa A. Connor. *They Died with Custer: Soldiers' Bones from the Battle of the Little Bighorn*. Norman: University of Oklahoma Press, 1998.
Sears, Stephen W. *To the Gates of Richmond*. Boston: Houghton Mifflin Company, 1992. Reprint, Mariner Book Edition, 2001.
Siebert, Wilbur H. *History of Ohio State University*. Columbus: Ohio State University Press, 1935.
Smith, Jean Edward. *Grant: A Biography*. New York: Simon and Schuster, 2002.
Smith, Robert Barr. "Benteen: Between a Rock and a Hard Place." *Wild West, The American Frontier* 23, no. 1 (June 2010): 28–37.
Stanley, David S. *Report on the Yellowstone Expedition of 1873*. Washington, D.C.: U.S. War Department, Government Printing Office, 1874.
Stedman's Medical Dictionary. 23rd ed. Baltimore, Md.: Williams and Wilkins Company, 1976.
Stevenson, Joan Nabseth. *Deliverance from the Little Big Horn: Doctor Henry Porter and Custer's Seventh Cavalry*. Norman: University of Oklahoma Press, 2012.
Stewart, Edgar I. *Custer's Luck*. Norman: University of Oklahoma Press, 1968.
———. *The March of the Montana Column: A Prelude to the Custer Disaster; Lt. James H. Bradley's Diary*. Norman: University of Oklahoma Press, 1991.
Stewart, Edgar I., and Edward S. Luce. "The Reno Scout." In *Custer to the Little Big Horn: A Study in Command; A Seventh Cavalry Scrapbook, #12*, compiled

and edited by Thomas O'Neil, 16–25. Brooklyn, N.Y.: Arrow and Trooper Publishing, 1991.

Stewart, Miller J. *Moving the Wounded: Litters, Cacolets and Ambulance Wagons, U.S. Army, 1776–1876*. Fort Collins, Colo.: Old Army Press, 1979.

Stiles, T. J. *Custer's Trials*. New York: Alfred A. Knopf, 2015.

Terry, Alfred H. *Field Diary of General Alfred H. Terry: The Yellowstone Expedition, 1876*. Bellevue, Neb.: Old Army Press, 1970.

Thornson, O. R. Howard, and William H. Rauch. *History of the Bucktails: Kane Rifle Regiment of the Pennsylvania Reserve Corps (13th Pennsylvania Regiment, 42nd of the Line)*. Philadelphia: Electric Printing, 1906.

Todish, Timothy R., and Todd E. Harburn. *A Most Troublesome Situation: The British Military and the Pontiac Indian Uprising, 1763–1764*. Fleischmanns, N.Y.: Purple Mountain Press, 2006.

Turner, Edward R. *The Negro in Pennsylvania: Slavery–Servitude–Freedom, 1639–1861*. Washington, D.C.: American Historical Association, 1911.

Unger, Arthur C. *The ABCs of Custer's Last Stand: Arrogance, Betrayal and Cowardice*. Battle of the Little Big Horn Series, no. 4. El Segundo, Calif.: Upton and Sons, 2004.

———. *Custer's First Messenger? Debunking the Story of Sergeant Daniel Kanipe*. New York: Custer 1876 Productions, 2011.

———. *Reno Court of Inquiry—Original Handwritten Trial Transcripts*. Audio CD in PDF searchable format. Hicksville, N.Y.: privately printed, 2008.

Upton, Richard. *Fort Custer on the Big Horn, 1877–1898*. Glendale, Calif.: Arthur H. Clark, 1973.

———. *The Indian as a Soldier at Fort Custer, 1877–1898: Lieutenant Samuel C. Robertson's First Cavalry Crow Indian Contingent*. El Segundo, Calif.: Upton and Sons, 1983.

Urwin, Gregory J. W. *Custer Victorious: The Civil War Battles of General George Armstrong Custer*. Lincoln: University of Nebraska Press, 1990.

U.S. House of Representatives. *Proposed Revised Army Regulations, March 1, 1873*. H.R. Rpt. No. 85, 42nd Cong. Washington, D.C.: U.S. Government Printing Office, 1873.

———. *Report on Management of the War Department, Rep. Heister Clymer, Chairman of the Committee*. H.R. Rpt. No. 79, 44th Cong. Washington, D.C.: U.S. Government Printing Office, 1876.

Utley, Robert M. *Cavalier in Buckskin: George Armstrong Custer and the Western Military Frontier*. Norman: University of Oklahoma Press, 1988.

———. *The Reno Court of Inquiry: The Chicago Times Account*. Fort Collins, Colo.: Old Army Press, 1972.

Vaughn, Jesse W. *The Reynolds Campaign on Powder River*. Norman: University of Oklahoma Press, 1961.

Viola, Herman J. *Little Bighorn Remembered: The Untold Indian Story of Custer's Last Stand*. New York: Times Books/Random House, 1999.
Walker, L. G., Jr. *Dr. Henry R. Porter: The Surgeon Who Survived Little Bighorn*. Jefferson, N.C.: McFarland, 2008.
Warner, Ezra J. *Generals in Blue*. Baton Rouge: Louisiana State University Press, 1964.
War Office, U.S. Army. *Regulations for the Army of the United States, 1889*. Washington, D.C.
———. *Regulations for the Medical Department of the Army, 1863*. Washington, D.C.
———. *Revised United States Army Regulations 1861 with an Appendix Containing the Changes and Laws Affecting Army Regulations and Articles of War to June 25, 1863*. Washington, D.C.
———. *War of the Rebellion: A Compilation of the Official Records of the Union and Confederate Armies*. Series 1, 1881–1884. Washington, D.C.
Welland, Francis. *Place That Plant*. Bath, U.K.: Parragon Publishing, 1998.
Wertenberger, Mildred. "Fort Totten." *North Dakota History* 34, no. 2 (Spring 1967): 125–46.
Wilbur, C. Keith. *Civil War Medicine, 1861–1865*. Guilford, Conn.: Globe Pequot Press, 1998.
Willert, James. "Another Look at the Reno Scout." *Research Review: The Journal of the Little Big Horn Associates* 14 (Summer 2000): 17–31.
———. *Little Big Horn Diary*. El Segundo, Calif.: Upton and Sons, 1997.
———, ed. *The Terry Letters*. Montclair, Calif.: Raul Brondarhit Printing, 1980.
Willey, P., and Douglas D. Scott. *Health of the Seventh Cavalry: A Medical History*. Norman: University of Oklahoma Press, 2015.
Windolf, Charles. *I Fought with Custer: The Story of Sergeant Windolf, Last Survivor of the Battle of the Little Big Horn, as Told to Frazier and Robert Hunt*. Edited by Frazier Hunt and Robert Hunt. New York: Charles Scribner's Sons, 1947. Reprint, Lincoln: University of Nebraska Press, 1987.
Work Projects Administration. *Graves Registration Project*. Washington, D.C., n.d.
The World Book Dictionary. 2 vols. Chicago: World Book, 1993.
Wyoming County Historical Society. "Charles and Wyllis DeWolf." *Lest We Forget: History of Wyoming County* 4, no. 1 (September 15, 1984): 35.
———. "Establishment of Wyoming County and Its Townships." *Lest We Forget: History of Wyoming County* 1, no. 2 (February 15, 1982): 1–8, 19.
———. *The Historical Development of Wyoming County, Pennsylvania*. Tunkhannock, Pa.: Northern Tier Regional Planning Commission, 1965.

Index

Abbis and Glen Alin, 86, 208n55
Abbotts, Henry A., 98, 107, 133, 217n21
acting assistant surgeon (civilian contract surgeons), 26–27
Aikison, David, 107
ambulances, 85, 102–3, 208n52, 219n35
American Indians, 14, 29–32, 102, 110, 114, 116, 118, 121
American Revolution, 3
antelope, 97, 102–3, 111, 113, 226n79
Appomattox, Confederate surrender at (1865), 12
Arapaho reservation, 34
Arikara (Ree) scouts, 125–26, 129
Arkansas River, 34
Army Medical Examination Board, 23, 73, 159, 174n81
Army of Northern Virginia, 10
Army of the Potomac, 8–9
Army of Virginia, 10
Army Service Record, DeWolf's, 6
Ashton, Isaiah Heylin, 37, 78, 80, 85, 89, 92–93, 103, 115, 202n35
Auburn, N.Y., 142. *See also* Fort Hill Cemetery

Babcock, Elmer, 106
Babcock, Orville, 56, 188n68
Bacon, Elizabeth "Libbie." *See* Custer, Elizabeth "Libbie" Bacon
Badlands of Little Missouri, 105
Baker, Stephen, 98, 113, 216n15
Baltic provinces, 4

band, Seventh Cavalry, 40, 78, 91, 95, 100, 102–3, 203n36
Bannock Indians, 14
battery. *See* Gatling guns
Battery A. *See* First Pennsylvania Light Artillery Volunteers
Baxter, Jedediah Hyde, 150, 231n1
Beaver Creek, Mont. (Camp No. 16), 112–13, 223n60
Beaver Dam Creek, Battle of (1862), 9–10, 167n20
Beland's Station, 40, 42, 178n27
Belknap, William W., 32, 42
Benteen, Frederick W., 87, 95, 104, 126; "his sweep to the left," 127, 134, 210n64
Bethesda Lodge of Freemasons, 173n73
Big Horn and Yellowstone expedition, 39
Big Horn Expedition, 34, 176n13
Bighorn Mountains, 30
Big Horn River, 38, 121, 142, 158
bighorn sheep, 123, 226n79
Bilroth's Surgical Pathology, 69, 193n95
Bismarck, Dakota Territory, 30, 38, 42, 48–49, 55, 62–63, 69; description, 70–72, 86, 92, 136–37, 193n1
Bismarck Tribune, 98, 104, 217n22
Blackhillers, 86, 209n59
Black Hills, 29, 31
Black Hills Expedition (1874), 30
Bloody Knife, 77, 129, 200n27
Boyer, Michel "Mitch," 125–26

Boyle, Robert [Owen], 107
Bozeman Trail, 13
Bradley, James, 90
Brady, James, 7
Brenner Crossing. *See* Davis Ranch (aka Sheyenne or Brenner Crossing)
Brenner [Bremmers], Ernest, 47, 64, 67, 98, 191n87
Brooklyn, Conn., 4
Brown, George B. Dandy, 71, 195n5
Brown, George C., 108
Brown, Mr. (DeWolf's first patient), 154
Brown, Nathan T., 41, 106, 178n28
Bryant, William E., 78, 203n38
buffalo, 114, 118–19, 121, 123, 226n79
Bull Run (Manassas), Second Battle of (1862), 10–11
Bull Run National Battlefield, 11
Burns, James M., 73, 197n11
Butler, James, 106
Byrne, Charles Borromer, 203n38

Cabin Creek, Mont., 113
Caldwell [Colwell], John R., 41, 106, 178n30, 220n44
Calhoun, James, 47, 60–61, 65, 68, 73, 98, 143, 184n52
Calhoun, Margaret, 184n52
Calhoun Ridge, 135
campaign hats, 84, 207n50
Campbell, Charles, 6–8
Camp Berry, Washington, D.C., 8
Camp Hancock, 38, 71–73, 86, 93, 196n7
Camp Lyon, 14–15, 159, 170n49
Camp No. 1 (Fort Abraham Lincoln), 213n1. *See also* Fort Abraham Lincoln
Camp No. 2, 95–96, 213n3. *See also* Heart River (Camp No. 2)
Camp No. 3 (Sweet Briar), 97, 214n9
Camp No. 4 (New Salem, N.Dak.), 97, 215n10
Camp No. 5 (Morton County, N.Dak.), 99, 218n26

Camp No. 6 (Head Hay Creek, Haymarch Town, N.Dak.), 100, 218n8
Camp No. 7 (Hebron, N.Dak.), 100, 218n29
Camp No. 8 (Young Man's Butte, N.Dak.), 102, 218n33
Camp No. 10 (Crow Ridge, South Heart, N.Dak.), 102, 219n37
Camp No. 11 (Belfield, N.Dak.), 105, 220n42
Camp No. 12 (Davis Creek, N.Dak.), 105, 220n43
Camp No. 13 (Davis Creek, N.Dak.), 105, 221n50
Camp No. 14 (Camp on the Little Missouri, Medora, N.Dak.), 109, 221n51
Camp No. 15 ("Snow Camp"), 110–11, 222n55
Camp No. 16 (Beaver Creek, Mont.), 112–13, 223n60
Camp No. 17 ("Badlands Camp," Mont.), 113, 223n63
Camp No. 18 (Cabin/Pennel Creek, Baker, Mont.), 113, 223n64
Camp No. 19 (O'Fallon's Creek, Mont.), 114, 223n66
Camp No. 20 (Powder River Camp, Locate, Mont.), 114–15, 224n68
camps on Little Big Horn Expedition, DeWolf's numbering system, 213n1
Camp Warner (New or Second), 15, 47, 123, 159, 171n53
card playing, 55
Cashan [Carpiti], William, 41, 106, 178n29
Chance, Josiah, 74, 200n26
Chandler, Zachariah, 32
Chappell, M. L., 146
Cheever, David W., 21
Cheyenne River Indian Agency, 38
Chicago Daily Tribune, 142
Chickahominy River, 10

Index 251

Christianity, 30
Chubb, Charles S. J., 73, 196n8
Cimarron River, 34
Civil War, 5–6, 9, 12
Clapp, Sarah "Sally," 13
Clark, Elbert Judson, 37–38, 73, 80, 85, 89, 92–93, 104, 197n13
Clear, Elihu F., 131, 133
Clymer, Hiester, 35
Clymer-Belknap Hearings, 35–36, 177n16
Coleman, John, 225n76
Colwell, John R., 41, 106, 178n30, 220n44
Confederate Army of Northern Virginia, 12
Connell, John, 100, 218n30
Cooke, William Winer, 89, 127, 143, 211n66
Couch, Mr. (DeWolf's patient), 156
coulee, 100, 103, 218n27
courts martial, at Fort Seward, 46, 184n51
Crane, Charles Henry, 19, 23–24
Craycroft, William Thomas, 44–46, 48–49, 51–52, 60–61, 68, 99, 106, 182n44
Crazy Horse, 30, 34, 38
Crittenden, John, 90, 98, 142, 216n16
Crittenden, Thomas, 83, 216n16
Crook, George: Big Horn and Yellowstone expedition, 38–39, 56, 59, 64–65, 86, 115; Rosebud fight, 117, 176n13, 188n69, 223n62; Snake War involvement, 15, 32; Wyoming Column, Big Horn expedition and Powder River, 34. *See also* Rosebud, Battle of (1876)
Crow scouts, 125–27
Crow's Nest, 126
Cushman, Herbert, 67, 193n94
Custer, Elizabeth "Libbie" Bacon, 35, 90; at Heart River camp, 95, 144
Custer, George Armstrong: arrival at Lincoln, 90, 95; attire on expedition, 98, 100, 103, 105, 109, 121, 125; at Battle of Little Big Horn, 126–34, 136, 142–43, 158, 160, 180n37, 182n43; Civil War brevet ranks, 30; at Crows Nest, 126; involvement in Clymer-Belknap Hearings, 34–36, 37–38, 40; stranded in snow on train to Bismarck, 42, 44, 48, 51, 56, 64, 80, 82, 84–86
Custer, Margaret, 184n52
Custer, Tom, 126, 143
Custer Battlefield National Monument, 160. *See also* Little Bighorn Battlefield National Monument

Dakota Column, 34, 36–38, 40
Dakota Territory, 29–30, 33, 37–38, 141
Dandy, George Brown, 71, 195n5
Davern, Edward, 131
Davis, John, 107
Davis Creek, N.Dak., 105
Davis Ranch (aka Sheyenne or Brenner Crossing), 40–42, 49, 178n26
Denver, 73, 76, 198n15
Department of California, 15
Department of Dakota, 24, 29, 56; postage accounting, 150
Department of the East, 19, 159
Department of the Gulf, 37
Department of the Interior, 31
Department of the Platte, 32–33
Devil's Lake, Dakota Territory, 33, 104, 219n41
DeWolf, Alice, 4
DeWolf, Amanda, 3
DeWolf, Amasa, 5, 8, 165n9, 167n18
DeWolf, Archibald, 3
DeWolf, Achsah Clapp, 3, 14, 169nn40–41
DeWolf, Balthasar, 4
DeWolf, Charles "The Hatter," 4, 165n8
DeWolf, Diantha Robinson, 5

Index

DeWolf, Edward P., 3
DeWolf, Edwin A., 3, 8, 167n18
DeWolf, Elizabeth Walbridge, 4
DeWolf, Erastus L., 3, 61, 63, 190n83
DeWolf, family origins, 3–4; Rhode Island branch, 4, 164n5
DeWolf, Francis "Fannie" Downing, 16, 33, 136, 143–44, 147, 158, 160; pension application, 173n63
DeWolf, James Madison, 3; assignment to right wing for 1876 expedition, 92; Bull Run, 11–12; childhood, 5; Civil War service, 5–12; death, 130–36; description of camps, landscape on Dakota expedition, 95–124; at Fort Abraham Lincoln, 71–94; at Fort Seward, 41–70; at Fort Totten, 27–28, 33, 37–38, 40; funeral, 145–46; grave site, 148, 152, 157–60, 212n75, 222n58; hints at life philosophy, 112; hospital steward post–Civil War, Camp Lyon, Camp Warner, 14–15; marriage to Fannie, 16; physical description, 6–7; preservation of his diary, 139, 143; Reno Scout diary, 116–21, 126; at Watertown Arsenal/Harvard Medical School, 19–20
DeWolf, Lafayette Erastus, 9
DeWolf, Mark Anthony, 3, 5, 12
DeWolf, Mary, 3
DeWolf, Moses, 165n7
DeWolf, Orman A., 3
DeWolf, William, 3
DeWolf-Robinson-Pearson cemetery, 6, 12
dispensary. *See* Fort Abraham Lincoln
District of Montana, 33
Division of the Pacific, 15
Division of the Missouri, 32
Dodd, Elijah, 147
Dodd, Verne Adams, 147, 160
Dodge, F. L., 15
Dogan Ridge, 10
Dorman, Isaiah, 130, 227n17

Downing, Elvira, 16, 172n59
Downing, Frederick, 16, 18
Downing, Nancy Wadsworth, 16, 172n59
Downing, Thomas Jefferson, 16, 172n57, 172n59
Drainsville, Battle of (1862), 9, 167n20
DuBray [DuBrays], Arthur William, 42–43, 46, 48–49, 51, 62–63, 65, 67–68, 70, 179n35
Duluth, Minn., 30
Dye, William, 106

Easton, Hezekiah, 8, 9
Edgerly, Grace Cory Blum, 89, 211n68
Edgerly, Winfield Scott, 84, 131, 207n51
Eighth Pennsylvania Regiment, 10
Eliot, Charles William, 23
elk, 119, 123
Ellis, Calvin, 20
Emory, William Henry, 63, 191n86

Fargo, Dakota Territory, 28, 52, 55, 61, 68–69, 72, 149
Far West, 76, 121–22, 136
Ferguson, Edna, 43, 50–51, 55–56, 60, 64, 77, 92, 152, 181n41
Ferguson, James, 28, 33, 43, 45, 55–56, 59–60, 67, 77, 91–92, 94, 115, 150, 181n41
Fifth U.S. Artillery, Battery C, 9–10
Fifty-First Pennsylvania Volunteer Regiment, 9
Finley Hospital, 11–12, 168n30
Finnegan, William, 196n9
First Pennsylvania Light Artillery Volunteers: Battery A, 6–12, 158; Battery B, 8–9; Battery G, 8–9
Fisk, Jonathan, 13, 169nn39–40
Fletcher, Mrs. William, 43, 50–51, 77, 90, 181n38
Fletcher, William, 60, 77, 202n31
Forbes, Amanda B., 46, 60–64, 183n48
Forbes, Jenni, 60, 62, 68, 183n48

Index

Forbes, William H., 183n48
Forkston, Penn., 5, 164n2, 165n8, 165n10, 166n11
Fort Abercrombie, 73, 90, 196n12
Fort Abraham Lincoln, 33–35, 37, 40, 56; as Camp No. 1, 213n1; DeWolf's sketch of, 89, 90, 92, 136, 141, 158, 160, 199n20, 206n47; dispensary at, 74; gardens at, 81, 86; horse stables, 87; life at, 73–94
Fort Buford, 38, 81, 86, 144, 206n45
Fort Custer, 142, 230n47
Fort Ellis, 39
Fort Fetterman, 34, 39, 86, 208n57
Fort Hill Cemetery, Auburn, N.Y., 142
Fort Laramie Treaty (1868), 29–30, 34
Fort Leavenworth, 143
Fort Lincoln. *See* Fort Abraham Lincoln
Fort McKeen, 74, 87, 199n21
Fort Peck, 158
Fort Rice, 37, 87, 90, 210n65
Fort Ripley, 37, 81, 205n44
Fort Seward, 37, 40–41; life at, 41–70, 148, 179n32
Fort Sisseton. *See* Fort Wadsworth (renamed Sisseton)
Fort Totten, 27, 33, 40, 177n25, 44, 54, 91–92, 94, 96, 143, 148, 150–51, 160
Fort Van Buren, 120, 225n75
Fort Vancouver, 14, 170n44
Fort Wadsworth (renamed Sisseton), 80, 204n41
Forty-Third Regiment of Pennsylvania, 7
Fourteenth U.S. Infantry, 13, 15
Fourth Infantry, 34
Frazier, Daniel, 155
Freemasons, 22, 54
French, Thomas, 96, 214n6
frostbite, 52, 186n61

Gaines' Mill, Battle of (1862), 9–10, 167n20
Galoon [Galvan], James, 106

gambling, 81–82, 206n46
"Garry Owen," 40
gas pockets, western Dakotas and eastern Montana, 110, 221n54
Gatling guns, 37, 89, 95, 119, 122, 224n72
Gerard, Frederic, 227n6
Gibbon, John, 33, 38–40, 86, 112–13, 115, 121–22, 135, 208n58, 222n59
Gibbs, Eugene Beauharnais, 98, 103, 149, 216n19
Godfrey, Edward, 133, 135
gold, 30
Gordon, Henry, 131
Grant, Orville Lynch, 36
Grant, Ulysses S.: reprimand of Custer, 36, 56; secret meeting for 1876 Indian campaign, 32–33, 35
Grasshopper Hills, 42, 179n33
Great Sioux Reservation, 29, 31, 34, 122
Greenfield, Mass., 50, 185n58
Grove Street Building, 21–22. *See also* Harvard Medical School

Hall, David T., 16, 27, 143, 145–48, 230n54
Hall, Emma Downing, 16, 18, 27, 145, 147–48
Hankey [Hauggi], Louis, 106
Harbach, Abram A., 60, 65, 190n82
Harding, James B., 6
hardtack, 115, 126, 224n71
Hare, Luther, 133
Harmon, William, 59, 190n80
Harrington, Henry Moore, 65, 72, 122, 192n90
Harrington, Weston, 106
Harrisburg, Pennsylvania, 6, 8
Harrison, William H., 106
Hartford, Connecticut, 4
Harvard Medical School, 19; Grove Street building and curriculum, 20–22, 51, 159
Heagner, Thomas [Francis], 107

Heart River (Camp No. 2), 95–96, 98, 101–2, 213n3
Heim, John, 107
heliotrope, 114, 224n69
Henderson, Zach, 108, 220n46
Henley, John S., 108, 220nn46–47
Henton, James, 47, 184n53
Hill, James, 113, 223n65
Hodgson, Benjamin Hubert "Benny," 96, 122–23, 125, 129, 133, 214n8
hospital stewards, 171n56
Howe, Henry Smith, 71, 72–73, 86, 193n2
Hughes, Robert Patterson, 98, 216n17
Hunkpapas, 30, 38
Hunt, Abby Pearce, 55, 57, 67, 86, 90, 95
Hunt, James C., 171n50
Hunt, Lewis Cass, 33, 43, 51, 55, 57, 67, 95, 181n40
Huxley's Physiology, 69, 91, 193n95

Idaho Territory, 14
Indian scouts, 89, 95, 104
instruments, 83, 152, 207n49. *See also* surgeon's kit
Interior Department, U.S. *See* Department of Interior
Iron Springs, Grasshopper Hills, 42, 179n33

Jamestown, Dakota Territory, 49, 51–52, 77, 186n60
Jenningsville, Penn., 5, 164n2, 165nn9–10
Johnson [Kennedy], Francis. *See* Kennedy, Francis Johnson
Jones, William B., 108, 220n48
Josephine, 76

Kane, Thomas L., 9
Kane, William, 112, 222n57
Kane's Rifles, "The Bucktails," 9
Kanipe, Daniel, 133
Kellogg, Mark, 98, 217nn22–23

Kelly, Arthur W., 47, 184n54
Kelly, M. J., 17
Kennedy, Francis Johnson, 108–9, 220n49, 220n52
Keogh, Myles, 96, 142, 214n5
Kimball, James Peleg, 56, 64, 73, 187n66, 197n14
Kinzie, Frank Xavier, 74, 98, 200n24
Klotzbucher, Henry, 227n14
Knight, C. W., 19

Laidley, Theodore (Thaddeus) Sobieski, 62, 191n84
Lakotas. *See* Sioux (Lakotas)
Lange, Henry, 107
Last Stand Hill (Custer Hill), 143
Lee, Robert E., 10
Leeper, Fredrick, 112, 222n57
Little Big Horn, Battle of, 38–39; early stages, 125–36, 141, 157
Little Bighorn Battlefield National Monument, 147–48. *See also* Custer Battlefield National Monument
Little Big Horn River, 125–26, 142
Little Missouri River, 102–3, 105, 109, 115, 127
Lobering, Louis, 106
Lohnes [Lunis], Edward H., 48, 59, 69, 185n56
Lomy, William A., 108
Lord, George Edwin, 38, 122, 225n77
Lounsberry, Clement, 71, 194n4
Low, William H., 74, 98, 200n23
Luce, Edward S., 147, 153
Lunis, Edward. *See* Lohnes [Lunis] Edward H.
Lyme, Conn., 4

Maize, William Reynolds, 42–43, 45–46, 49, 62–63, 65, 68, 83, 180n36
Mason, Henry S., 108
McAnn, Patrick, 108
McCall, George A., 8–9
McClellan, George B., 9–10
McCue [McHugh], Philip, 106

Index

McDougall, Alice M., 43, 50, 60–61, 68, 90
McDougall, Thomas Mower, 43–46, 48–49, 51–52, 57, 61–63, 68, 82, 87, 90, 95, 98, 107, 182n42
McGuire, Edward, 95, 98, 213n4, 217n20
McIntosh, Donald, 130, 143
McLaughlin, James, 69, 193n96
McWilliams, David (DeWolf's patient), 114, 223n67
Mechanicsville, Battle of (1862), 9–10, 167n20
Medicine Lodge Treaty (1867), 34
Mehoopany, Pennsylvania, 3; settlement and name, 5, 153, 164n2, 165n10, 166nn11–12
Mehoopany Creek, 3
Michaelis, Otho Ernest, 90–91, 98, 212n70
Middleton, Johnson Van Dyke, 74, 77, 91, 93, 95, 199n19
Mills, Reverend, 146
Missouri River, 29, 37, 72, 86
Mitzpah Creek, Mont., 117–19
Monroe, Mich., 144
Montana Column, 177n22
Montana Territory, 30, 34, 39
Moon [Moonie], George A., 107
Moylan, Myles, 77, 81, 202n32
Myers, William D., 131

Nebraska, 29–30, 33
New Salem, N.Dak. (Camp No. 4), 215n10
New York City, 13, 23, 159
New York Herald, 86
New York World, 177n19
Ninth Infantry, 34
Ninth Pennsylvania Reserve Regiments, 10
nontreaty Indians, 30, 32
Northern Cheyennes, 34, 135
Northern Pacific Railroad, 30–31
Northern Paiute Indians, 14

North Platte River, 30
Norwalk, Ohio, 16, 143–45, 147, 158
Norwalk Experiment, 144, 230n55
Norwalk Reflector, 55, 145, 187n65
Nowlan, Henry James, 86, 211n67

O'Connel [O'Connor], Patrick, 107
O'Fallon's Creek, Mont. (Camp No. 19), 114, 223n66
Oglalas, 30, 38
Ohio State University Hospital, 147
O'Keefe, David, 77, 201n30
Omaha Republican, 97, 215n13
123rd Ohio Volunteer Infantry, 16
Oregon Territory, 14–16, 47
Oregon Trail, 13

pack trains, mules, 37, 116, 176n13, 177n23
Page, Mrs. Isaac, 154
Panic of 1873, 30
pannier, 82, 152
Patterson, John H., 42, 46, 62–63, 65, 179n34
Patterson, Mary Elizabeth Forbes, 58, 183n48, 189n75
Pedro Club, 60, 64, 190n81
Pennsylvania Reserve Corps, Army of the Potomac, 6, 9
Pequossette Lodge of Freemasons, 22, 54, 145, 173n73, 230n53
pericarditis, 66, 192n92
Perkins, William, 15
Plains Indians. *See* American Indians
pleurisy, 69, 77, 201n29
Pope, John, 10
Porter, Henry Rinaldo, 37–38, 71, 73, 93, 103–4, 121–22, 125–27, 134; letters to Fannie DeWolf, 136–38; recovery of DeWolf's diary, 139, 143, 157–58, 194n3, 220n49
Porter, James Ezekiel, 74, 81, 84, 198n17
Powder River, 34, 113–16
Powder River Fight, 34

Pumpkin Creek, Mont., 117, 119

Ransom, Dunbar R., 10
Red Cloud's War (1866–68), 29
Redd, Robert George, 74, 79, 81, 91–92, 94–95, 198n18
Reed, Harry Armstrong, 110, 221n53
Reese, William, 107
Reily, William Van Wyck, 65, 72, 74, 77, 83, 143, 192n90
Reno, Marcus, 78, 89, 92–93, 96, 100, 104, 124, 126–27; charge of the village at the Little Big Horn, timber fight, retreat, 129–31; defense hill, 134, 157, 203n37, 228n21
Reno court of inquiry, 228n21
Reno Creek, Mont., 127
Reno Hill (Reno-Benteen Defense site), 134–35, 148
Reno Scout, 115–21, 224n70
Revolutionary War (American), 3
Reynolds, Alfred, 59, 189n78
Reynolds, John F., 10
Reynolds, Joseph J., 34
Reynolds, "Lonesome" Charley, 86, 97, 125, 209n61, 215n11
Robinson, Alice, 155
Robinson Cemetery (Forkston, Penn.), 165n8
Rose, Peter E., 106
Rosebud, Battle of (1876), 39
Rosebud Creek, 112, 119, 123–25, 152
Rosebud River, 38
Rugar, Henry H., 44, 55, 57, 60–61, 63, 66, 68, 183n45
Russian Baltic provinces, 3–4
Ryan, John, 130–31, 136–37

San Francisco, California, 15, 47
Sanger [Sanford], Louis A., 74, 200n25
Schele, Henry, 108
Second Cavalry, 34, 38
Seidletz Powders, 48, 184n55
Seip, Robert Cloud, 90, 212n71

Seminary Street, Norwalk, Ohio, 146, 148
Seven Days Battles (Peninsula Campaign, 1862), 9
Seventeenth Infantry, 37, 80, 98, 204n41
Seventh Cavalry, 31, 33, 35; companies for the final expedition, 121, 126, 160; Company E medical list, 107, 109; Company L medical list, 106; comprising the Dakota Column, 37; order of Dakota Column, 95, 98–99, 104; Reno Scout, 116–19; in southern reconstruction, 62–63, 74, 77, 84, 87, 89
Seventh Infantry, 33, 38
Seymour, Truman, 10
Sheridan, Michael V., 141, 158
Sheridan, Philip H., 32–33, 36; letter to Fannie DeWolf, 143–45; plan for retrieval of remains Little Big Horn casualties, 140–42
Sherman, William Tecumseh, 32, 59
Sheyenne. *See* Davis Ranch (aka Sheyenne or Brenner Crossing)
Shields, William H., 108
Shoshone Indians, 14
Simpson, John G., 6, 10
Sioux (Lakotas), 29–32, 34, 125, 126–27; at Little Big Horn, 126–35
Sisseton. *See* Fort Wadsworth (renamed Sisseton)
Sitting Bull, 30, 38
Sixth Infantry, 37, 98
Slaper, William, 130
slavery, in DeWolf family, 4, 164nn5–6
Sloan, William J., 80, 93, 204n40
Smith, Algernon Emory, 65, 143, 192n89
Smith, Edward Worthington, 74, 77, 83, 98, 198n16, 216n18
Smith, John, 122, 225n76
Smith, Rodney, 150, 231n2 (App. A)
Smith, William, 73, 96, 196–97n10
Snake River, 14

Index

Snake War (1864–68), 14
Southern Cheyennes, 34
St. Louis Republican, 85, 97, 208n54, 215n13
St. Paul, Minn., 57, 59, 80, 90, 141, 149–50
Stanley, David S., 31
Stanley's Stockade, 90, 112, 211n69
State Historical Society of North Dakota, 148
Stein, Charles Andrew, 86, 209n60
Stella, Alexander, 108
Stempker, Henry C., 101, 218n32
Stewart, Alexander Turnery, 66, 84, 192–93n93
Sully's Hill, 208n55
sunstroke, 123, 225–26n78
surgeon's kit, 83, 152, 207n49, 217n24
Susquehanna River, 3
sutures, 99, 217n24
Sweet Briar River (Camp No. 3), 97, 214n9

Tarbox, Byron, 106
Terry, Alfred H., 32, 34, 36–38, 40, 56, 83, 86, 89–90, 95, 98, 100, 103, 105, 114; arrival at Little Big Horn, 135, 140–42, 187n67; orders Reno Scout, 115
Third Cavalry, 34
Thirteenth Pennsylvania Reserves, 9
Thompson, Peter, 71, 195n6
Thompson, Richard Edward, 96, 195n6
Timman, Henry, 148
Tongue River, 38, 119
Tweed, Thomas, 106
Twentieth Infantry, 37, 81, 205n44

unceded areas, 30–31
Union, 76
Union Pacific Railroad, 29
U.S. Naval Reserves, 147

Varnum, Charles, 125, 131

Walker, Edward, 50, 185n57
Wallace, George, 131, 133, 157
War Department, 23, 142
Warren, John Collins, 20
Warren Anatomical Museum, 20
Washington, D.C.: Army headquarters move to, 59, 80, 82, 189n79; Custer's sojourn to (1876), 35–36
Washington Territory, 14
Watertown Arsenal, 19, 23, 61, 173n67
Waterville, Ohio, 147
Weir, Thomas, 77, 79, 81, 91, 97, 134, 201n28
West Point, N.Y., 142
Weston, John Francis, 86, 210n62
whiskey, 122–23, 225n76
White, James C., 23
Williams, John W., 37, 90, 92, 95, 98, 104, 109, 121–22, 140, 212nn76–77, 220n49; use of travois at Little Big Horn, 229n33
Wilson, George A., 71, 195n6
Windham Township, Pennsylvania, 3, 164n2, 166n11
Wolf Mountains, 126
Woodlawn Cemetery, Norwalk, Ohio, 146–48
Wyoming Column, 32–34
Wyoming County, Ia., 13
Wyoming County, Penn., 3; U.S. Census of, 5, 158, 166n12
Wyoming Republican, 167n14
Wyoming Territory, 29–30, 33
Wyoming Valley Massacre (1778), 3

Yates, George, 81, 86, 95, 143, 213n2
Yellowstone Expedition, 1873 Northern Pacific Railroad survey, 31
Yellowstone River, 30–31, 99, 110, 112, 115, 121, 142
Young Man's Butte (Camp No. 8), 101, 218n33

Zimmerman, George, 41, 106, 178n31, 188n74

www.ingramcontent.com/pod-product-compliance
Lightning Source LLC
Chambersburg PA
CBHW031431160426
43195CB00010BB/691